CW00446531

Dress Code
Interior Design
for Fashion Shops

Frame Publishers
Amsterdam

Birkhäuser — Publishers for Architecture
Basel - Boston - Berlin

Contents

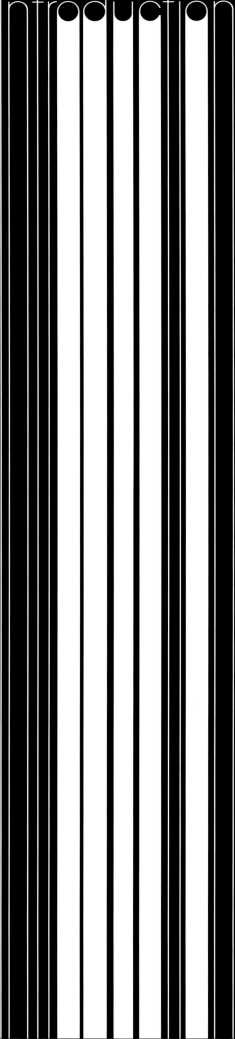

Dress Code
The Architecture of Fashion

Text
Shonquis Moreno

Humans live inside clothes. Since time immemorial, clothes have been our second defence – the first being our own skin – against the elements. Buildings have been our third.

Buildings and garments mediate and buffer our experience of the world outside our bodies, something reflected in the fact that fashion designers and architects have been borrowing from each other for eons by sharing the same materials (bark, grasses, hide, steel) and techniques (weaving, pleating, folding, draping) at different scales. Both work with scale and geometry, texture, colour and ornamentation, volume and voids and are increasingly using technology to do so. While designing the high-tech but voluptuous Miele boutique in New York's Meatpacking District, Hani Rashid and Lise Anne Couture of Asymptote used computer studies of fabric cuttings from the floor of Miele's design studio to convey both the sensuality of the body and the tectonics of clothing construction. 'We wanted to find out if we could structure pattern for space the way you structure pattern for the body,' Rashid explained. In Tokyo, designer Steve Lidbury created an architecture for the men's section of the Addition boutique that, with its diaphanous layers of glass, polyurethane, reflections and light, resembles a textile in its own right. Over and over again in recent years, we have been reminded that while clothes are miniature dwellings, buildings are vast garments; we can dress ourselves in architecture and take shelter in our clothes. And if we don't want to hide, architects and fashion designers can also use structure and surface – silk, seams and thread as much as marble, beams and cable – to create interfaces between people, tools that communicate without talking. Architect Shuhei Endo who created the Roden-stock Galerie de Brille shop in Tokyo, compared eyeglasses to architecture. Located 'in between', between people and their environments, both connect our inner and outer worlds and hold up a lens to our surroundings and our selves.

In alliance with the fashion industry, whose most exclusive houses were swallowed up by behemoth international conglomerates during the 1990s, retail architecture has become a tool in the manufacture of individual and group identity (particularly in urban areas) as well as an expression of corporate identity. Now, garments have become characters that perform on an architectural stage and the theatrical quality of both creates a dia-logue between the two that is all about the brand. In fact, retail designers are finding fertile creative ground by refusing to draw distinctions between art, architecture, fash-ion and commerce. The increasingly vigorous and synergistic exchange taking place amongst these disciplines has become more conspicuous in the retail environment today. 'To me, a clothing store is a more accessible kind of gallery,' says contemporary design curator Ellen Lupton, 'a place where I can walk away with some art in my shop-ping bag.'One no longer merely browses, tries on and buys clothes. In a boutique, above all, a shopper has an experience that is contrived through architecture: you enter a different world or are thrust into a very real world you might not otherwise have had the opportunity (or wanted the opportunity?) to enter. You find a fly-postered city in London shop, Firetrap. You enter a white forest in Seoul's T.odo boutique, wander through the tarpaulin-clad lean-tos of a homeless community in Tokyo's Bernhard Wil-helm store. Indeed, Manhattan's entire Meatpacking District has become a theme park of fashion boutiques, hermetic fictions linked by a single goal: to sell expensive clothes.

Fabio Novembre
'Architecture and fashion design
are not about function but
about communication.'

How can architecture help to sell clothes today? Ten years ago, it was expected to recede in favour of the fashions. Not so any longer. With the proliferation of choice today, offering a product, even a chic product, isn't enough. Retailers and fashion houses feel pressure to offer something bigger. Dutch firm 3D Projecten redesigned a Mayke shop in the Netherlands, not structurally or even functionally, but to evoke the brand through the atmosphere of the space. Today, according to 3D architect Peter Robben, architecture and fashion are expected to reinforce one another in exactly this abstract, ambient, wholly explicit manner. The accessories of retail architecture remain the same: a till, fitting rooms, display systems (racks, tables, shelves, cupboards), a storefront – but they must resonate with shoppers' fantasies in a way that lasts long after they leave the shop. A pair of trousers, a frock, become the souvenirs of an experience and tokens of a larger, ongoing narrative that is the brand. 'Architecture and fashion design are not about function but about communication,' says designer Fabio Novembre. 'Attaching some clothes to some rails is not really a difficult function to solve. Seducing people with a beautiful spatial story is what it is all about.'

Stories
The word design means 'to conceive or fashion', 'fashion' means 'to give shape or form to', architect, 'to form or devise'. These words denote a family of makers. What is being made today by designers of both disciplines are stories. Most (stories and interiors) are built to last even if the fashions aren't. Fashion is ephemeral but endurance has always been architecture's virtue. When it comes to ephemerality, however, Rei Kawakubo's guerrilla Comme des Garçons outposts and, more recently, Bernhard Wilhelm's in-mall Tokyo boutique designed by artists item idem and Muti Randolph's Galeria Melissa in São Paulo, challenge the notion of static retail space. Although architecture has yet to match the speed and totality with which fashion shifts, Kawakubo's guerrilla shops differ radically from place to place and have preset expiration dates in case we become too attached to them. Wilhelm's shop is an art installation where clothes are sold; the entire interior will change twice a year. Made in its initial incarnation from trash and found objects, its 5800-euro price tag makes this frequent overhaul unprecedentedly feasible.

Sometimes retail architecture's story is as simple as making the shopper feel at home (in the Platonic ideal of home, perhaps) as Laur Meyrieux has done with her Fukuoka shop, Le Ciel Bleu which resembles a bright Mediterranean living room. Other times, it is a story about technology. Technology hasn't yet transformed the shopping experience as the publicity machines of Prada and Koolhaas once hoped, but it has helped us to change the shape of our clothes and our architecture. Ammar Eloueini's Pleats Please boutique designs for Issey Miyake in Berlin and Perpignan celebrate form and composition as much as the couturier does and the computer has allowed him to do so in a new way.

At other times, it is a story that is meant to pleasantly confuse, instead of clarify, the shopping experience. In Robin Elmslie Osler's design for B8 in New York City, the darkness of the space amplifies its exclusivity – coming in off the bright street in summer, shoppers feel as if they've entered a secret jewel box. By layering mirrors, screens and translucent material, Osler obscured the edges of the space. 'In the fashion industry,

you're working with vanity because that's all that fashion is,' says Osler, who worked as
a model for ten years before training to become an architect. 'It's a powerful tool that
you can use to manipulate how others see you. So we were manipulating how visitors
perceive the space.'

Many of the boutiques in Manhattan's Meatpacking District use metaphors from nature
as a way to provide a recognizable and tranquil place to spend time and money or to
offer shoppers a new world that must be explored and discovered. If the Stella McCart-
ney boutique is a topographical map, the adjacent Alexander McQueen shop, a glacier complete with crevasses and caverns, and Balenciaga, to the north, a desert, the
neighbourhood seems to be evolving into a cabinet of curiosities. The Catherine Malan-
drino shop, designed by Christophe Pillet, evokes a lush garden. A hillock of a sofa has
sprouted leather sod and garments hang in a profusion of mossy knits and leafy silks
from racks that might be hedgerows. The branches of a chandelier are weighted with
pendulous Murano glass bulbs, beneath which a path wandering through the shop
creates tiny openings and closures. This is how Eden looked after the apple was eaten.

One of the more recent phenomena of retail architecture is the opulent flagship store
which, pioneered by Rem Koolhaas and Herzog & de Meuron for Prada, has become a
total declaration of brand as well as a provocation: Has culture sold out to commerce?
At the other end of the spectrum, as artists item idem did for the Bernard Wilhelm store,
some designers are foregoing luxurious materials in favour of elevating or recycling the
very humblest of materials (trash, in the case of item idem) to dress a boutique. Guy
Zucker's design for Delicatessen manages to redeem lowly linoleum. Using only linoleum
and cardboard tubes, the designer sheathed the space in a thin 'garment' that forms
the store's furniture: display racks, a fitting room, a cashier's desk and a storefront. With
a change of season, change of mode or change of the owner's heart, this garment
can be replaced, the interior keeping pace with the latest fashions. The entire project
cost a mere 2500 euros (830 euros of which went for materials). By cutting, folding, rolling, stacking and wrapping his materials – almost as a fashion designer might – Zucker
spun pedestrian, ephemeral, readymade stuff into something fine, reminding us, as our
mothers once did, that it is not the clothes that make the man. Zucker's resourcefulness
poses a challenge to retail architecture and to fashion, itself. If builders can embrace
the ephemerality of the fashion industry, if designers can alter our notions of what is
precious and what is poor, we may be able to invest in imagination over material.
Mind over matter, my mother always said.

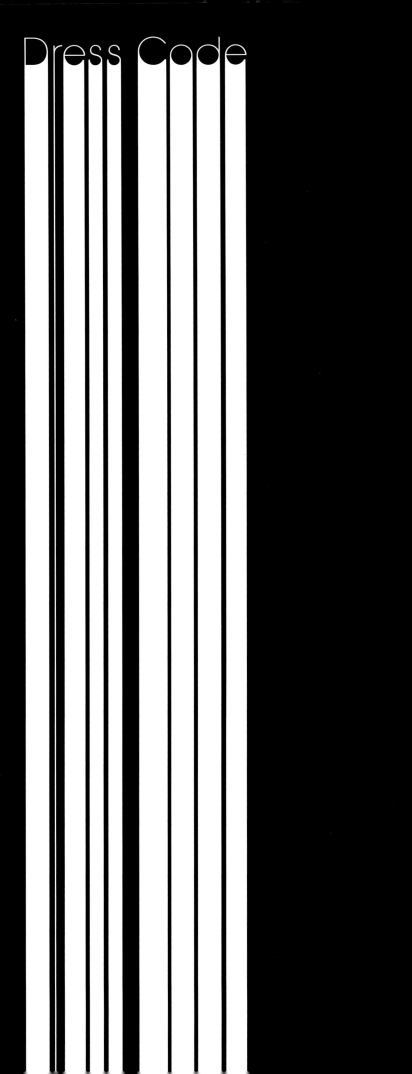

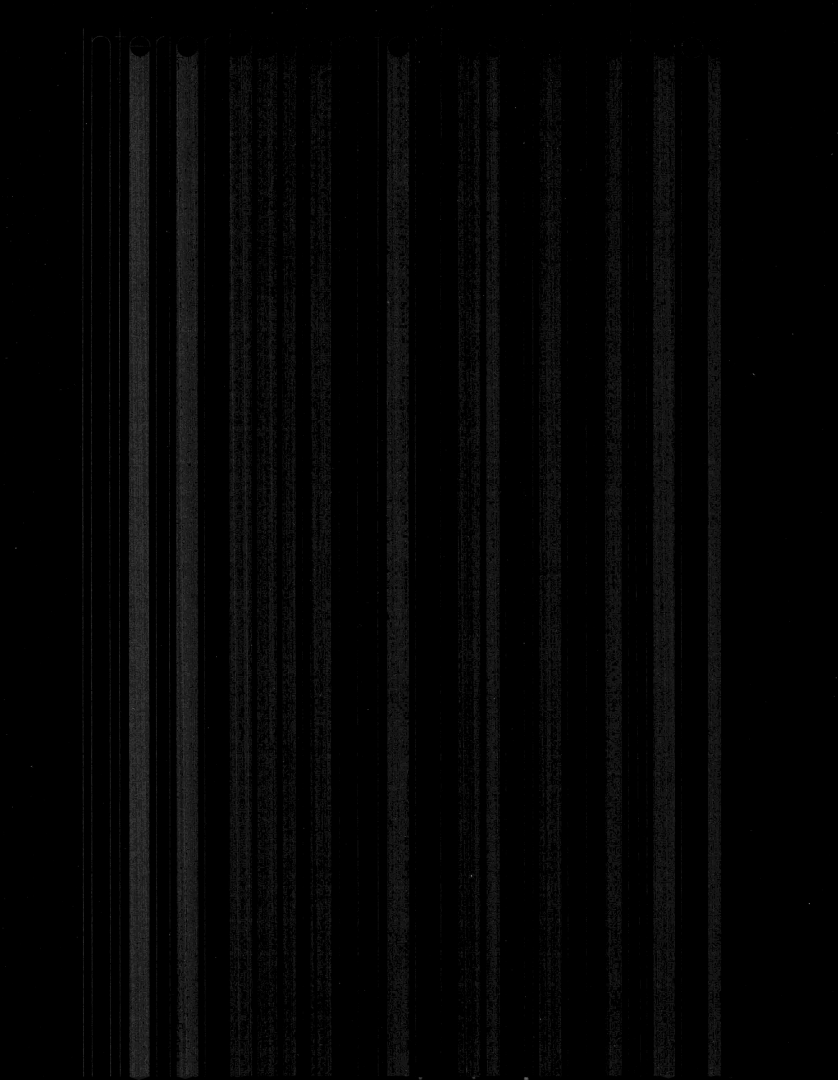

Store
Lanvin

Location
Tokyo, Japan

Architect
Hiroshi Nakamura

Hiroshi Nakamura
'Today's shops provide
experiences. People go shopping
to be entertained.'

Text
Masaaki Takahashi

Photography
Daici Ano

Adorning the façade and interior of Tokyo Lanvin is Hiroshi Nakamura's playful polka-dot light show.

Hermès, Christian Dior, Prada, Louis Vuitton . . . these are only a handful of the super-brands that have commissioned renowned architects to design stunning outlets in Tokyo, to shape skilful interpretations of well-known retail images in an attempt to attract even more customers. A recent addition to the list is Lanvin, who brought in young Japanese architect Hiroshi Nakamura to design its flagship store in the sumptuous Ginza district of Tokyo. Although perhaps not as swank as many of its neighbours, Nakamura's contribution to this shopper's paradise has an air of subtlety that is precisely what makes it a noteworthy project.

In his function as architect for Kengo Kuma & Associates, Nakamura had headed a project devoted to photographer Roland Kirishima's Plastic House. A visitor to Plastic House, who happened to be designer Alber Elbaz of Lanvin, was intrigued by the architect's work, and the rest is history. Elbaz commissioned Nakamura to revitalize the legendary brand name by giving it a fresher, more youthful image. Later, in Paris with Nakamura, Elbaz took the young man on a tour of the city that touched on everything from opera to perfume, a stimulating experience that flooded the architect's mind with the sensations of France. His specific brief was to come up with a retail design that took its cue from the modern residence of fashion designer and brand founder Jeanne Lanvin. Two weeks later Nakamura unveiled his concept, a design based on the insertion of a two-storey dwelling into the existing building in Ginza, an interior that reflected the 'family theme' vital to Lanvin's origins: a mother making clothes for her only child. Won over by the idea, Lanvin rather unconventionally asked Nakamura to design the shop both inside and out. Standing among the glazed façades of the posh boutiques that line the streets of Ginza, an establishment that could have sprung from the pages of Virginia Lee Burton's *The Little House* must come as a great surprise to urban shoppers.

Perforating an attractive façade of black Corten steel are 3000 holes in three diameters: 5, 6 and 7 cm. Filled with a transparent acrylic resin, they provide a glimpse inside the shop. Nakamura says it was not at all easy to plug the holes, which are formed by short metal pipes, while maintaining a smooth overall surface. He used two 4.5-mm-thick panels of Corten steel, welding them into place along with the pipes. After sandblasting the edges of each hole, on both sides of the wall, workers inserted plugs of acrylic resin, chilled to -40° C, into each opening. Once it had thawed

and expanded, the resin filled the holes completely. The job required precision work, as the difference in size between the resin plugs and the metal pipe sleeves meant working with margins of error measured in thousandths of millimetres. A mistake could lead to a plug that expanded to the point of fracture or that was too small to prevent leakage.

How does Nakamura explain his approach to the façade? First of all, he wanted a pure surface only with light, despite the holes. 'I wanted a façade that would stand up to rain, wind and heat without using devices such as drip mouldings to get rid of rainwater.' Conventionally framed windows often detract from the architecture, he says. He was aiming for something different, but he didn't like the idea of using an adhesive to fill the holes with resin. He went to Takahashi Kogyo for help, the company whose welding technology had been crucial in building the kelp-like steel structural columns for Toyo Ito's Mediatheque in Sendai.

'Today's shops provide experiences,' says Nakamura. 'People go shopping to be entertained. The retail designer has to make a space that allows the customer to have fun, while also making her brand-conscious and familiarizing her with the latest collection. It's this kind of thinking that prompts major brands to commission well-known architects. What I've done for Lanvin by replacing the conventional display window with a façade of clear acrylic peepholes is to shrink the shop window to a more interesting size. It invites passers-by to peek through the openings – to play an active role – and it raises their expectations about what's inside.' During the day, the façade is an invitation. After dark, however, an illuminated interior scatters pinpoints of light across the black steel façade, turning it into the 'fabric' of a diamond-embroidered Lanvin evening gown.

Although in many cases the interiors of super-brand boutiques are left to in-house design teams, Nakamura was in charge of creating the atmosphere inside Lanvin as well. Illuminated partly by light that streams in through the acrylic-resin apertures, the three-storey shop envelops customers in an environment that changes along with the natural light that enters from outside. Nakamura took particular interest in the nine fitting rooms, bestowing each with a name – such as Jazz, Chanson, Vivaldi, L'Opera and, Versailles – as well as with theme music and a distinctive scent. Picture frames used on tables, counters and furniture for displaying merchandise reflect the notion of family.

Lanvin

This page
Light enters through 3000 holes, casting
a dotted pattern on the floor and creating
an illusion of small illuminated globes
floating inside the shop.

Floor plans and section
1. Entrance
2. Front display area
3. Womenswear
4. Menswear
5. Cash desk
6. Fitting room
7. Office
8. Stockroom
9. Tailoring room / atelier
10. Salon
11. Staff room

Opposite top
To waterproof the façade with its 3000 perforations, he adapted a method used in shipbuilding. Transparent acrylic tubes-cooled to an extremely low temperature were inserted, while still cold, into holes made in the façade, which consists of sandwich paneling clad in steel sheet. The tubes expanded as they warmed, filling the holes completely.

Opposite bottom
View of the entrance area from inside the boutique; this buffer zone provides space for displaying merchandise not shown in the shop window.

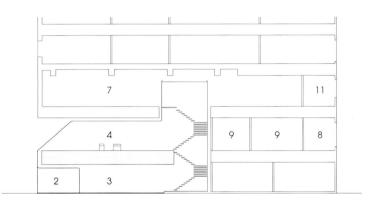

Section AA[1]

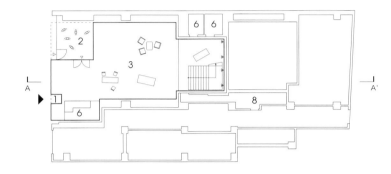

Ground floor

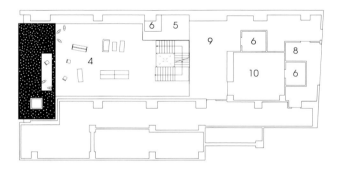

First floor

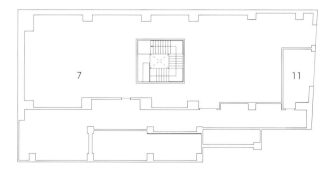

Second floor

This page
The stairway is reflected in a wall of
mirrors in the ground-floor fitting room.
White doors in the red-carpeted space
create an amazing visual effect.

Opposite
Above the gypsum-board ceiling,
mortar and steel plate coated
with fluorocarbon resin coating
3 millimetres thick forms two layers.

Lanvin

Store
Alexander McQueen

Location
Divers

Architect
William Russell

William Russell
'I wanted the customer to step off the
pavement into another world, which they
could take their time to explore.'

Text
Shonquis Moreno

Photography
Frank Oudeman

Architect William Russell and fashion designer Alexander McQueen join forces to produce shops in Milan, London and New York that are both intimate and frostily ethereal.

The architecture of the Alexander McQueen flagship in New York City's Meatpacking District pays homage to the ineluctable power of gravity. Designed by architect William Russell in collaboration with McQueen, himself, it is an architecture of the ceiling which has served as a blueprint for additional shops that have also opened, with negligible contextual variations, in London and Milan.

The structure of the Manhattan shop appears to have derived wholly from an overhead deluge. Columns, dripping heavily from the ceiling, never achieve the floor. Instead they resemble miraculously regular stalactites. Stripped of straight lines, the visual unity of walls and display units gives the impression that everything has formed from dripping condensation originating from a humid pool above and then frozen there, codifying the cool conceit of the fashion industry itself. Columns anchored only to the ceiling create a bright, vacant space, an elegant reticence that is a pleasure to behold. 'The pieces hang naturally, as gravity would intend,' McQueen explains. 'By making the ceiling the focus, I have made a conscious move away from a purely static environment.'

Indeed, it is a glowing, 335-square-metre cathedral of ice that one might imagine moving, imperceptibly, at the pace of a glacier. The walls of the shop are the chill colour of the particularly exquisite and (normally) inaccessible cleavage of a crevasse, a white which, under varying light, can appear opaquely and brightly white or just barely, greenly, sheer. Partly for this reason, this is a retail interior that feels deliciously anomalous on a stickily humid New York summer afternoon. Lit by a single, 30-cm-wide stripe of light embedded in the walls just above head level, the store's illumination becomes a part of the architecture instead of prosthetic to it. Threading through the space, this effulgent collar wraps even interior columns. 'The space was conceived as if carved or hollowed out of a solid block rather than constructed piece by piece,' says Russell. 'Therefore, conceptually there are only two surfaces – the ceiling/wall and the terrazzo carpet. The walls curve seamlessly into the ceiling, which in turn arcs down to form the floating display cabinets as if they are all from the same homogenous block.'

At the heart of the boutique, a structure that the designers call 'the mother ship' holds three fitting rooms lined in a black walnut veneer and couture pieces displayed in a Victorian cut-glass vitrine. This element – with its hemispherical shelves – resembles a windowed eastern mosque in a warmer but equally extreme climate. These niches are carved out of its flanks and into surrounding columns in a staggered, Mondrian-like profusion. The shop feels both well-proportioned and tight-fitting, tailored crisply around its contents. We can picture the garments searing their way into the walls powered by their own fashionable heat. McQueen's creative tapas.

The London shop adds to this New York model a wider frontage, a nautilus-like stair that spirals more elliptically than helically, and vast sculptural columns that punctuate the interior. They are less like stalactites and more like pendulous drops of cream that have, at long last, reached the floor and rippled upwards to form either the seat of a bench or the arcing, tilting hood of a display rack.

The Milan shop loses some of the intimacy of the other two and with it some of their power. Instead, it takes on the grandiosity of the Arctic, evoking polar sky, cliffs sheering off periodically into icebergs, and anorak-clad humans who are properly diminished beside the holy austerity of the landscape. The architecture wins too wholly in Milan and, in this case, becomes more pedestrian.

All in all, however, the Russell-McQueen collaboration has resulted in dynamic spaces that feel unexpectedly contrary, interiors that are both blankly clean and formally rich, massive without losing visitors in volume. The contradictions successfully reflect those within McQueen's brand: tradition balancing modernity, softness balancing sharpness, craft balancing the mass-produced. Echoing a retail trend that has emerged over the past decade, McQueen visitors are allowed to discover the sparsely distributed merchandise. 'I wanted the customer to step off the pavement into another world, which they could take their time to explore,' Russell says. 'Despite the fact that it is a substantial space, I wanted to create a sense of intimacy and ethereality.'

Alexander McQueen

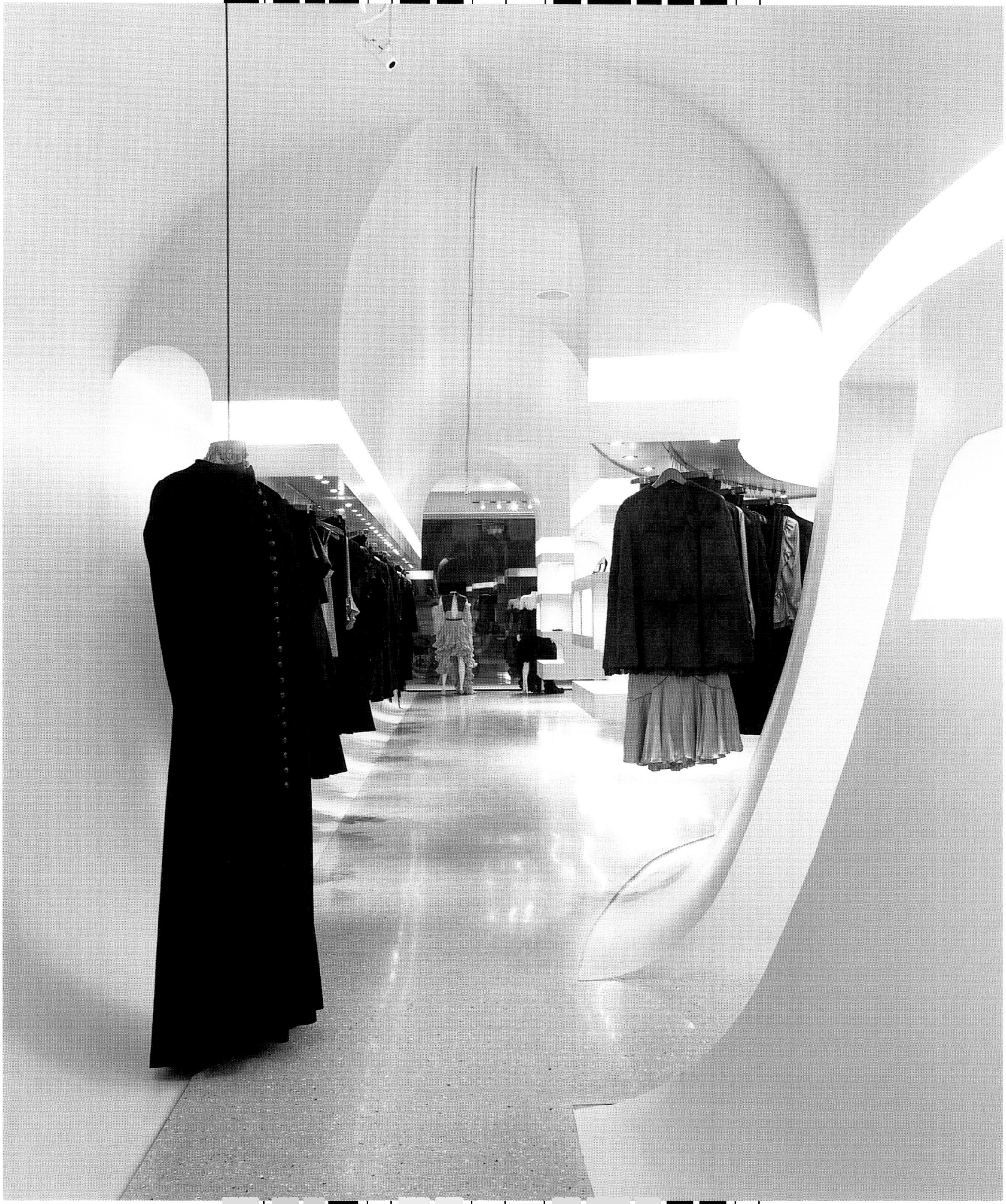

Preceding page
In New York, a sinuous geometry
juxtaposes hard lines and soft curves
in the Alexander McQueen flagship.
Working with McQueen, architect
William Russell suspended garments
just above the terrazzo floor.

Below and opposite
Virtually the whole 335-square-metre
store is one custom-designed element. The
painted-plaster ceiling drops to form hanging units, embedded with a strip of light,
from which accessories and clothes are displayed. As these units are the same colour
as the ceiling, they appear to be carved
from the same homogeneous block.

This page
The Milan McQueen lacks the unusual lighting of the other two shops but is even more monumental formally.

Opposite top and below
The London shop closely parallels the outlet in New York, although the lighting is somewhat more kasbah than crevasse and the floor displays a warmer shade of terrazzo.

Alexander McQueen

Store
TroisO

Location
Tokyo, Japan

Architect
Ito Masaru Design Project / SEI

Masaru Ito
'As contemporary boutique design
becomes more uniform in quality,
creating something that merely looks
good is no longer enough.'

Text
Masaaki Takahashi

Photography
Kozo Takayama

Kitsch, decadence and eroticism are key to the universe that Ito Masaru Design Project / SEI crafted for TroisO in Aoyama, Tokyo.

'When I am designing a boutique, I see myself as an artisan shaping a frame that will set off the tableau of fashion in the store,' says designer Masaru Ito. 'The interior designer and his client, the fashion designer, work together as equals, in a collaboration to mould a single universe.' It should come as no surprise that Ito has been the creative force behind more than a few boutiques and that he counts a number of top designers among his friends.

Tatsuya Okonogi, fashion designer and owner of the boutique in question, is one such friend. As a designer starting out at Issey Miyake's atelier, Okonogi had already made the acquaintance of Masaru Ito. Housed in a former restaurant, TroisO was conceived as a place to display Okonogi's Pantalogue range of stretch pants, garments designed to show off ladies' legs to their best advantage. At first he simply called the shop Pantalogue, but after deciding to use the boutique as a showroom for his entire range of TroisO couture, he gave the shop the same name. Although located in busy Aoyama, a hotbed of fashion, the store is tucked away in a quiet alley just off the Aoyama Dori thoroughfare.

During brainstorming sessions aimed at a concept for the store, Ito and Okonogi hit upon the idea of creating something with the same kitsch and precious appeal of sculpture by Louise Bourgeois. Her immense iron spider, towering delicately over Roppongi Hills Plaza, has fast become a symbol of Roppongi and a well-loved Tokyo landmark. Ito explains that he and Okonogi pictured a space that would 'embody a blend of the same elements of decadence and eroticism that is found in Louise's work'.

As a first step towards the chosen atmosphere of wantonness and decay, the designers called a halt to renovations and stripped away sections of tiling inside and out, revealing the bare concrete underneath. Plans to insert a mezzanine into the high-ceilinged interior were dropped. Instead of installing an aluminium window frame near the entrance, Ito added a feeling of weight by opting for a steel frame. After custom-made tiles had gone up, walls were sprayed silver, with the exception of ten steel-faced tiles scattered randomly across the surface.

Highlighting the interior is a selection of vintage materials, including chandeliers, hefty antique doors that partition the space, and furniture used to display TroisO merchandise. Functioning as a counterpoint to the antique theme is a square, futuristic table in transparent acrylic placed at the centre of the boutique. Rather than leading to a sense of incongruity, the mix of eras and materials only adds to the appeal of the space.

To bring out the desired ambience of tacky affectation, Ito used flowers as a motif throughout the interior. Artificial blooms sit behind the glass surfaces of the cash desk, and a striking floral pattern – partly the work of the owner, it seems – was hand-stencilled onto the bare concrete of the exterior walls. These additions soften the stark impression of the boutique by giving a feminine touch to what had been a fairly masculine space.

Towards the rear of the store, three side-by-side doors are not quite what they seem. The two outer doors, made to look like entrances to toilets, actually lead to men's and women's fitting rooms, while the middle door opens to disclose nothing more than the curious shopper herself, reflected in a full-length mirror. Another such witty trick, of which there are many at TroisO, is the design of wall sconces in the form of mannequins' hands. Ito has hidden items both cute and strange all over the shop. Even the inclusion of a glowing Casper doll from one of his excursions is calculated to spark conversation between staff and clientele.

Painted white, the real rest room features yet more hands reaching out from the rear wall. These hold business cards, flyers and other notices, transforming the surface into a message board. TroisO is also used as an event space and a gallery, and the glass-walled entrance area acts not only as a show window for goods displayed on chairs, but also as a spot for announcing upcoming events.

'As contemporary boutique design becomes more uniform in quality, creating something that merely looks good is no longer enough,' says Ito. In the designer's quest to amuse as well as to enchant, he has provided visitors with a multitude of devices that give a little something extra in the way of visual entertainment. 'The world of fashion is going to keep on changing,' he continues. 'Because each dress code is born of a certain social context, it's a code that means something only within the philosophical framework of a specific time period. When fashions are mixed together, as they are today, things get increasingly diverse and complex in a way that allows you to subvert the very meaning of "fashion code". There's a need to reflect on how these codes influence spatial design, in terms of what's on show, as well as of what's hidden.'

This page
After stripping the tiled walls of the former restaurant, Ito Masaru Design Project / SEI and fashion designer Tatsuya Okonogi brought the bare concrete to life by spray-painting the surface with a floral pattern.

Right
Highlighting the heart of the store
is a fusion of acrylic and antique doors.

Opposite top
Artificial blossoms add colour to
the glass-fronted cash desk.

Opposite bottom
Without a mezzanine, the retail interior is
a high-ceilinged, single-level space.

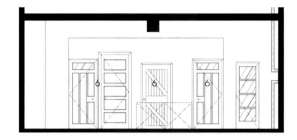

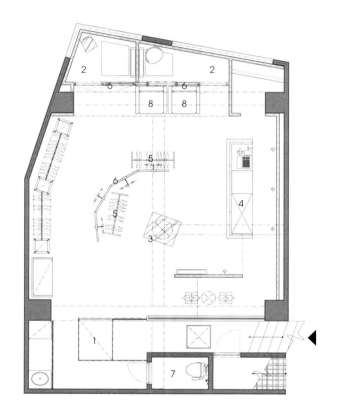

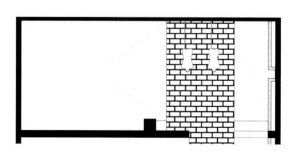

Store
Albrecht 7

Location
Graz, Austria

Architect
PURPUR.ARCHITEKTUR

ChristianToedtling
'In the showcase, the shoes are bedded
on pillows almost like jewels, heroizing an
object of utility as luxury.'

Text
Matthew Stewart

Photography
Hertha Hurnaus

Footwear freaks can indulge their fantasy with shapely stilettos, sandals and slip-ons inside a slick shoebox in Graz by Purpur.Architektur.

When opposition forces stumbled onto Imelda Marcos's collection of more than 3000 pairs of shoes (size 8½), true shoe aficionados everywhere felt secret pangs of empathy; like Marcos, they could see the uniqueness and importance of every single pair. Ditto *Sex and the City*'s Carrie Bradshaw, who calculated the value of her collection of Manolo Blahniks to be $40,000, all amassed on a writer's paltry salary. What is it about shoes that captures the imagination of fashion watchers in such a primal way? Rivalled perhaps only by handbags, shoes have a totemic power to establish status and position the wearer, a power as seductive as it is mysterious. A shoe can define a moment. Creating the right environment in which to retail footwear is a matter of creating something au courant but resistant to the tug of trends, something able to act as a blank canvas for hundreds of bright-coloured, tasselled, feathered, beaded and otherwise-adorned fetish objects. Albrecht 7, a shoe shop in Graz, Austria, is just such an environment. Tucked away in a galleria space off a pedestrian strip linking Graz's public-transport hub with the main town square, the footwear boutique designed by Purpur.Architektur is a structurally engaging space that doesn't upstage the elegant wares within.

In developing Albrecht 7, Purpur.Architektur's design team looked at the context of the shop from a bird's-eye view. To generate the desired 'self-confident stance in urban space', as they describe their goal, the designers employed a bold gesture at street level to distinguish this store, housed in a 250-year-old building, from those surrounding it. They broke the plane of the glazing along the pavement façade of the boutique with a low-slung rectangular box which pushes through to the inside of the store.

Embedded with several coloured-Plexiglas display units along the pavement side, the box grabs the attention of passers-by while obstructing the view below eye level of the interior within, which is visible only through the glass plane that forms a thin seam above the display case and the entry doors on both sides. Instead, visual attention comes to rest on the select few shoes on display. 'In the showcase, the shoes are bedded on pillows almost like jewels, heroizing an object of utility as luxury,' explains Christian Toedtling of Purpur.Architektur. Inside the store, the back of the box becomes a monumental piece of furniture lined with dozens of drawers that contain Albrecht 7's stock of shoes. A sleek update of an apothecary cabinet, the anthracite-faced wall of drawers quietly screens out above-eye-level activity on the street outside. Thanks to the

showcase, says Toedtling, 'customers are immersed in the very limited intimate space'. Because it breaks the plane of the façade (where we typically understand the division of shop and street to lie) and reads as a single element existing partly within the shop and partly on the street, the showcase simultaneously creates and unites separate zones.

Its freestanding nature also serves as a handy and harmonious way to introduce strong new design moves into the historical building. Furthermore, the awkwardly angled floor plan and several ceiling protrusions (which seem to come bundled with these types of antiquated spaces) required this ingenuity of thought regarding decoration and form. Of course, for Purpur.Architektur, which has designed three other boutiques with the same client, all in the area, this thinking has become second nature.

A similar sort of dexterity is visible in the second major element the design team introduced: an angular folded display system comprising a steel frame covered in white fabric. Cantilevered glass shelves hang off the crystalline volume displaying the merchandise, while portions of the same element jut out to serve as seating areas for customers trying on shoes. Appearing to float in space, the complex illuminated form contrasts starkly with the smooth dark plane of the showcase box, while deftly handling the difficult shape of the ceiling. Mirrored walls on both sides visually extend the structure, as well as the strip of space between it and the drawer wall, to infinity, making the 70-sq-m shop feel markedly larger than it actually is.

These form-gestures are strong enough to define the interior of the boutique and engage the street, but they do not challenge the internal skin of the location. The designers simply polished the concrete on ceilings and floor, and even embellished the classical look with a gold and crystal chandelier. Of course, it goes without saying that an old inner-city property such as this is a listed building, a status that necessitated these types of detached spatial interventions.

The strong positioning of the shop in relation to the street, as well as its delicately crafted internal environment, demonstrates Purpur.Architektur's multidisciplinary scope, which reaches well beyond the field of retail. 'The starting point in creating the space was not a real image or a special vision of the ideal shop,' says Toedtling. Instead, the solution greeted challenges on scales both macro and micro, from questions posed by the urban situation to those at the product level, and drew inspiration, he says, from the 'irony of attaching such great importance to fashion accessories'. Success on all levels adds up to a small shop that makes a big impression.

Preceding page
Mirrors at either end of the shop visually
stretch the narrow, efficient space into
infinity. The bright crystalline form of the
steel and fabric display structure toys
withthe wall and ceiling boundaries of
the interior.

Floor plan and elevation
1. Entrance
2. Shop window area
3. Stock drawers
4. Display system
5. Rear area

Opposite
The designers at Purpur.Architektur bridge
the divide between street and shop interior
by breaking the plane of glazing with
a multifunctional building unit. Coloured
Plexiglas boxes within this unit display a
selection of merchandise.

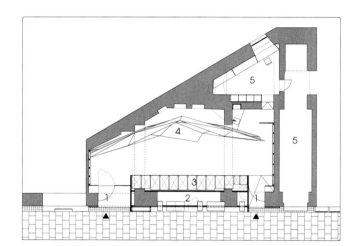

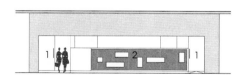

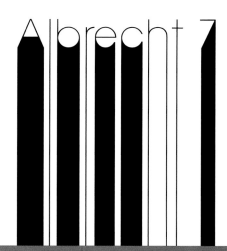

Albrecht 7

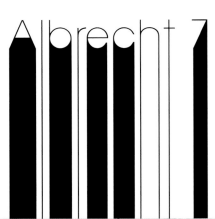

Albrecht 7

Below and opposite
Anthracite-faced drawers, a nod
to the old-fashioned apothecary,
contain the entire stock of the shop.

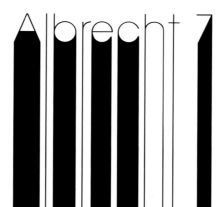

Albrecht 7

Store
Le Ciel Bleu

Location
Kobe, Japan

Architect
Keiko + Manabu Uchiyama

Keiko Uchiyama
'Shops are not just boxes for displaying
merchandise. They are more like magnified
images of merchandise.'

Text
Masaaki Takahashi

Photography
Nobuaki Nakagawa

Keiko + Manabu Uchiyama's design for Le Ciel Bleu in Kobe led to an unexpected dialogue between the fashionable merchandise and its architectural surroundings.

Having originated in Kobe, Le Ciel Bleu is popular all over Japan, but especially in the Kansai region. In an almost unheard-of move, the company once responded to the ever-increasing demand from customers outside its target area by actually reducing the number of stores. Later, however, a new business plan led to a revival of the brand, which included the opening of a flagship store at the very heart of Kobe's business district, close to Sannomiya Station. The project also included the remodelling of Le Ciel Bleu's sister brand, Restir, as both labels are part of the same company. A French designer brought in to create the retail concept was originally assisted by a Japanese colleague, Keiko Uchiyama, who was ultimately entrusted with the design of the flagship store in Kobe together with Manabu. They were given this responsibility by the president of Le Ciel Bleu's parent company, who had seen the work of both.

In 1868, Kobe opened its port to foreign trade, a decision that attracted people from all over the world and turned the city into an international hub of commerce. Many foreigners settled in a part of town whose streets were soon lined with 19th-century European-style mansions – an area that eventually evolved into a popular tourist spot. Strict building regulations were put in place to preserve the authenticity of this historical zone. Preservation also meant stagnation, however, and the earthquake that destroyed much of Kobe in 1995 did not help matters. The brief for the new store, which is located close to this commercial area, called for an eye-catching design that would play a role in a revitalization project targeting this area.

The existing 40-year-old building comprises four narrow floors, each with a floor area of only 75 square metres. Situated on a street corner, the building has two exterior walls in full view of both pedestrians and motorists. The Uchiyama's used this 'double exposure' to good effect by creating a glittering surface across the face of the entire building. Cladding the façade are reflective, stainless-steel panels alight with blue LEDs set into holes 6 cm deep. In considering the reputation that Le Ciel Bleu enjoys throughout Kobe, they rejected the idea of a logo or even a shop window. 'Shops are not just boxes for displaying merchandise,' Keiko says. 'They are more like magnified images of merchandise.' She believed that

everyone in the city would recognize the building itself – blue lights beckoning – as the home of Le Ciel Bleu. 'Designing shop windows is difficult, because they always have to attract attention,' she continues. 'As far as I can see, not many of them are exceptionally well done.'

They positioned the ground-floor entrance area at right angles to the street. With only one stairway leading from floor to floor in the narrow building, the Uchiyama's gave high priority to a plan for good circulation. The solution was to keep the stairway free of objects wherever possible. Shoppers entering at ground level feel as though they are in a gallery. To accentuate this concept, the designer created frames illuminated by bright light for displaying products as though they are works of art. Fashion designers at Le Ciel Bleu fell in love with the idea, which even prompted them to create new merchandise to match the ambience and colour scheme of the refurbished interior. On the first floor, which greets the visitor with a great many garments on hangers, the Uchiyama's wanted to achieve a clean, uncluttered look. Focusing on the design of the floor to get the desired result, they opted for a surface covered with sheets of film printed with graphics, taking their cue from an advertising strategy used in recent years on the floors of Japanese train and metro stations. Keiko and Manabu chose an enlarged black-and-white image of the sparkling ripples of the ocean off Kobe at sunset and had printers adjust the brightness of the graphic design. Boxy fixtures (each 300 x 80 cm) that hang from the ceiling and mirrors reflect the surface of the floor, making the space seem larger and more attractive. They explain that the treatment of this area transformed a rather two-dimensional environment into a three-dimensional shopping experience.

The second floor accommodates a sister outlet, which they have injected with a sense of privacy without removing its function as a boutique. It can be described as an Alice-in-Wonderland walk-in closet that invites customers to shop in luxurious surroundings.

Each floor has a distinctively designed fitting room. Here, as elsewhere in the building, Keiko and Manabu had the full cooperation of the people at Le Ciel Bleu. 'There was a lot of communication between us and the brand's designers,' Keiko says. 'At one point we made a joint decision to use a see-through curtain made of five different materials. Collaborating with them – even on the fine points – made the job go well.'

Le Ciel Bleu

Preceding page
Cladding the façade are reflective, stainless-steel panels alight with blue LEDs set into holes 6 cm deep. Uchiyama believed that everyone in the city would recognize the building itself – blue lights beckoning – as the home of Le Ciel Bleu.

This page
On the first floor, a great many garments on hangers greets the visitor with a clean, uncluttered look. The design of the floor is an enlarged black-and-white image of the sparkling ripples of the ocean off Kobe at sunset. Boxy fixtures (each 300 x 80 cm) and mirrors that hang from the ceiling reflect the surface of the floor, making the space seem larger and more attractive.

Opposite bottom
Subdued interior lighting accentuates merchandise in the display frames and, combined with other light sources, makes the framed products appear to be two-dimensional – like a painting.

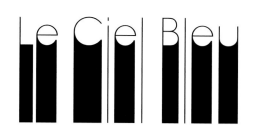

Le Ciel Bleu

Floor plan
1. Cash desk
2. Display frames
3. Hanging display
4. Stairs
5. Stockroom

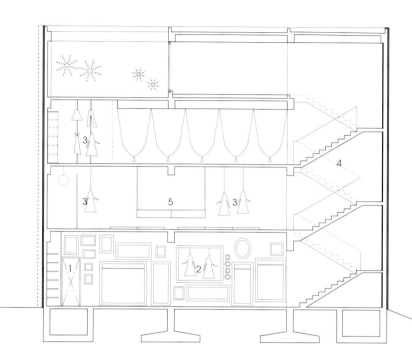

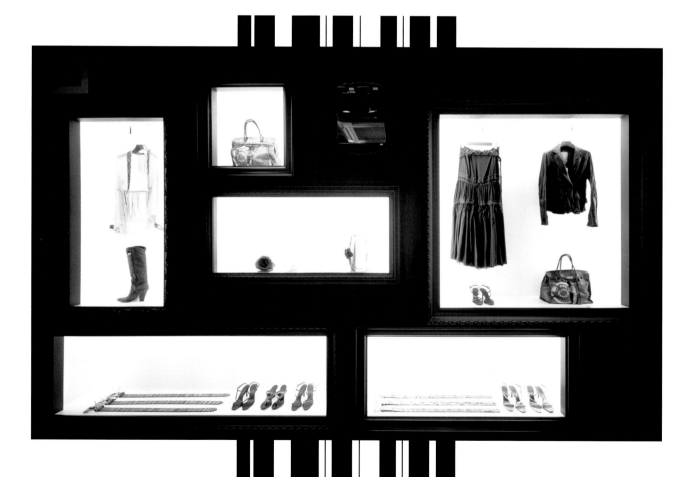

Opposite bottom
The second floor resembles a secret closet that could have been plucked from the pages of Alice's Adventures in Wonderland.

Opposite top
Restir, a sister outlet of Le Ciel Bleu, occupies the second floor, a space characterized by gently draped black-lace curtains.

This page
Highlighting the stairway to the second floor is shiny wall panelling adorned with graphic images.

Store
Missoni

Location
Antwerp, Belgium

Architect
B-architecten

Evert Crols
'Where do you draw the line between the
display of merchandise and the creation
of a concept?'

Text
Joeri Bruyninckx

Photography
Vercruysse & Dujardin

In Antwerp, the two faces of a boutique for Italian fashion label Missoni pay tribute to B-Architecten's big-impact, low-budget approach to retail design.

September 2005 marked the moment that shoppers on Frankrijklei, a thoroughfare at the commercial centre of fashion-conscious Antwerp, were first confronted with a surprising sight. At the end of a street whose countless display windows vie for the attention of passers-by is the glazed façade of the Missoni boutique. The Italian label looks out at the world in refreshing style. Not only because its largely glazed corner location appears to vanish in thin air, but also and primarily because Missoni's window presents greenery rather than garments. The work of Antwerp-based B-architecten, the boutique illustrates the innovative approach with which this team continually reinvents both the existing environment and itself. The objective is to make the greatest impact on the lowest budget.

Missoni's new interior began with a corner office building designed by Antwerp architect Leon Stijnen in the 1960s: an undeniable testament to the splendour of modernist linearity, raw concrete construction and spacious glazed façades. Filled with the frivolous zig-zags and whimsical patterns of the Missoni collection, however, the space becomes a stripy poetic composition of lines. 'The type of building was a vital factor in our design of the interior,' says Evert Crols of B-architecten. And building and interior do seem to be made for each other.

B-architecten tries to gear its interior designs to site, merchandise and clientele, even though 'the three elements often differ from one another in the extreme', according to Crols. 'And that demands the appropriate response.' He mentions the existing glass walls, which connect two sides of the shop with the street and with passers-by, and which would seem to offer a perfect basis for the design of a boutique. Here, however, the walls were more challenge than reward. Neither Missoni nor its clientele associate the brand with come-hither display windows brimming with merchandise. Of course, a retail interior should be aimed at intriguing window-shoppers and making them potential customers. 'But when you fill the display window from top to bottom, you quickly relinquish the qualities of that space,' Crols continues. As an architect, he asks himself: 'Where do you draw the line between the display of merchandise and the creation of a concept?'

Consequently, the design of the boutique is an exercise in balance that comprises the transparency of the building, the visibility of the shop from the street and the sense of intimacy required for an exclusive interior. B-architecten is keen to make use of all existing elements. Here, a barrier of plants shields customers and retail space from the busy traffic artery outside – the window area was originally designed to support a winter garden – while the immense windows around the corner, rising from waist height, offer a full view of the interior. It's something like the game of hide-and-seek: one window nearly conceals the space behind it, while the other bravely exposes the entire shop. And from both angles passers-by catch sight of a striking element whose presence overpowers the screen of green, as well as the mannequins around the corner, rousing the curiosity of all who glance at these façades. The ceiling inside the shop is completely covered by a grid of large inflatable balls that appear to cast an atmospheric light on the interior. Illumination so bright that in the early evening passers-by moved by the magic of the lighting are drawn into a shop they might have been able to resist earlier in the day.

And there you have it: bright orbs, big impact, low budget. An idea as simple as it is brilliant. The balls lower the high 'office ceiling' and their compact arrangement hides a series of ordinary fluorescent bulbs. The ceiling is one of the architects' few conspicuous interventions. 'Too many ideas lead to nothing but fragmentation,' says Crols, implying the loss of an effectual design language. Their aim was 'to develop a good idea as strongly, as extremely and, in any case, as consistently as possible' in order to create an element that could support the entire interior. Remarkably, the antithesis between a down-to-earth approach and a seemingly light-as-air idea is not an antithesis at all and, in practice, works very well. Little was done to the existing interior: the floors were left intact and the concrete walls touched up and, at certain places, covered with an inexpensive but flattering fabric. The same rule that applied to the existing '60s furnishings in a boutique for Veronique Branquinho and in a parking garage for Walter Van Beirendonck – earlier projects by B-architecten for major fashion designers – applied here, too: if it's good, don't change it.

More than anything else, the sober interior provides a calm backdrop for Missoni's colourful, extrovert apparel. The use of curtains from the Missoni Home Collection contributes to a display system that allows garments to 'float in space' and hence to determine the appearance of the interior. Collections change with the seasons, and the look of the space changes along with them. It's a uniform environment that subtly blurs the line between collection and interior, which are different but complementary. The shop illustrates B-architecten's ideology: reinforce your ideas throughout the design process and they will eventually . . . float.

Preceding page
The transparency and location of the building were vital in determining the retail concept. The resulting combination of visibility and invisibility rouses curiosity.

Below
Taking a matter-of-fact approach to the interior, B-architecten created a display system featuring hooks and transparent fishing line that inconspicuously vanishes between the Missoni curtains, leaving garments to float in midair.

Opposite
A mix of the straight lines that characterize the concrete structure and the meandering lines of the display installation generates a sense of tension in the interior. By dressing the shop in the Missoni Home Collection, which changes with the seasons, the architects provided the fashion brand with an interior that wears a brand-new look from time to time.

Missoni

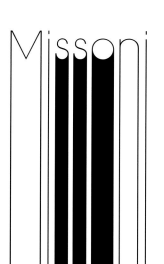

Missoni

Opposite
An inflatable ball in the fitting room refers to the ball-covered ceiling. An inexpensive white tablecloth with a geometric motif accentuates walls and doors.

Below
Little has been done to modify the existing interior. Granite floors have been maintained, as have hidden radiators. The busy thoroughfare outside is partially hidden from view by a 'winter garden'.

Store
Firetrap

Location
London, England

Architect
Brinkworth

Kevin Brennan
'We convinced the client that sometimes
if you want to be somebody, you have
to upset somebody.'

Text
Shonquis Moreno

Photography
Lara Gosling and
Louise Melchior

London-based Brinkworth turns the urban environment into a retail space, pissing off local authorities, preserving street archaeology and embracing grass-roots expression in the process.

Indians on the plains had smoke signals, Victorians had the telegraph, and city kids today have graffiti and flyposting. Enshrining the youthful compulsion towards self-expression, promiscuous communications and occasional bad behaviour is Firetrap, a shop that opened in the autumn of 2004 as the company's first standalone store.

The architects convinced their client that sharing the culture and tools of groups native to the street could give the label credibility. 'We looked at the client's advertising campaigns and their website and understood the label as trying to tap into an urban vibe,' says Brinkworth design director Kevin Brennan. 'The images they were using were very gritty and urban, so we created a 3-D look out of what Firetrap was trying to achieve in a 2-D medium.' To bring the street in from the street, Brinkworth used austere, street-related materials: concrete, stone, plywood, steel, graffiti, billboards and posters. Indeed, Brinkworth imagined the shop as 'a living billboard'. Posters can be changed out to keep up with trends in pop culture, from film and music to art and fashion.

Brinkworth worked with a London company called Diabolical Liberties, the UK's leading ambient communications agency, to create the posters that paper the walls of the store. 'Flyposting is a subject that we've been interested in for a long time,' explains Brennan. 'It's almost like civil disobedience.' Unless Londoners have got loads of money, there's little outlet for posting information on the street. In an effort to clean up the city, the Camden Council (along with other borough councils) has made it illegal to advertise a local event with posters. Brinkworth's design for Firetrap taps into the idea that the independence of people to convey information in public places is being threatened. The location of the store in Covent Garden is on the front line of the controversy. 'We convinced the client that sometimes if you want to be somebody, you have to upset somebody,' says Brennan. 'The clientele Firetrap is looking for is going to respect them for that.'

With seemingly acrobatic inspiration, the designers managed to squeeze the most out of a diminutive site (together, ground floor and basement areas totalled only 93 square metres) and to negotiate a myriad of regulations. To work around the limitations, they turned the ground floor into a floating mezzanine with the use of glass pavement blocks. Shoppers enter the space at the corner, where a graded ramp ascends to the 93-square-metre concrete-and-glass floor plate. This floor-cum-canopy allows passers-by to see 'the denim pool' – the jeans section of the 59-square-metre basement area, with its black-stone flooring – while doubling the height of the lower level and providing display space along Earlham Street for visual merchandising and art shows. The street outside continues in the interior, where the back of a large billboard is clad in Douglas fir. Bespoke stainless-steel furniture and Georgian wired glass are reflected in a high-gloss Barrisol ceiling. Backing the raw wooden stairway that leads to the basement is a tilted black-glass wall pierced by a window with a view of a graffiti 'masterpiece'.

When the client took over the site, Brinkworth discovered a piece created by local graffiti artist INSA. Around the time he had been showing work at an exhibition down the road, the street artist had broken into the building to create a black-and-white mural. The architects preserved it and placed it behind a black glass wall. 'It was about contemporary archaeology,' Brennan says. 'It was about not covering it up, but taking it on.' They also commissioned artist Louise Melchior to take stark black-and-white photographs of public conveniences – urinals, a record shop, city buses – which were made into the digital-photographic wallpaper that highlights the fitting rooms, each of which represents a different street environment: one is a public toilet, another a record store. 'It wasn't a precious project,' says Brennan. 'We said, "Let's get people in to play," and it set the mood for the opening. Shops don't start their life until they open. When Firetrap opened, it was almost as if it had been around for a long time. It felt established.'

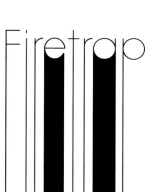

Firetrap

Below
To tap into urban youth culture,
Brinkworth used fly posters to make
the Firetrap façade a nearly seamless
continuation of the street.

Firetrap
"THE BAND THAT RE-INVENTED PUNK...TWICE." 8/10
"EXHILARATING"
"AN AUDACIOUS ARTISTIC
GREEN DAY
PRESENTS
american
THE ALBUM
WWW.GREENDAY.COM
TYPICAL ME
INCLUDES THE UNDERGROUND SMASH P'S & Q'S
FEEDER
PUSHING THE SENSES
THE NEW ALBUM
Ferdinand
SING SING
FIRETRAP
STONEBRIDGE
2CD Deluxe Edition
Out 24.01.05
good for nothing
LANGUAGE
KAISER CHIEFS
A NEW SINGLE
OUT ON FEB 21st
MYLO
FIRETRAP
2CD Deluxe Edition
Out 24.01.05

Firetrap

Left
The architects envisioned the shop as a 'living billboard'. They worked with Diabolical Liberties, the UK's leading ambient communications agency, to collage the posters.

Floor plans
1. Entrance
2. Shop-window display
3. Retail area
4. Display units
5. Cash desk

6. Fly-poster wall
7. Shoe area
8. Jeans wall
9. Fitting room
10. Rear area

Opposite
The design makes the most of a tiny site and deftly negotiates a myriad of regulations. Brinkworth turned the ground floor into a floating mezzanine using glass pavement blocks. The canopy gives shoppers a view onto 'the denim pool' and doubles the height of the lower floor.

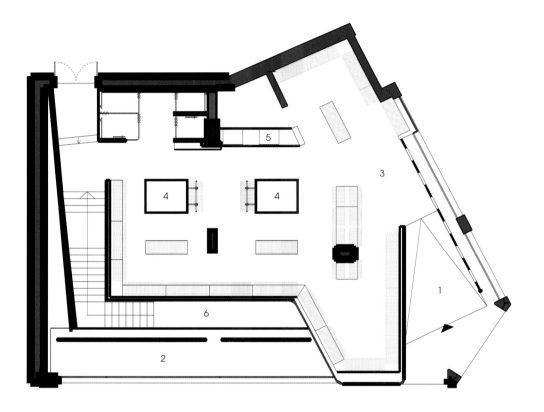

Ground floor

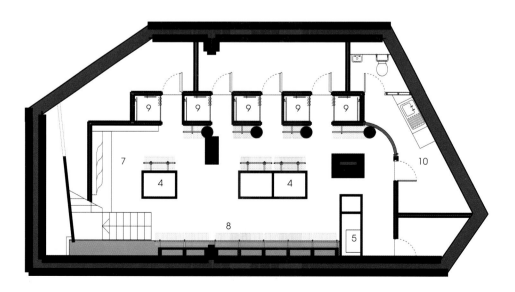

Basement

Firetrap

Store
Restir

Location
Kobe, Japan

Architect
Laur Meyrieux

Shoppers appear to have discovered a
secret place where fantasies play out in
a ritualized choreography

Text
Shonquis Moreno

Photography
Kozo Takayama

It's Laur Meyrieux's deft combination of austerity, dim lighting, old-world opulence and comfort that make Kobe's Restir a place out of time – and a place that stirs the emotions.

Kobe's Restir boutique, designed by Tokyo-based Frenchwoman Laur Meyrieux, follows on the heels of a sister shop in Tokyo's tony Ginza neighbourhood, while having the distinction of being almost twice the size. For all the emphasis the Japanese give to trendiness and all the energy the fashion industry devotes to cultivating an intriguingly mercurial temperament, Restir has the distinction of looking like a durable environment.

A fascinating juxtaposition of details and the shop's chiaroscuro palette are foreshadowed by a dark, oversized façade – its glazing clad in a sheer black film – unexpectedly paired with a sweetly florid, delicately thread-like logo. (The company's graphic design has also undergone renovation, a collaboration between Meyrieux and Mote Sinabel.) Taking her inspiration from a photography studio, Meyrieux has also given black dominion over the interior of the 950-square-metre shop. Banisters, ceiling-hung spotlights and light stands are all fruits of the notion that light can be best understood in its (strategically planned) absence. The conspicuous clutter of theatre lights tracked on the ceiling above table-like displays of garments contrasts with the sleek minimalism of the tables themselves. The lighting is laser-focused, and its effect is powerful: it establishes an expectant, sensual moodiness and brings together a red-light-district cloak of darkness and the product considered most desirable, most sublime. Shoppers appear to have discovered a secret place where fantasies play out in a ritualized choreography, as fantasies do in the house of masked women that mesmerizes the viewing audience in Stanley Kubrick's *Eyes Wide Shut*. Restir is a place where, momentarily, we are elevated by our own desires.

And Meyrieux is an expert when it comes to inducing a hunger for more. Targeting the highest-end clientele, the shop has two retail floors, a bar/lounge and a pair of luxurious VIP rooms, one at each level. The designer 'drew' different patterns on the ceilings of each room using white LED lights that are reflected in the surrounding glass walls. The LEDs are Meyrieux's answer to illuminating a lounge area furnished with a sofa and a table. The LED drawings serve as a flattened, contemporary version of the classic chandelier. Meyrieux inserted a VIP room into the very centre of the second floor, defining its boundaries with a glass wall backed with a black film

that generates reflections throughout the space. This room-within-a-room resembles a vast shop window of the type seen at posh department stores; here, however, both custom mannequins and clients are on display.

'Because the space is bigger than what we had to work with in Ginza,' says Meyrieux, 'I wanted a layout that would make clients feel as if they are in a private, exclusive environment.' She rejected the notion of something 'visually big like a department store'. The bar and lounge area feels even more intimate than the rest, with its black vinyl floor, black carpeting beneath black leather furniture, black painted and papered walls, and black-lacquered bar counter. Certain elements have been articulated with a hairline of metallic gold paint, the effect of which is carefully brightened and heightened by the lights.

Layered over the shadowy bits of the shop are decadent materials that include leather, horsehair, crocodile, high-gloss or matte paint, and transparent film. Against one wall a mural features a flower pattern and women's faces. The mural, with its obvious reference to classical art, has a pixelated effect that is roughly the quality of newsprint. The union of the frieze, the antique-looking wallpapers and pendant lamps wrapped in Renaissance art with canvases of colour-washed neon (the colour of which will change seasonally), pragmatically mobile furniture and mirrored display plinths culminates in an artful result that was not at all easy to achieve. Every bit of Restir looks remixed. The space is a nuanced synthesis of geographies and eras that removes visitors from both time and place. What could be more modern and more desirable?

This page
Meyrieux inserted a VIP room into the
centre of the second floor, defining its
boundaries with a glass wall backed with
a black film that generates reflections
throughout the space.

53

Opposite top
Cylindrical pendant lamps draw on
classical references: in this case, a
Renaissance painting of Botticelli's
The Birth of Venus.

Opposite bottom
Despite the generous size of the space,
Meyrieux's well-considered floor plan
heightens the illusion of an intimate interior
and avoids the generic volumes of the
department store.

Floor plans
1. Shop window area
2. Cash desk
3. Movable
display system
4. VIP room
5. Lounge
6. Bar counter
7. Fitting room
8. Stockroom

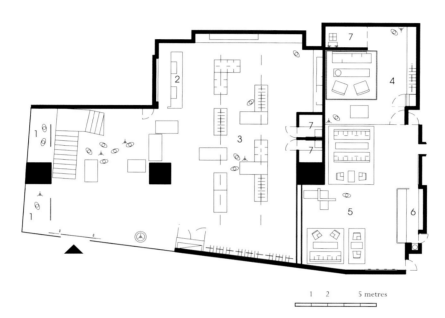

1   2   5 metres

Ground floor

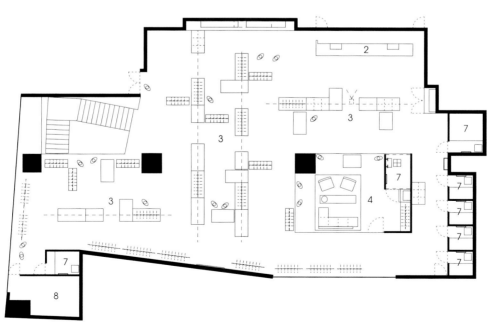

First floor

This page
Restir's spare, strategic use of light both obscures and reveals the merchandise in a moodily seductive way. Each mobile vignette becomes a discovery, even though it is displayed in plain sight.

Below
A canvas of coloured light accents the
darkness and changes with the season or
at the whim of store managers.

Store
Hussein Chalayan

Location
Tokyo, Japan

Architect
Block Architecture

The rhythmic pattern of poles and ropes might remind shoppers of a *Shinto* ritual that takes place on building sites before construction work begins.

Text
Masaaki Takahashi

Photography
Leon Chew

The Cypriot roots of fashion designer Hussein Chalayan play an important role in the interior of his Tokyo outlet, a design by London-based Block Architecture.

Despite his Mediterranean heritage and close ties with the UK, when it came to opening a boutique of his own, Hussein Chalayan headed straight for Tokyo. Arguably the individual with the most overtly philosophical leanings of the designers to exhibit at the Paris collections, Chalayan had strong ideas about the look of his new undertaking. The result of his collaboration with Block Architecture of London is a shop interior that epitomizes the fashion designer's distinctive vision transposed onto a Japanese context.

Born in Nicosia in 1970, ten years after Cyprus gained its independence from British rule, Chalayan was four when the island nation was invaded by Turkey and split in two, with the Islamic population in control of the north and Cypriots of Greek descent occupying the south. At the age of 12, he emigrated with his father to the UK. His early preference for architecture gradually evolved into an even greater interest in fashion as he began to see clothing as architecture on a more intimate scale. To further validate his degree from London's prestigious Central Saint Martins College of Art & Design, at the school's graduation show the young designer presented an astonishing series of garments that had been buried underground for two months. The entire collection was bought up by Browns, the famous London boutique, which gave his fashions pride of place in its window display for the season.

In 1994, only a year after graduating, Chalayan launched his eponymous brand. He has taken part in every major Paris fashion event since the Spring/Summer Show in 2002. His designs often contain architectural references and reveal glimpses of his philosophical bent – the same references and glimpses that appear in the design of his flagship store.

The retail concept is 'omnipresence'. The design incorporates elements that suggest Chalayan's Cypriot roots, while also exhibiting structural components based on the theme of aviation. The gently sloping ramp leading from the door into the women's section of the boutique is patterned with red and black triangles, their narrow, tessellated forms reminiscent of a backgammon board. This is the first in a series of references to Chalayan's background and his continued engagement with the country of his birth. One display area consists of a flush-fitting, two-storey-high surface of steel panels modelled on the fuselage of an aeroplane, complete with flaps

that open to form shelves. The panelled wall extends into the upstairs' space, thus working as a connecting feature that unites the two floors. Directly opposite the entrance is a wall of display boxes, labelled in the manner of a filing system and filled with T-shirts from Chalayan's well-known Airmail range. Provided with built-in lighting, the wall was designed with traditional post-office pigeonholes in mind to reinforce the notion of 'airmail'.

The ground floor was designed along the lines of a garden in Cyprus. Olive trees planted under the wooden floor appear to grow directly out of its herringbone surface. Light bulbs dangling from the ceiling shine as brightly as the fierce Mediterranean sun. Posts marching in rows across the floor are connected by smooth lengths of rope. Specially designed hangers transform this 'washline' installation into a display for Chalayan's creations. Holes sunk into the parquet at regular intervals allow the configuration of these poles to be changed in an instant, making for a highly adaptable display. Spotting the rhythmic pattern of poles and ropes, some Japanese shoppers might be reminded of a *Shinto* observance that takes place on building sites before construction work begins. The ritual begins when four slender bamboo poles are thrust into the ground and connected by rope to form a square, in preparation for a religious ceremony held to purify the site.

On a landing halfway up the stairs leading to menswear, a large blackboard displays a message from Chalayan in both Japanese and English. A new welcoming note from the fashion designer introduces each season of the year. At the centre of the upper level, chairs made of wood imported from Cyprus are arranged in rows which recall the outdoor-movie theatres that the designer loved as a child. Films shown here fall into one of two categories: short features directed by Hussein or images of his collections. Display units looking very much like flight attendants' carts line one side of the room, while blinds suggesting an airport shade the windows on both floors. Designer Zoe Smith of Block Architecture says they wanted to create a space with a 'juxtaposition of the modern against the classic', one imbued with 'a sense of timelessness and charm'.

The shop is located in Daikanyama, an up-market section of Tokyo populated by embassies and not a few exclusive boutiques. The area is also home to Hillside Terrace, a mixed-use complex designed by celebrated architect Maki Fumihiko. Rather than taking centre stage in this fashion wonderland, however, Hussein Chalayan's shop is found down a side street on the bottom two floors of a vaguely neoclassical building.

Hussein Chalayan

Preceding page
Apparel is presented on clotheslines,
while display cases suggest traditional
post-office pigeonholes.

Floor plans
1. Entrance
2. Retail area
3. Cash desk
4. Olive tree
5. Hanging display
6. Display cabinet
7. Trolley for tea and coffee
8. Fitting room
9. Stockroom
10. Rear area

Opposite
Block Architecture wanted the ground-floor
womenswear department to exude the
air of a Cypriot garden. The backgammon-
board pattern of the entrance ramp hints
at border disputes betweennations.

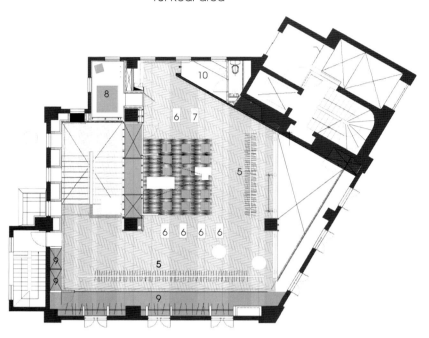

First floor

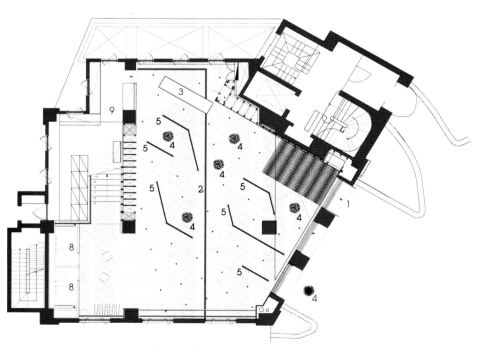

Ground floor

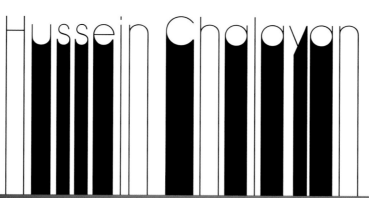

Hussein Chalayan

Opposite top
The stairway to the first floor. On the landing wall, Chalayan's handwritten message addresses visitors in both English and Japanese.

Opposite bottom
An area at the centre of the menswear department on the upper level recalls Cypriot outdoor-movie theatres of the past, complete with chairs made of wood shipped to Japan from Cyprus.

Below
The double-height entrance has the appearance of an aircraft, with stowaway shelves that fit into the walls like in-flight dining trays. Flooring throughout the interior is made from plywood panels laid in a traditional herringbone pattern.

Store
Little Red Riding Hood

Location
Berlin, Germany

Architect
Corneille Uedingslohmann
Architekten

Yves Corneille
'What we created for Little Red Riding
Hood is really a made-to-measure interior.'

Text
Brigitte van Mechelen

Photography
Joachim Wagner

Step into the light-filled interior of Little Red Riding Hood in Berlin, where CUE Architekten moved beyond fairy tales and fashion to express a creative philosophy.

It all began with display tables that Corneille Uedingslohmann Architekten (CUE Architekten) of Cologne developed for Olymp & Hades, a shop in Dortmund, Germany. After spotting these elegantly flowing objects, which rise from the floor or hang from the ceiling, the Little Red Riding Hood fashion label invited CUE Architekten to pitch a proposal for the brand's new flagship store in central Berlin.

Based in Cologne and featuring the work of designer Tara Kanon Kikkoman, Little Red Riding Hood steers a middle course between reality and fantasy. Fashion journalists use terms like 'surreal dream world' and 'modern, multilingual fairy tale'. The collection launched at the opening of the flagship in Berlin Mitte, for example, was dubbed 'Another Superhuman Tall Tale'. It formed the final episode of the brand's 'Tales of Tomorrow' trilogy.

The store on Berlin's bustling Friedrichstrasse is divided into two levels. The visitor is drawn into the world of Little Red Riding Hood with an almost tangible force: a large projection screen and mannequins sporting wolfs' heads lure the shopper into the 330-metre-square street-level space. If the name on the label evokes images of a setting for a guileless little girl, a big bad wolf and a bedridden grandmother – birch-lined paths, log cabins and wicker baskets – be forewarned that Kikkoman's cosmos is unlike any traditional ideas you might be nurturing.

Once inside the store, you are a modern-day Alice in Wonderland, surrounded by a fairy-tale world that has nothing in common with the street life and the avalanche of stimuli you've just escaped. Dominating the ground floor are gleaming white walls that curl, recede and protrude to form niches, alcoves and silken-smooth shelving. 'We could never have produced this effect with traditional building materials,' says Corneille. 'We opted for glass fibre reinforced plastic (GRP), a lightweight material that takes its shape from moulds and that's frequently used for building boats and aeroplanes.'

Freestanding units within this retail area function as seating and display surfaces. Reinforcing the surreal effect is the contrast between all these white surfaces and the 'open' ceiling, in which mechanical systems and lighting are exposed for all to see. An unpolished floor of epoxy resin modestly defers to the splendour of the walls, whose ebb and flow forms a continuous loop that was assembled on site from 7-metre-long GRP sections. Structural columns are also clad in GRP. The proportions and the way in which each section fits into the next exhibit perfect workmanship. The omnipresent white is interrupted here and there by flashes of colour from the fashions displayed, as well as by the scarlet cushions on the seats and the brand's red logo.

Not just a boutique, Little Red Riding Hood is seen by the management as a forum for new talent in the areas of fashion, art, music and modern media. Artists and other creative spirits are invited to play a role in the multilingual, multicultural world of Little Red Riding Hood. The sales concept – a symbiosis of the themes highlighted in the forum – emerges from these ideas. The latest of Little Red Riding Hood's prêt-à-porter collections is accompanied by carefully selected music, accessories and literature. Illustrated story books rub shoulders with magazines like *Alert* and *Parkett*, and various exhibitions take place at the store. The challenging and often surprising mix of fashion, art and media can be experienced throughout the shop, which offers a generous amount of space for the display of art.

'What we created for Little Red Riding Hood is really a made-to-measure interior,' says Corneille, 'but we also see it as a prototype. We approached the commission as though it were a pilot project that would help us find out whether or not we could develop digital processes for controlling the entire procedure – from the first sketch to the manufacture of spherical surfaces – by means of computers.'

Preceding page
Positioned as islands within the 330-metre-square space are display modules thatdouble as seating; these volumes are made from glass-reinforced plastic (GRP).

Below
View of the interior. Walls made from GRP form niches, alcoves and shelving for the presentation of merchandise (left) and a cash desk (right). A centrally positioned stairway lends access to the retail space downstairs. A red background grabs the eye in this primarily white interior.

Bottom
A view from the opposite angle. White display tables scattered throughout the shop also function as seating. Mannequins wear fashions by Tara Kanon Kikkoman.

Little Red Riding Hood

LITTL
E
RED
RIDIN
G
HOO
D_

Floor plan and sections
1. Entrance
2. Freestanding seating-
   and display unit
3. Display unit
4. Fitting room
5. Cash desk
6. Rear area

Opposite top
Corneille Uedingslohmann Architekten
developed a continuous loop of GRP
walls that curl, recede and protrude to
form niches, alcoves and silken-smooth
shelving. The manufacture of this structure
was computer-controlled from start to
finish, a technique almost unheard of
in customized work.

Opposite bottom
Here and there the white walls protrude to
form display surfaces. GRP is also used in
the manufacture of boats and aeroplanes.

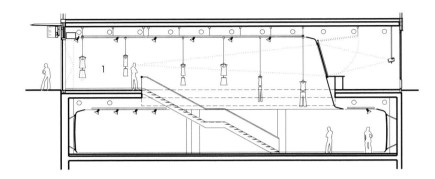

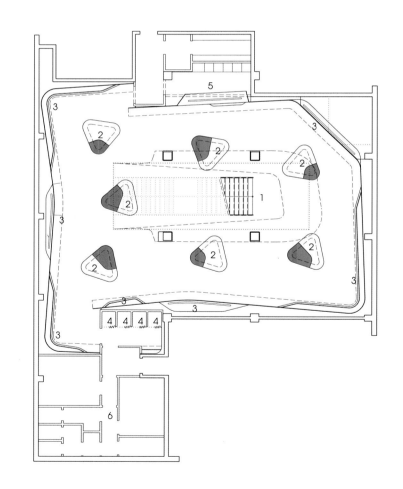

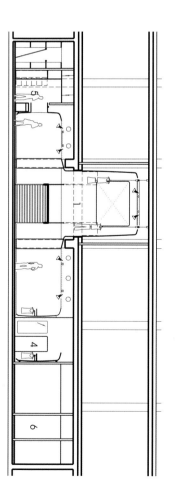

Little Red Riding Hood

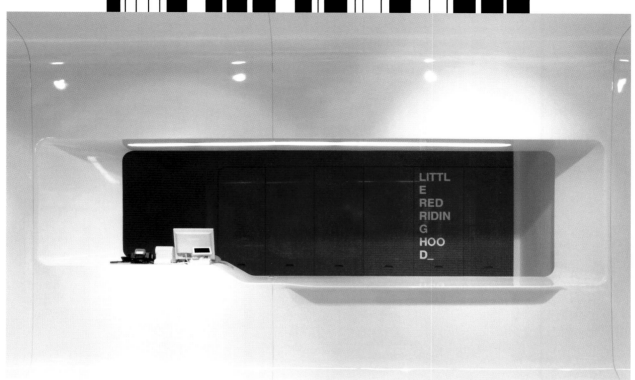

Store
De Bijenkorf

Location
Maastricht, Netherlands

Architect
Merkx+Girod

Evelyne Merkx
'I've certainly developed a feel for retail
design, but a lot depends on the client's
overall goal.'

Text
Edwin van Onna

Photography
Roos Aldershoff

By playing with light, colour and decoration, Merkx+Girod creates an airier, more spacious floor show at de Bijenkorf, a department store in Maastricht.

The well-organized display of a wide assortment of clothing brands on one floor is a challenge for any interior architect. Especially when the floor area is asymmetric and one section is designated as a café. This was part of the brief that de Bijenkorf, Holland's most fashionable department store, presented to Dutch architects Merkx +Girod, the firm commissioned to renovate the branch of the store in Maastricht. Merkx+Girod transformed the space in question into a richly variegated floor show with linear routing that leads to a chic café overlooking the street. White ceilings, white floors and brightly coloured accents disguise the relatively low ceilings.

Merkx+Girod has had considerable experience in retail design. Previous projects include the successful new look of another Dutch department store, HEMA, as well as outlets for Anna van Toor, a chain of boutiques. Nor was this the firm's first project for de Bijen-korf, for whom the architects had designed several shops-in-a-shop. 'I've certainly developed a feel for retail design,' says architect Evelyne Merkx, 'but a lot depends on the client's overall goal. In the renovation of a department store, fashion is just one part of the whole.'

The redesign of the Maastricht store turned out to be a fairly complex job that was plagued by a string of restrictions. 'The floors are shallow layers with ceilings you can almost reach up and touch. That caused problems,' explains Merkx. 'We deliberately set out to create a lighter and more spacious store.' Hampering their aim was a building that had to be shared with V&D, a less exclusive depart-ment store. The enclosed roof terrace was reserved for V&D's La Place Restaurant. All mechanical systems serving the restaurant are installed in the ceiling of the top floor of de Bijenkorf, which neces-sitated the use of lowered ceilings throughout the store.

The presence of the restaurant also had major consequences for lighting in de Bijenkorf. 'We wanted to include a skylight that would have drawn daylight into the various levels of the store,' says Merkx. 'But the roof terrace put an end to that idea. Nor were we permit-ted to enlarge the existing void, an intervention that the client saw as a waste of valuable floor space.' Complicated circumstances demanded new choices. Initially, the escalators were key to the architects' plan for in-store circulation. The definitive design, how-ever, features a linear organization that benefits the space as a whole, while deftly dealing with the asymmetric shape of the floor.

To solve the problem of illumination, Merkx+Girod designed a ver-tical lighting element for the void that embraces the escalators.

Characterizing the redesign of the first-floor women's department are long axial views and eye-catching 'trend islands', which are complemented by strikingly designed fitting rooms. 'The translucent fitting rooms we created for the central area are clearly distinguish-able in form and colour from those tucked discreetly into a quiet side area that is immersed in off-white,' says Merkx. 'Thanks to the translucent material, the staff can see when the fitting rooms are occupied and can better prevent theft.'

An important feature here is Café B, which borders an exterior wall and is flooded with daylight. Is this not the ideal spot for displaying apparel? 'A logical conclusion,' agrees Merkx, 'but the architect of the building was dead set against window displays. And a prac-tical reason for not displaying garments here has to do with back-lighting, which spoils the desired effect.'

The serene ambience pervading Café B is enlivened by splashes of colour. A highlight is the uninterrupted line formed by the back-rest of a long seating element clad in a traditional fabric whose pink design is shot with silver threads. Hanging from the ceiling, above freestanding chair-plus-table ensembles, are four colossal lamps whose serrated aluminium ribs are lined on the inside with red-copper-coated cardboard. Light reflecting on the copper surfaces spreads a warm glow throughout the space.

Merkx points out that the furniture arrangement was no accident. 'People like to look outside or, more specifically, to watch pedes-trians as they pass the window. That preference is expressed in the placement of tables and chairs. And sitting across from each other is much nicer than sitting side by side.'

The entrance to the café is marked by a large block with a deco-rative surface boasting pink accents. This angular volume houses space for washing dishes and storing supplies, functions aestheti-cally hidden by perforated walls with little integrated lamps that form a charming rose motif. 'The rose motif represents innovation in store design,' says the architect with obvious pride. 'Ornamented architecture is ubiquitous today, but we've been using decoration for ten years. Take our work for de Bijenkorf in Amstelveen, where we sandblasted a damask pattern on the window. I'm not claim-ing that Merkx+Girod is a trendsetter; I'm just emphasizing our ongoing fascination with decoration.'

Preceding page
A vertical lighting element in the void disperses light throughout all departments of the store and is attractively reflected in the brushed-metal sides of the escalators.

Below
View of Café B on the first floor, where visitors seated along the exterior wall can watch the comings and goings of passers-by.

Opposite
In Café B, a colossal lamp with serrated aluminium ribs casts a warm glow on freestanding chair-plus-table ensembles. The uninterrupted line of the backrest of a long seating element, upholstered in a patterned pink fabric, closes off one wall.

De Bijenkorf

Below
A serene ambience in off-white immerses visitors to the women's department on the first floor.

Opposite top
Basement eye-catchers are orange boxes of translucent plastic that function as fitting rooms in the menswear department.

Opposite bottom
The outer walls of the fitting rooms are used as display surfaces for shirts and other articles of clothing.

Store
Pleats Please
Issey Miyake

Location
Divers

Architect
AEDS

Eloueini's interiors are meant to reflect
Miyake's sculptural approach to fashion
design while maintaining the shopper's
focus on the clothes

Text
Shonquis Moreno

Photography
Christian Richters

Ammar Eloueini's Digit-all Studio (AEDS) uses polycarbonate, computer software, and CNC technology to design two interiors in Berlin and Perpignan that reflect Japanese fashion designer Issey Miyake's sculptural approach to clothing design while maintaining the shopper's focus on the clothes.

He's used a similar technique to create the set for a modern dance performance and an installation intended to resemble an artificial sky. He used it to craft a creased surface for video projection, to drape a catwalk for a fashion show in Chicago and to design his MU chair. Architect Ammar Eloueini of Chicago and his Paris-based Ammar Eloueini Digit-all Studio (AEDS) have now used translucent polycarbonate, software, and CNC technology to design two shops for Japanese fashion designer Issey Miyake's Pleats Please line in Berlin and Perpignan, and they are working on a third in Paris. These interiors are meant to reflect Miyake's sculptural approach to fashion design while maintaining the shopper's focus on the clothes.

For both projects, Eloueini built fitting rooms and storage spaces whose faceted walls are composed of two overlapping pieces of aluminium-framed polycarbonate panelling. The 127-x-254-x-1.27-cm sheets of aluminium (which the designer and his team sought to make as discreet as possible) were cut using water jets; the sheets serve as scaffolding for the 16 sheer 61-x-244-cm polycarbonate panels, as well as for display racks and a table. The curvilinear polycarbonate surfaces were modelled as a single crumpled form on a computer and then unfolded in a process that relies on 3-D modelling software. The unfolded sheets were fabricated in Chicago using a router CNC (computer numerically controlled) machine, shipped abroad and assembled on site. Thanks to the lightweight materials – including the plastic zip ties that fasten all components together – the walls were inexpensive to ship and easy to assemble.

In both shops, the overall effect of the faceted screens is one of gleaming, milky moiré, as the eye of the observer records what seem to be softly shifting images moving across the modelled polycarbonate surfaces. And, as the internal qualities of the material 'shift', the panels appear to be creased as well. 'The effect that we are looking for is lightness,' says Eloueini, who explains that the desired impression emerges when light reflects off the irregular polycarbonate forms. Eloueini opted for Softimage XSI to model the definitive shapes of the walls. Their form is the result of combining, as the designer phrases it, 'constraints and intentions'. He was constrained, for instance, by the dimensions of the CNC router machine and the polycarbonate panels, by the use of water jets

to cut the aluminium sheets, by the fact that the forms had to be manufactured in Chicago and shipped to Berlin and, finally, by the necessity for walls that had to be fireproof. 'The intentions and constraints created a framework inside which I worked with different geometries until I defined the form. The decision about when the form is right is highly subjective.' Eloueini stresses that the idea was to achieve a folded, translucent surface that would multiply each reflected beam of light. 'This is where we started exploring the idea that overlapping surfaces could create intimacy without having to deal with doors.'

Much of Eloueini's work involves exploration: the exploration of computer modelling, of CNC milling, of lightweight transport, easy assemblage (often using zip ties) and faceted surfaces. He sees the process as an in-depth study of digital architecture that takes him from computer modelling through representation to fabrication. As opposed to designers who begin with cardboard-and-paste models, scan them into the computer with 3-D scanners and rework the images digitally, Eloueini designs objects and spaces that can be traced, for the most part, directly to their digital origins, with no detours along the way. 'We've seen many digitally produced projects and images in the last decade, but few of them were built successfully,' is his comment. 'The transition between the screen and reality is not an obvious one.' Perhaps ironically, he attributes the difficulty involved to 'the infinite possibilities and ease of modelling with 3-D software', adding that designers may be in the 21st century in terms of representation, but the building industry seems to be stuck in the previous millennium. Needless to say, Eloueini and AEDS are hoping the situation will change – sooner rather than later.

Preceding page, below and opposite
Ammar Eloueini of AEDS used polycarbonate, software and CNC milling technology to design Pleats Please shops in
Berlin, Germany, and Perpignan, France.
The shops take their cue from Issey Miyake's sculptural approach to design, while
anchoring the visitor's focus on the clothes.
Faceted panels that create an illusion of
softly shifting images hang on aluminium
frames and serve as fitting room, display
and storage space.

79

Pleats Please Issey Miyake

This spread
'The effect that we are looking for is lightness,' says Eloueini, who modelled the panels in Softimage XSI. The architect explored the notion that overlapping surfaces could create intimacy without doors.

PLEATS
PLEASE
ISSEY MIYAKE

81

Store
Stash

Location
Maastricht, Netherlands

Architect
Maurice Mentjens

Maurice Mentjens
'How often do designers find themself
working as a sort of upgraded decorator
rather than as a designer?'

Text
Brigitte van Mechelen

Photography
Arjen Schmitz

With a clever but simple solution, Maurice Mentjens magnetizes shoppers at Stash Bags and Accessories in the southern Dutch town of Maastricht.

Initially it's not his most well-known project, but it's Maurice Mentjens' favourite all the same. What makes Stash so special? 'Stash is totally my kind of thing. How often do designers find themself working as a sort of upgraded decorator rather than as a designer? Not only did I come up with the concept for Stash; I was also able to implement my plan. Without having to defend the design in the endless sparring match that's known as "making concessions".'

Mentjens' contribution to Stash Bags and Accessories, a shop in the centre of the southern Dutch town of Maastricht, was a new display system. Because bags hang on the arm, from the shoulder or in a diagonal line across the chest, Mentjens wanted to see them displayed in a hanging position and not on a shelf, stuffed with wads of paper to prevent them from collapsing or losing their shape. But how? The solution lay in steel walls combined with magnets. Each bag – a popular model in Stash's collection is the messenger bag or carry-all – contains one or two strong magnets sealed in a plastic envelope. Walls are completely clad in steel panelling. Voilà.

Mentjens had previously used magnets for a trade-fair stand featuring Count It, a counter cashing system that Inbase had developed for iMac. Gaining entry to the 'cage' that highlighted the stand was a matter of pushing through a curtain-like fringe of colour-changing tubing, after which the tubes – anchored to an overhead rail and to a corresponding base in the floor by industrial-strength magnets – snapped quickly back into their upright positions, leaving the visitor in an enclosed space.

At Stash, walls reaching from floor to ceiling and from entrance to rear wall function as a display system. Shoppers pluck any bag that catches their eye from the wall, inspect it, and stick it back up wherever they like. Quite a handy idea for a shop as small as Stash, which has a retail area of only 33 square metres. An efficient use of the space was one inescapable requirement of the brief; another was a clever response or two to the need for more display possibilities.

Descending from the ceiling deeper in the interior are two rectangular volumes covered in the same gleaming red steel as that on the walls. These suspended elements hang above two rectangular display units designed to present bags selected for extra attention.

The positioning of these units creates two aisles that impart an illusion of greater depth to the premises. A large mirror at the end of these aisles doubles the effect. Another suspended volume, again with a display unit beneath it, is in the shop window. The combination of these two elements draws the eye to the store, while also forming a partition of the cash area, preventing passers-by to look into the cash register. Figuratively speaking, the red, powder-coated steel panelling on walls and ceiling also has a 'magnetizing' effect on passers-by. Not only that, but experience has shown that red functions well as a backdrop for the hip bags that Stash sells.

A layer of grey polyurethane provides floor, counter and display units with a seamless coating, a uniformity that is further accentuated by the smoothly rounded corners of the various grey volumes. 'It's as if you're ensconced in a big bag yourself,' says Mentjens, who does not only retail design, but also domestic, office and health-care interiors – including a recent project for a gynaecologist – as well as exhibitions. Incorporated into his design of 'Smaak/On Taste', an exhibition hosted by Maastricht's Bonnefanten Museum, was an aroma laboratory, an opportunity to taste cheese, a smoking salon, a water and oxygen bar, and two water- and perfume-related exhibits. And there's more: Mentjens also designs furniture, lamps, vases and wristwatches.

The best ideas are simple. 'The innovative display method with magnets is original, breaks free of the traditional model of a shop for bags, and is the kind of idea that we would have liked to come up with ourselves,' concluded the jury of the Dutch Design Awards in the autumn of 2005. Mentjens has given the client and his customers a design with 'added value', continued the jury, backing up these words with the award for Best Retail Design.

Preceding page
Throughout the shop, walls clad in powder-
coated steel panelling offer an extensive
display surface. Thanks to the use of
magnets, bags stuck to the walls can be
removed for inspection and reattached
at random.

Floor plan and sections
1. Entrance
2. Shop-window display
3. Cask desk
4. Display table

Opposite
Large floor-to-ceiling mirrors – even bags
have to be 'tried on' – make the small interior seem larger than it is. Two freestanding
units positioned beneath two rectangular
volumes suspended from the ceiling provide
the 33-square-metre space with extra room
for special displays.

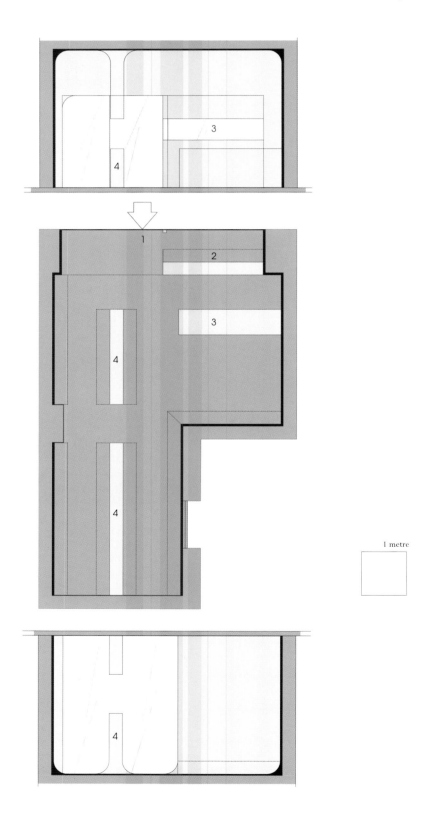

1 metre

Stash

Opposite and this page
Two centrally positioned steel volumes
hang above a pair of display modules;
the ensemble forms a strong architectural
element and creates two aisles that end in
a large mirrored wall, making the shop appear much longer than it is (this page). Red
walls and ceiling shout a warm welcome to
passers-by and make a perfect backdrop
for the trendy bags sold at Stash.

Store
m-i-d Press Room

Location
Tokyo, Japan

Architect
Fumita Design Office

Akihito Fumita
'Attracting customers sometimes
takes a statement that expresses
aloofness or even tension. Presenting
merchandise in the right way can
also increase its value.'

Text
Masaaki Takahashi

Photography
Nacása & Partners

To create a sense of duality and distinctiveness in Tadao Ando's concrete building, Fumita Design Office crafted a transparent light box for m-i-d Press Room's boutique-cum-showroom.

In describing the enigmatic aspect of boutique design, Akihito Fumita says that 'the notion of a place being boutique-like is highly ambiguous. You're striving to create a space that is not a boutique, a place that is used for something else, but it's this very quality that makes it a boutique. In considering the options available for displaying clothes, you have three basic choices: hang them, fold them or drape them on a mannequin. Unless you invent a unique way to display them, you're limited to these three. Getting that special boutique "look" is a matter of arranging hangers, shelves and mannequins in a nearly empty space.'

Having said that, Fumita points out the absence of strict form- or style-related conditions for designing a boutique. He cringes at the thought of designers who approach the space – regardless of dimensions or location – mount a horizontal pole, install a fitting room, and hang up the merchandise. Although even a professional can do little to change the basic conditions of an interior, he would hope that the designer in question would insert a few innovative details and complete the picture with an interesting intervention or two, as that is 'the only way to differentiate'.

The m-i-d Press Room, highlighted here, occupies the ground floor and basement of a Tadao Ando building faced in architectural concrete. The area currently enjoys a minimum of pedestrian traffic, but more is anticipated as a neighbourhood redevelopment project nears completion. Plans for the showroom called for a high-impact interior that would stand out from those around it. Tenants played no role in the design of the building, however. The space functions as both showroom and media-relations centre for m-i-d, a firm with headquarters in the Kansai, a cultural area of Japan. An executive office is adjacent to the showroom, but the main area – a flowing series of rooms – reflects Fumita's previous designs at other m-i-d offices. Although not aimed at customers or the general public, the interior, similar to a boutique, radiates an air of mystery that transcends merchandise and brand. The high-end designer appeal of the showroom was intended to trump the look of a regular shop.

The earlier-mentioned redevelopment project, scheduled for completion in 2006, includes Omotesando Hills, another design by Tadao Ando. Here in Tokyo's Harajuku district, this large-scale commercial complex replaces apartments which, when torndown in 2003, had been a vital part of the neighbourhood for 76 years. Featured in the showroom are walls consisting primarily of two layers of clear glass. Sandwiched between the layers and positioned at equal intervals are 400 lamps made from high-precision stainless steel: the result of a lost-wax casting technique. Each lamp is 16 cm long and 10 cm in diameter. Light is reflected throughout the space on floors, walls and ceilings, multiplying its sources and immersing everything in radiance. Which point of light is real, and which is a reflection? Individual luminaires, real though they may be, cannot be identified from a distance. A sense of duality defines the space, underlining Fumita's remarks on ambiguity and his pursuit of new ways of expression. He mentions seeing a North Korean nuclear facility on television. 'When you think of that plant as the possible inspiration for the m-i-d Press Room, the space takes on a somewhat dangerous aura. Looking at televised images of the control rods being carefully inserted and removed, I felt an amazing amount of tension.'

In their unfurnished state, Fumita-designed boutiques often have the appearance of art installations. The observer does not get an impression of a designer who gives a great deal of forethought to technical or architectonic matters. In reality, however, at the outset of a project Fumita carefully considers factors such as location, internal circulation, shelf heights and the arrangement of display units.

Not every store is backed by a super-brand that draws shoppers with much-publicized products and an established interior design. Less well-known companies like to explore new and perhaps unorthodox avenues of architecture and retail design. 'Shops are not simply places designed for comfort,' says Fumita. 'Attracting customers sometimes takes a statement that expresses aloofness or even tension. Presenting merchandise in the right way can also increase its value.' His design philosophy is based on a good understanding of what kind of elements stimulate customer traffic and of what kind of floor plan makes the ideal shopping environment. Moving through his retail-scapes, however, the average shopper is completely unaware of Fumita's clever devices.

Although his portfolio bulges with boutiques – projects already realized, as well as those in development or nearing completion – Fumita asks to be respected for the insight needed to create well-thought-out interiors, rather than being assigned to the category of boutique design: a reasonable request backed by the oeuvre of an exceptional talent.

Below
Media office, president's office and
reception room are on the ground floor.

Floor plans
1. Entrance
2. Press office
3. Meeting area
4. Office
5. Counter
6. Hanging display
7. Showroom
8. Fitting room
9. Stockroom
10. Rear area

Bottom
The basement is used as a showroom
and for business meetings.

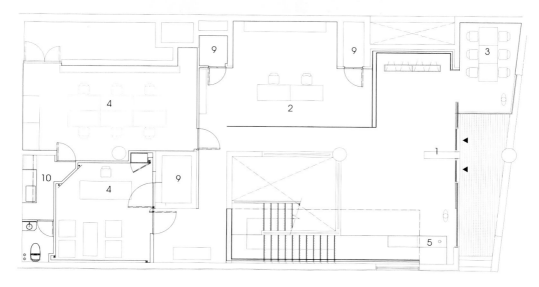

Ground floor

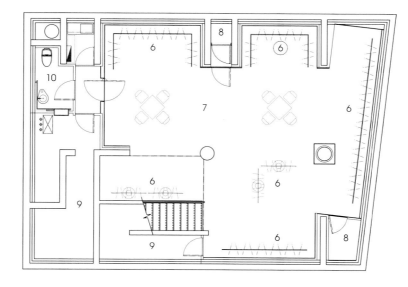

Basement

Below
Equipped with compact florescent
bulbs, custom-made lighting units for
the glass walls are 19 cm long and
12 cm in diameter.

Opposite top
This project occupies the ground floor
and basement of a building by Japanese
architect Tadao Ando. Omotesando Hills,
a complex also designed by Ando, is in
the same part of Tokyo.

Opposite bottom
Despite restrictions regarding the
preservation of Ando's original interior,
Fumita exercised his own style.

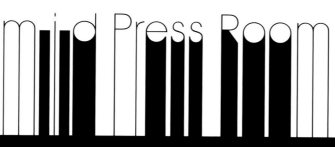

Opposite top
Appearing to float within the glass wall
of the ground-floor reception area are
lights that refer to the core rods of a
nuclear reactor.

Opposite bottom
The view from just inside the ground-floor
entrance. At first glance, the light-filled
space has an office-like atmosphere.

Below
Thick concrete columns in the showroom
downstairs are clad in half-mirrored glass
to make them inconspicuous.

Store
Karen Millen

Location
London, England

Architect
Brinkworth

Carl Nichols
'Our design allows an interactive
geometry of surface area, window and
internal display, giving the appearance
of one surface both outside and in.'

Text
Shonquis Moreno

Photography
Louise Melchior

Crowning 16 years of work for a single client is Brinkworth's design of Karen Millen's Regent Street flagship, where the firm's interior architects have once more raised the bar on quality in fashion retail.

Sixteen years after the completion of its inaugural project, the first Karen Millen boutique, Brinkworth can look back on the design of over ten dozen outlets for its esteemed client, including the 300-metre-square flagship on Regent Street in London. An extension of the tony boulevard outside and a product of the many preceding designs, this Millen interior combines antithetical materials to lavish effect. The fourth flagship for the label shares some of its materials with previous Millen projects, most notably the Vegas-inspired cut glass (used throughout the stores, but in varying shades) that has become a Brinkworth signature. It also shares a clean geometry and a strategy of juxtaposing materials in bands, which evokes a surprisingly inviting and glamorous chic. 'Regent Street is a pretty high-specification street,' says Brinkworth design director Carl Nichols. 'The store needed to reflect that.' He paints the picture of an interior whose architectural statements generate the desired effect – including an air of accessibility – by mixing glitzy materials with natural stone. 'It's a balance between sophisticated richness, which is inspirational, and the high street. The materials reflect the sophistication of the brand.'

Like the previous (award-winning) Gateshead shop designed for Millen, the new flagship demonstrates how architecture can transform a limited space by working with its inherent organization, using diagonal lines and loops of materials to create product areas. This Regent Street site, with its listed status, was particularly difficult, as the exterior could not be touched. Brinkworth's designers have made a deliberate distinction between the historical façade and a fresh interior that is formally spare but materially sumptuous, expressing the dynamic personality of the brand. Windows line one side of the boutique, helping to illuminate the interior but also cutting down on display area. The architects erected a series of backdrop walls just behind the frontage, leaving enough room for mannequin displays facing the street and a background for clothing racks on the other side without blocking out light. Atop a plinth of wide, unfinished planks that runs the length of the store, mannequins catch the attention of passers-by. 'Our design allows an interactive geometry of surface area, window and internal display,' says Nichols, 'giving the appearance of one surface both outside and in.'

The team was able to reinvent a very constrained space by wrapping loops of contrasting materials, both traditional and highly contemporary, over floor, walls and ceiling. Shoppers step from the pavement into a soft sandstone loop before passing through loops featuring milky glass walls and high-gloss, white-quartz floor tiles. The white sections blend lucidly with the displays that hem the side of the space. In a herringbone configuration, display units made of layered slabs of glass contain racks and surfaces through which hanging garments are visible, simultaneously precious and available. The pale but warm colour of sandstone against the walls complements not only the quartz floor, the transparent displays and the glossy walls, but also a ceiling sheathed in illuminated Barrisol glass for a sleek diffuse light. In general, synthetic materials are balanced by matte, natural stone and gentle light, a combination that reflects the character of Millen's fashions, which often mix satiny or sparkly fabrics with the natural look of distressed denim, big knits and plush leather. 'I like the palette of materials,' says Nichols. 'That's what sets the store off.'

A wall at the back of the shop gleams with another sparkly material: Vegas glass. Reminiscent of the Hollywood regency period that has been brought back into vogue by the likes of Brinkworth and Jonathan Adler, Vegas glass is made by cutting and faceting strips of glass, after which they are used to clad curved walls. The result is diffuse lighting and a cacophony of reflection. Here the wall adds sharp contrast and drama to the rather soberly designed loops, ups the glamour content of the boutique, and creates a strong focal point at the rear to draw eyes, bodies and pocketbooks through the space towards the shoe department and the fitting rooms. The designers were very generous with the fitting rooms, which boast an adjoining lounge area complete with globe lamp, white benches, large mirror and Arne Jacobsen's white-leather Swan chair. The Barrisol ceiling and faceted mirror nearby bathe the lounge in a subdued light. This microcosmic salon-like scenario defines the area and infuses it with a touch of personal drama. Through its years of investigations, the Brinkworth team has clearly found a very economical but ebullient way to tell the story of its favourite brand.

Floor plan
1. Entrance
2. Shop-window display
3. Retail area
4. Display units
5. Cash desk
6. Shoe department
7. Fitting rooms

Bottom
A clean geometry of diagonals marks the composition of the 300-metre-square Karen Millen flagship on Regent Street in London. Brinkworth combined a diversity of materials in its design, which forms an extension of the boulevard outside.

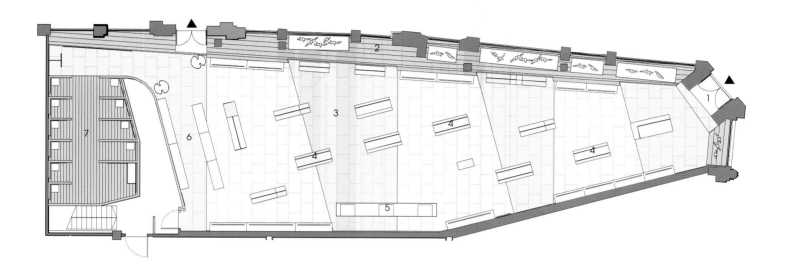

Karen Millen

Preceding page
A cash desk dressed in fluted strips of Las Vegas-inspired cut glass stands out from loops of sandstone, milky glass and white quartz that ribbon through the shop.

Below
A shoe area right outside the fitting rooms feels both swank and residential. The Vegas glass reappears along a curved wall, generating reflections – and glamour.

Opposite
Walls posing just behind the glazed façade leave a narrow corridor floored with unfinished timber for mannequins and displays that run the length of the shop.

Store
Rodenstock

Location
Tokyo, Japan

Architect
Shuhei Endo

Shuhei Endo
'Top priority in this interior is the function
and nature of the merchandise.'

Text
Masaaki Takahashi

Photography
Nacása & Partners

Looking through the eyes of Japanese architect Shuhei Endo, one can see his interpretation of German *Sachlichkeit* at Rodenstock, an eyewear store in Tokyo.

Body language and speech aside, eyes are a prime source of communication. And those who can't see without glasses or contact lenses are even more aware of the importance of eyesight. Shuhei Endo, architect of German brand Rodenstock's new spectacles shop in Tokyo, puts it this way: 'Glasses and architecture are similar phenomena. Both are situated in between, forming the necessary connection between the outside and inside worlds.' Compared with the amazing evolution of our clothing and our overall appearance, glasses look much the same as they did many decades ago. In designing the interior of Rodenstock Galerie du Brille Ginza, Endo based his retail concept on the idea that eyewear is a tool that more or less merges with the body when worn.

Established by Josef Rodenstock in Würzburg, Germany, in 1877, the eyewear company bearing his name is well known in Japan, especially among the older generation. The popularity of the brand was underlined when the first shop in the world with an exclusive offering of Rodenstock products opened not in Berlin or Frankfurt, but in Tokyo. The 21st-century 'rebranding' of Rodenstock, a move aimed at drawing the attention of a younger target group and thus expanding the company's market share, began in 2005 on the first floor of a building in Ginza. Like other rebranding strategies in Japan, the project was based on design.

'When I was developing the concept for this store,' says Endo, 'the first thing that popped into my mind was the German word *sachlichkeit* and the style of modern architecture known as *Neue Sachlichkeit*.' Endo explains that his interpretation of *sachlichkeit* is what prompted him to stress the special physical characteristics of materials used in the interior. In addition to *sachlichkeit*, he wanted to illustrate the subtlety and high quality that he associates with Rodenstock products.

Endo aimed for a minimalist exterior that would highlight the company's logo while reflecting the characteristics of the brand. Inside the store, a 5-mm-thick carpet of emerald green covers the floor. Because the carpet yarn is relatively long and not pile cut, the surface looks like a lush lawn of natural grass. Endo wanted the flooring to be a soft expanse of green that would appeal to the city shopper's love of nature and sense of touch. Inspired by 'the famous moss-covered grounds of the Saihoji Temple in Kyoto', he

tried to re-create the delicate mossy surface at the new Rodenstock store. His quest to match the high quality of Rodenstock design begins at the customer's feet.

An illuminated ceiling clad in milk-glass panels that distribute light evenly throughout the space is symbolic of the glass lenses that Rodenstock produced in its earlier years. In a setting of sensory delight, seamless white walls feature round niches that vary from 15 to 40 cm in diameter. Clad in differently patterned steel mesh, each small alcove contains a revolving display table with mirrored underside: a platform just large enough for a pair of spectacles. A pale blue light fills the niches, creating a coolly futuristic polka-dot motif that contrasts with the white walls and grass-green floor. Danish furniture by Finn Juhl, Hans Wegner and Arne Jacobsen – selected because of its association with Germany's early-20th-century modernist movement – completes the picture.

'I created an environment for people to experience,' says Endo. 'This shop is an ongoing field of interaction between walls and floor, displays, eyewear and customers. In German design, function dictates form. Top priority in this interior, therefore, is the function and nature of the merchandise.' He tells of designing a building for a specialist in Oriental medicine and learning about *ki*, which is an internal force that flows through the body like a weak electric current. Impressed with the notion of *ki*, he started looking at the design of interiors from the Oriental viewpoint of spatial awareness. Although most of his projects involve architecture rather than retail design, Endo believes that the main difference between the two is the importance of artificial light in shop interiors. Otherwise, he says, architecture and interior design are basically the same. Always looking for a challenge in terms of both style and construction, he often opts for the unusual, such as the use of corrugated steel where another architect might employ concrete. 'We wear T-shirts for normal everyday activities,' he explains. 'There's no need for a suit of armour. We're not going into battle. Why, then, should we live and work in conventional concrete boxes – far too solid, far too heavy – when we can get by with much lighter and simpler structures?'

Preceding page
Plastered white walls feature round
niches that hold revolving display tables
with mirrored undersides. The rear surface
of each niche features a patterned
metallic mesh.

Rodenstock

Left
Clad in randomly stacked panels made from cracked milk glass, the suspended ceiling distributes light evenly throughout the space.

Opposite
The retail interior is a conceptual fusion of German and Japanese themes. Accentuating the simplicity of the waiting room are lamps designed by Frank Lloyd Wright.

Floor plan
1. Display units
2. Display table
3. Cash desk
4. Lounge
5. Examination room
6. Rear area

Bottom
A 5-mm-thick carpet of emerald green is Endo's reference to the moss-covered grounds of the Saihoji Temple in Kyoto.

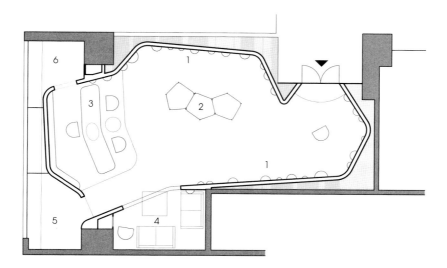

Store
Marithé + François Girbaud

Location
Divers

Architect
Kristian Gavoille

Kristian Gavoille
'You can't tell story in five or ten minutes.
After all, the customer is there to buy.'

Text
Chris Scott

Photography
Myr Muratet

Fascinated by new materials and technologies Kristian Gavoille incorporated them in the shop designs for Marithé + François Girbaud.

Designers Marithé and François Girbaud are forerunners in jeans-wear. They are responsible for such well-established classics as stone-washed and distressed-ripped jeans. Often referred to as 'jeansologists', they rethink and redesign the garments, inventing new industrial processes and constantly reviewing materials, structures and shapes. Everything that can be done to a pair of jeans – and more – has been and is still being done by these 'jeansetic engineers'. Their approach and their attitude are unlike those of any other fashion label. Inevitably, therefore, they selected some-one special to design their retail outlets. That someone is designer and architect Kristian Gavoille.

The first time they met, François and Gavoille clicked immediately. They talked about everything but shop design. A long and success-ful collaboration began that day, a synergy that has grown over the years and that continues to develop. Upon asking Gavoille how many retail outlets he has designed, one gets a somewhat vague response: 'Around about 30-something.' It's difficult to keep track of the number of boutiques, franchises and 'shop corners' he's created. Disregarding the Girbauds' worldwide presence, approximately 30 shops and 2000 smaller outlets are spread across Europe alone.

Gavoille's first commission was the flagship store on rue Etienne Marcel in Paris. It opened just over ten years ago, marking François and Marithé's return to France after a period of living in the USA. They viewed their return to Paris as a renaissance. François, who is particularly involved in the creative side of the company, has never given Gavoille more than a minimal brief. At the outset of a project, François discusses the direction he would like the work to take, his current fashion activities and sources of inspiration. He says a few words, perhaps draws a sketch, and the rest is in Gavoille's hands. No interruptions. No change of plans. François may occasionally make an inquiry, but Gavoille is basically free to translate the Gir-bauds' spirit into the new surroundings.

The Girbauds are renowned for their futuristic, progressive use of materials, which is invariably reflected in their retail interiors. Equally fascinated by new materials and technologies, Gavoille incorporates them into his work. Examples are luminous silicone poufs with a veined surface, designed for the rue Mahler shop; specially coloured mauve shelves in Avonite Crystelle by Oberflex,

made for the Cherche Midi shop; and a vertical garden that forms a wall covering at the Osaka store.

Ideas come from a variety of sources, including Francois's long-time obsession with cowboys and Indians, his love of rock music, and Marithé's earth-mother tendencies. Themes such as human nature, landscape and 'techno-nature' vibrations emerge in both clothing and interiors. Combined with a love of experimentation, materials and technology, these themes have led to some inter-esting results. The cocoon concept, which has appeared in a number of retail interiors, was introduced at the Etienne Marcel store, where Gavoille worked with the rounded shapes and plastics that François prefers, as well as with natural materials like wood, which are very much Marithé. As the cocoon concept developed – 'same words, different nature' – the cocoon began to open, and the organic elements gradually appropriated more space.

For the New York store, also based on this concept, the wish for something stronger and more provocative prompted them to crack the cocoon. In Osaka, the cocoon was shed and the but-terfly within examined. Butterfly wings and the scales of a snake's skin provided inspiration for the Osaka design, which features a wall covering of aluminium panels in graduated shades whose scaly appearance is repeated in felt-covered chairs. The colours of the Osaka shop reflect the colours of the Colorado desert that impressed both the Girbauds and Gavoille on their trip to that region of the United States. Overall, the retail interiors express a love of nature and suggest a strong interest in the environment. Although the briefs seem to give Gavoille carte blanche, he is aware that the fashions have priority and that the Girbauds like to display a lot of clothing, as at a bazaar, rather than to highlight single items. They want customers to have an instant understand-ing of the interior. 'That doesn't just happen,' says Gavoille. 'You can't tell a story in five or ten minutes. After all, they're there to buy.' He hopes, however, that certain features of the space will linger in the minds of customers after they leave.

Scheduled for 2006 are the opening of a new shop in Moscow and the revamp of the Etienne Marcel flagship store, which will probably coincide with the launch of another Marithé + François Girbaud line. In the words of Gavoille, 'The story of the Girbauds is far from finished.'

Marithé + François Girbaud

Opposite top
At the rue Cherche-Midi outlet, Gavoille took yet another approach: 'The ceiling comes down; the furniture goes up.' Equipped with built-in lighting and made from Barrisol, the upper section display table seems to connect the suspended display table with the ceiling.

Opposite bottom
Fitting rooms are made from oak-veneered MDF. Chairs with an organic design, here in front of the mirrored partition, have metal frames and leather upholstery.

Below
The latest stage of evolution at M+F Girbaud's Osaka shop has a 'techno-nature' vibe. Organic elements take over the interior: scaly green columns resemble trees, and hanging displays look like tree trunks (left). The backdrop for clothes presented on the 'tree trunk', a display table of veneered-MDF (right), is a green wall of fake plants.

Store
Reiss

Location
New York, USA

Architect
D_raw associates

The chandelier's more formal
function is to act as a metaphoric
'building within a building'

Text
Shonquis Moreno

Photography
Eric Laignel

The vast chandelier that d_raw associates designed for UK retailer Reiss provides more than illumination.

The chandelier, as well as contemporary translations of the chandelier, has been making a comeback for the past decade, but the flagship store that UK fashion retailer Reiss recently opened in New York may be the apotheosis of this trend. Reiss SoHo is a vast chandelier in itself. Reiss's first US store – which opened last spring alongside Donna Karan, Dolce & Gabbana, and Alberta Ferretti – is the work of d_raw associates.

To further the label's ambitions for international expansion and to mark its entry into America's big-time retail scene, d_raw gutted and converted a five-storey, yellow-brick building that was once a garage. The 465-square-metre, ground-floor boutique is located beneath loft apartments, studios and offices. As shoppers enter, they are greeted by the first of several monumental 'details' in the form of heavy, pivoting, solid-oak doors inset with huge glass panels. Beyond, the retail space is reminiscent of Philip Johnson's iconic rod-crowned bar at the Four Seasons Hotel in midtown Manhattan; Reiss's interior is more intricate and more luminous, however, and has greater depth and texture. The stunning effect is the result of a shop both crowned and divided by what the architects claim is the biggest chandelier in the Western hemisphere. The immense lantern is made up of long, slender glass rods beaded together sparsely on pale cables and suspended like flawless stalactites from the 6.5-metre-high ceiling in a centralized grid. The architects inserted the rods into illuminated slots in the matte surface of a dark-grey drop ceiling that emphasizes the sleekness of the rods, which also emit light from their fibre-optic tips. In addition to illuminating the shop floor, the row upon row of 2-metre rods create a dramatic approach to the retail area and inject a fractured focus (or a pleasant shattering of the focus) to the interior. The chandelier's more formal function is to act as a metaphoric 'building within a building' or, in the apt words of the designers, as 'an architectural edifice in itself'. Pouring downwards, the glass rods draw the shopper's attention to the centre of the space, act as partitioning, suggest circulation around merchandise, and provide a sense of veiled intimacy and privacy. The hub of the shop is an illuminated cash desk made from resin; radiating outwards from this volume are clusters of merchandise arranged in strategically grouped categories. It is a scheme that maximizes the scale and varies the texture of the shop. 'The clustering of fixtures and merchandise was a running theme and helped us achieve a strong spatial identity, visual focal points and ease of manoeuvre for the shopper,' says d_raw's creative director Dorrien Hopley. 'This separation of visual areas creates maximum visual impact and provides definition – important when dealing with both men's and women's collections.'

The designers have successfully married contrasting materials and finishes – with no sense of jarring – against the coarse box of the original space. Unrefined brickwork (revealed beneath layers of fuel exhaust and grime) and structural steel function like crude settings for jewels made of glass and mirror-polished steel. The strategy strikes a balance between luxury and accessibility. 'In enticing high-street shoppers, the impact has to work from outside as well as inside,' says Hopley. 'The aim was to create an aspirant shopping environment in line with the brand's signature style – aspirant yet affordable – an aim that informed all our design decisions.'

The combination of contrasting qualities and textures continues throughout the space. Temporary graphics were applied to glass panels that sheath the brickwork. The texture of natural materials – recycled Khors Canadian maple flooring and carved walnut tables – contrasts with synthetic pieces: rails of polished stainless steel; shelving made from UV-bonded, bronze-tinted, opti-clear glass; and handmade tabletops of translucent resin. Enriching the glossy elements in the fitting-room area, d_raw used bespoke seating, rugs and curtains, as well as a rococo Mylar and lavender wallpaper. In this way, they maintained the integrity of an old space while overlaying it with a spectacle of modernity. 'These days, more people than ever have a sophisticated sense of design, and it's important to respect that,' says Hopley. 'Also, in a climate where high-street shopping is having to increasingly compete with online retailers, I think it's more important than ever to create retail spaces that are both exciting and relaxing and, as far as possible, interiors that appeal to the senses.'

As Reiss clothing isn't unique in the neighbourhood, it's safe to say that the shop design will prove a good investment for the company. To date, sales have been double those predicted. Apparently, the accomplishment is being acknowledged: d_raw will design not one but two more shops in Manhattan. And, one assumes, will continue to spread the light from there.

Below
Computer sketches of graphic patterns
for screens featured at Reiss.

Bottom
Computer sketch showing how a
graphic pattern influences the lighting.
The centralized grid of the chandelier
is clearly visible.

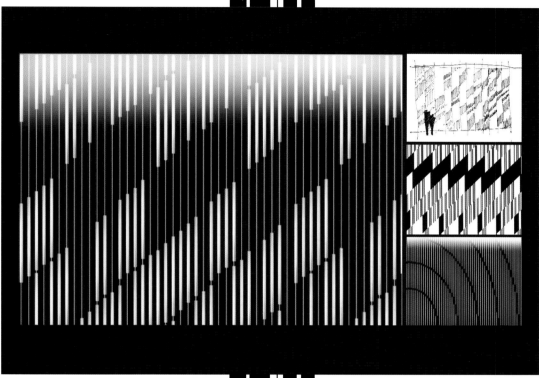

Floor plan
1. Entrance
2. Shop-window area
3. Women's retail area
4. Men's retail area
5. Accessories area
6. Cash desk
7. Display table
8. Women's fitting room
9. Men's fitting room
10. Stockroom
11. Rear area

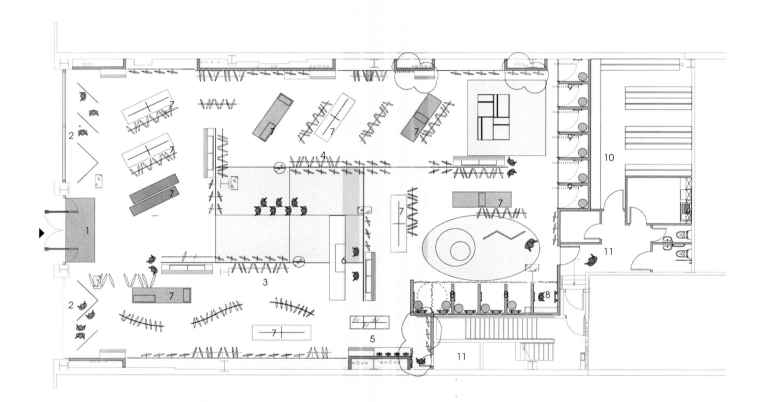

Preceding page
Beaded with fluted acrylic rods, tensioned stainless-steel cables between floor and ceiling draw the shopper's attention to the centre of the space, act as partitioning, suggest circulation around merchandise, and provide a sense of veiled intimacy.

Below
Enriching the glossy elements in the fitting-room area, d_raw used bespoke seating, rugs and curtains, as well as a rococo Mylar and lavender wallpaper, thus maintaining the integrity of an old space while overlaying it with a spectacle of modernity.

Opposite
The immense lantern is made up of long, slender glass rods beaded togethersparsely on pale cables and suspended like flawless stalactites from the 6.5-metre-high ceiling in a centralized grid.

Store
Costume National

Location
Los Angeles, USA

Architect
Marmol Radziner + Associates

Ron Radziner
'We saw some of the clothes Costume
National were working on, as well as many
pictures of the space where they worked.
We felt it was important to understand how
they worked and why they came up with
the clothes they did.'

Text
Matthew Stewart

Photography
Benny Chan / fotoworks

The phenomenon of light bouncing off fabrics in the client's collection was the basis of Marmol Radziner + Associates' retail design for Costume National's new Los Angeles outlet.

Costume National might be the biggest name with a small ego. With modest fanfare (but a strong customer base), designer Ennio Capasa has mounted show after show of delicate, innovative, sexy and subtle looks for both men and women. It's Armani with an edge, Versace without the vulgarity. Their low profile is due in part to their dedication to the craft of fashion, with subdued advertising and highly select retail outlets. The latest location, in Los Angeles, became only their fourth store presence. While the other outlets in New York, Milan, and Tokyo have successfully parlayed the label's sultry, dark look into gritty, urban settings, the latest shop, developed by LA-based architecture firm Marmol Radziner + Associates, brings a brighter – dare we say Californian? – outlook to the shopping environment.

Marmol Radziner + Associates' work for Costume National puts light at the centre. Principal Ron Radziner traces this inspiration not only to the LA setting, but also to Costume National's own approach to design. 'They play a lot with the way light bounces off of fabrics,' says Radziner. 'Like them, we were interested in how light gets absorbed into the materials or gets reflected.' Building in a former restaurant space on LA's bustling Melrose Avenue, Marmol Radziner + Associates increased the glazing on the street-facing façade to reach from floor to almost ceiling. With the large windows and several skylights, the store is flooded with the maximum amount of natural light. Inside, the surfaces were finished not simply in white, but in several shades of grey and putty to toy with the incoming light, in unexpected ways. Natural light was enhanced with artificial, primarily through fluorescent tubes that serve as backlighting for white lacquer panels behind the rows of clothing that seem to float from a series of dividing walls. Finally, LED lighting built into the glass and white lacquer display case the team created for the shop brings an uncanny glow to selected merchandise within. With LED lights optics, says Radziner, 'you can bring light to the most remote places without putting bulbs in, creating these wonderfully ethereal effects.'

The large street-facing windows reveal much of the shop at a glance, an important aspect to the designers. 'We tried to connect this place to the city and the urban environment that exists on Melrose, and to the city as a whole,' explains Radziner. 'Connecting to the street is something that we often don't do enough in LA,' he adds. Nevertheless, the shop doesn't unfold completely at first glance. Instead, once the customer enters, a series of dividing walls along the left side conceals much of the clothing, making it visible only as one progresses deeper into the shop. The long display case along the right ferries customers to walls of Lucite shelving which display the brand's coveted shoes; getting customers to the shoes without obstacle was a key part of the program. A white lacquer sales counter at the back is flanked by two flat-screen monitors, one to display the men's runway shows and the other for the women's.

The boxy furniture with low centres of gravity are contrasted by the odd angles of the display walls and the rear walls. The unusual geometry was the team's response to the ceiling of the space, which slopes downward from the glazing wall into the shop. The sharp angles turn the slab forms into Richard Serra-like sculptural elements, their minimalism appropriate both to the rest of the space and to the clothing.

While much of the solution can be attributed to the space the team inherited and to their fascination with light, Radziner also drew inspiration from the label's designers and methods. 'We saw some of the clothes they were working on, as well as many pictures of the space where they worked. We felt it was important to understand how they worked and why they came up with the clothes they did,' says the architect. The store's brightness and openness shares much in common with the Milan atelier inhabited by Costume National's creatives. Furthermore, Radziner believes the solution works because of common traits shared by the two cities. 'There's a similarity between Milan and LA: they're both big and messy cities. In your work you're trying to carve out some sense of clarity within that city.' Flooded with light, trim and clean, Costume National's LA store is clear as day.

Costume National

Preceding page
The design team increased the height of street-facing glazing to let in the maximum amount of light and to foster a seamless connection between the boutique and its surroundings.

Below
Inspired by the geometry of the ceiling, which slopes down and back from the window-walls, Marmol Radziner + Associates introduced partition walls at jutting angles to break the space into discrete chunks.

Opposite
Featuring white lacquer and glass, and illuminated with embedded fibre-optic lighting, the squat, compact display case is firmly grounded in an otherwise airy shop.

Below
From the entrance, customers are either
ferried along the display case to Lucite
shelves at the back of the space bearing
the shop's hottest merchandise (shoes
and accessories) or left to meander
among racks of clothing concealed
by partition walls.

The Costume National boutique is a study
in light. In addition to a flood of natural
light, fluorescent tubes behind the white-
lacquer panels of display walls provide
merchandise with an ethereal, buoyant
atmosphere.

Store
Nike iD Studio

Location
New York, USA

Architect
Lynch / Eisinger / Design

Street culture meets high
culture – and giggles

Text
Shonquis Moreno

Photography
Paul Warchol

Nike's 'Individually Designed' website, which touts the company's young retail-design space, offers this tantalizing come-on: 'The invite-only Nike iD Studio in New York is a one-on-one customization experience with access to exclusive colours, styles and materials available nowhere else. You never know when 255's doors might open for you. Check back often for your chance to get an appointment. Just Do It Yourself.'

Everything at Nike iD's 'design clinic' at 255 Elizabeth Street in Manhattan has been custom-designed by architects Christian Lynch and Simon Eisinger. Lynch / Eisinger / Design's customization echoes the purpose of the clinic: to allow invited clients to design their own trainers not only with the aid of a consultant but also without a huge mark-up in price. Although Nike's effort feels somewhat limited – at last count, visitors had fewer than a dozen shoe styles to choose from and 13 'exclusive' colours – the architecture does not disappoint. Nike is purporting to bring design to the masses without giving clients the full range of tools needed to genuinely 'design' their own shoes. The studio provides visitors with niceties (a seasonal palette and a genial consultant), while withholding more generous gestures (choice of any colour, the ability to shape the shoe to an individual's anatomy and so forth). Fans of architecture, however, won't mind any of this very much, having been won over by the nicest nicety on offer here: the design of the design clinic itself. Given carte blanche to shape the space as they saw fit, Lynch and Eisinger customized everything in sight with wit, chic and an obvious respect for the anatomy of their client. Fronting what was once a fishmonger's shop, iD's unassuming digs are faced with tall panes of glass that obscure the clinic, which began life as an exclusive appointment-only experience but now caters to anyone willing to make an appointment 24 hours in advance. Visitors enter to find floor-to-ceiling racks of lacquer-white, powder-coated aluminium and walnut designed by architects who first studied Nike's pattern-making and the construction of sneakers. The racks consist of modules with radiused corners, the halves of which can be fitted together in varying configurations. Lynch and Eisinger also used their pattern-making knowledge to detail furniture and finishings. Leather furniture in the reception area, for instance, features the double-stitching more commonly found on sportswear.

Peppering the space are sport metaphors and witticisms that are not tinny, puerile or merchandise-y. The drollery begins with trompe l'oeil wallpaper in the reception area. Andy Walker designed this sylvan series of papers (one is flocked) by abstracting athletic motifs – basketballs, trainers set sole-to-sole, silhouettes of players

making lay-ups – that resemble vintage opulence from afar. Shoes have the appearance of fleurs-de-lis, and only after a second or third look is it possible to make out the other forms, which are inevitably more mundane than they appear at first glance. Against the wall in the main room, just beyond reception, is a heavy mirror whose black frame mimics carved gilt frames of the kind that normally hold Old Masters; this one, however, is made from cast resin and moulded with baroque images of different types of athletic shoes. Street culture meets high culture – and giggles.

Although architecture is, by definition, static, the designers have used our eyes to lend apparent speed to the space. Every pattern or texture in the 102-square-metre interior turns a corner, forcing our gaze to give the architecture the athleticism it necessarily lacks. Behind three banquettes or 'design pods', where consultants jog clients through their design experience, an illuminated vitrine displays a history of trainers taken from the archives at Nike's Portland, Oregon, headquarters and complete with designers' notations on heels and uppers. Facing the historical design models and suggesting a future based on Nike's past, a tall walnut cabinet, floating off the wall across the room, contains the blank-grey 'ghost' shoes that clients use to experiment with the styles and sizes available to them. Between the past and the future is a present that remains in constant flux; at this spot a walnut bench displays samples of shoes designed by previous clients.

At the rear of the clinic, hiding the 250-square-foot storage and office space, a wall is filled with a work by UK artist Shiv. Printed on pivoting square panels, Shiv's graphic illustration features the 13 colours from Nike's current shoe palette. The panels peel down to hold shoe samples designed by visitors, revealing identical but colourless images beneath. Like an Advent calendar, the 'open doors' add depth to the back of the clinic, while also showcasing the products. 'The colour is being sucked out of that wall and placed into the shoes,' says Lynch. Clinic or gimmick, iD's interior exemplifies creativity and self-expression – a concept stated more articulately by the architecture than by the brand for which it was designed.

Preceding page
Peppering the space are sport metaphors
and witticisms, including Andy Walker's
trompe l'oeil wallpaper in the reception
area, a bit of vintage opulence when
viewed from a distance.

Below and bottom
The façade of the design clinic features
dark wood strips and a window displaying
its *raison d'être*: highly designed trainers
on radiused modular racks (see detail).

Opposite
Inside, walnut cabinets contain pale grey
'ghost' shoes used by visitors for sizing and
style selection.

This spread
At the centre of the space is a 7-metre-long cantilevered display bench whose massive walnut top floats on – and off – a steel base painted white. The back wall of the studio comprises 132 panels designed by U.K.-based artist Shiv.

Nike iD Studio

Store
Jan Comme des Garçons

Location
Tokyo, Japan

Artist
Jan De Cock

Rei Kawakubo
'I didn't commission Jan to design a
shop. The point was to use his artwork
as a frame for the shop.'

Text
Masaaki Takahashi

Photography
Yasuo Kobayashi

A temporary blend of Japanese fashion and Belgian creativity, Jan Comme des Garçons is a boutique disguised as an art installation.

On Kotto-dori, the small street in Tokyo's trendy Aoyama district where Rei Kawakubo first launched Comme des Garçons, a new two-storey shop opened in April 2005, another of the fashion designer's temporary projects. In a neighbourhood where buildings and shops come and go virtually unnoticed, the 27-year-old brown-brick building would be labelled 'old', not to mention inconspicuous. Enter Kawakubo and her latest 'retail designer': Belgian artist Jan De Cock.

The shop may not stand out immediately amidst the visual clutter of Aoyama, but the passer-by who steps back to take a good look will see a striking construction of interlocking chipboard niches and boxes wrapped around the exterior. All painted white and arranged in the now-familiar De Cock style, the ensemble embraces an area that resembles an outdoor café. Almost big enough to park a car, this 3-metre-deep recess fronts a shop window made of two-way mirrored glass that offers a view of the interior, where clothing displays have been designed and positioned to lure shoppers inside. Surprisingly, however, potential customers looking for the entrance are stopped in their tracks. The wall of glass is uninterrupted by a doorway. To enter the shop, they have to go around the corner to the side of the building, away from the busy street and its incessant flow of pedestrians.

Occupying the narrow space immediately beyond the cash desk are numerous stacked display modules. Like the panelling used to clad the remainder of the space – floor, walls and ceiling – the displays are made from chipboard. De Cock wanted to give the ground floor what he calls a 'mix-and-match feeling', which he compares to the backstage area of a theatre. Leaving first-time visitors to the shop a bit bewildered was part of a carefully conceived plan to welcome them into an environment that feels more like an installation than a shop.

Readers familiar with Raf Simons' stall at the Dover Street Market in London will surely recognize the hand of De Cock at Comme des Garçons in Aoyama. It was actually Raf Simons who introduced De Cock to Kawakubo. She was immediately taken by the Belgian's rebellious nature and his dismissal of any preconceived notions of what a shop should look like. For his part, De Cock says that 'Kawakubo takes a stand with her fashion design, always reviewing the parameters, always ignoring what people expect of her'.

Soon the two were hatching plans for the building on Kotto-dori. Standing in front of it, Kawakubo pointed to the blank brick exterior and asked the artist to make it beautiful. When Jan De Cock reviews a possible commission, he often accepts or declines the offer on the basis of how much freedom the client gives him. But because Kawakubo was already familiar with the artist's reputation and had anticipated his need for independence, the plans for the Tokyo store took shape smoothly. Says Kawakubo, 'I didn't commission Jan to design a shop. The point was to use his artwork as a frame for the shop.'

Sculpture that doubles as architecture is not new to De Cock. His installation at the Henry van Velde University Library in Ghent, Belgium, is another work of art that attached itself to the spaces it occupies and which responds to the functional needs of the user. But more than that, it sets off the beauty of the library interior itself. Thinking along similar lines, Kawakubo envisaged a shop whose interior would be a work of art, rather than a shop to which art would be applied as ornament. Painted white, the chipboard is the same colour ordinarily used for museum walls. It's a colour that lends the clothing and accessories on display – no doubt intentionally – the status of precious objects in a gallery. 'I don't feel as though I've designed a shop,' says De Cock. 'I have created a work of art, which was what Rei Kawakubo wanted. I don't think many fashion designers would be willing to give me the freedom she did.'

Those who want to experience first-hand a delightful duet between two trailblazers in the worlds of fashion and art had better grab their credit cards and head straight for Kotto-dori. The temporary sculpture-cum-shop is scheduled to disappear in spring 2006. Fashions come and go, and so do works of art.

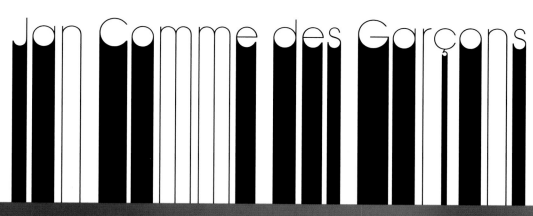

Preceding page
Recessed a full 3 metres, the completely
glazed façade at ground-floor level draws
the attention of passers-by. To enter
the shop, they must go to the side of
the building.

Below
De Cock compares the ground
floor, with its grid of low-cost chipboard
shelves, to the backstage area of a
theatre. Boundaries within the largely
white space are blurred.

Opposite
Tiled surfaces on the first floor of the
27-year old building possess a new charm.
De Cock enclosed the outdoor terrace
with a wooden structure whose openings
allow a glimpse of the surrounding city.

Below
From inside the boutique at ground level,
shoppers can see people looking through
the long narrow windows that face the
public space. As a whole, the store is part
architectural sculpture, part retail design.

Opposite
An arrangement of chipboard
components envelops the first-floor terrace
and serves as a signboard for Jan Comme
des Garçons. The interior of the upper floor
is furnished with a grid of steel pipes.

134

Jan Comme des Garçons

HO'ME

13

Store
Le Ciel Bleu

Location
Fukuoka, Japan

Architect and
interior designer
Laur Meyrieux

Laur Meyrieux
'I imagined the garden as a continuation
of the retail space. My idea was to display
clothes in the branches of the trees.'

Text
Shonquis Moreno

Photography
Kouji Okamoto

French designer Laur Meyrieux uses domestic icons, Brigitte Bardot
and summertime in southern France to create an intimately chic boutique
in Japan.

The design of the Le Ciel Bleu boutique in Fukuoka is as simple, and
as simply miraculous, as a blue sky dotted with fluffy white clouds.
French interior designer and artist Laur Meyrieux, whose practice is
in Tokyo, combined a roof terrace, a wallpapered stairwell, a rear
garden, simple drapery and Persian-carpeted floors to evoke the
sense of a comfortable yet refined domestic environment. Though
few living rooms are as flawlessly and pleasingly aesthetic as Meyrieux's evocation, the design as a Platonic ideal rather than as
reality is no less effective. Isn't fashion all about ideals? Where the
metaphor of home is thin, the designer gives visitors such a deft
combination of blank space, warm colour, clean composition and
engrossing depth of field that shoppers couldn't care less whose
living room they are in or how much that tank top costs.

This was Meyrieux's first opportunity to design an entire building.
The shop is in a quiet old neighbourhood of small streets, few cars,
traditional houses, restaurants – and a smattering of new shops. By
making Le Ciel Bleu a house, she situated it nicely within its transi-
tioning context, relating it to both the sleepy traditional area and
the tonier shopping district arising in its midst.

The two-storey, 140-square-metre shop glows white after dark. The
ground-level box is wrapped in 4-metre-high glass panels of varying widths and veiled with gauzy white curtains. A white façade
recessed above and behind the display window is embedded
with diamond-shaped mirrors that reflect the sky, animate the face
of the store and frame the depth of the glassy retail space below.
Looking at the 'house' during the day, passers-by glimpse the
crowns of parasols on the terrace, which hint at a life of Mediterranean tranquillity, the kind of eternal summer that emerges from the
photography of Jacques Henri Lartique. Pedestrians peering into
the front windows and through the entire street-level shop can see
in the distance a garden that carries the long space into greenery.

Inside, the rule is rich simplicity. By using brightly ornate carpets
and two layers of diaphanous drapery that can be drawn across
the width of the space to play with the notion of privacy, Meyrieux
gives visitors a sense of being in a chic, mid-20th-century living
room furnished in the modernist style. Throughout the space,
sparsely displayed garments hang like fruit on trees. Differing
materials and colours cohabitate here: pastel pieces share the
interior with distressed denim and bright white blouses. This subtle
contrariness, which is echoed in the combination of industrial elements (aluminium racks, concrete on floor and wall) with softening
touches (carpets, blond woods, warm shades of paint that accent
the patrician white), manages to cultivate a simultaneously airy
and intimate environment.

In this ménage of complementary opposites, the interior can also
be seen as a modern interpretation of the Greek house of antiq-
uity, which was built around an outdoor atrium. Meyrieux's atrium
is a waterless pool defined by three shallow steps that double as
display surfaces. Visitors enter the shop at street level and follow
a catwalk-like path before descending into the pool, if they so
choose. In most cases, the 'living room' furniture and display surfaces are configured to outline this path of circulation and to con-
centrate activities at the centre of the shop.

All of this cultivates a feeling of embracement and a somewhat
intimate shopping experience within a space that is actually exposed and lofty. This is not just any living room. It is chic, it is strategically planned, it is patrician, and, not least, it is irresistibly inviting.
While designing it, Meyrieux imagined Brigitte Bardot moving
through the Malaparte House in Jean-Luc Godard's Le Mépris.
Shoppers can actually watch a second iconic Bardot film, Roger
Vadim's Et Dieu Créa la Femme, which is screened on a wall upstairs. Here Bardot gives what Meyrieux calls 'a lesson in femininity'.

Fitting rooms at the centre of the space are simple white modernist cylinders that look like old-fashioned facilities for donning one's
bathing costume on the beach in Nice. Display shelves with blond-
wood exteriors contain cubbyholes of varying sizes painted orange,
bordeaux or black inside. Garment racks – simple metal pipes of
the type used for scaffolding – provide vertical continuity between
floor and ceiling. Beside the cash desk, Meyrieux begins to overlap
interior and exterior, lining a section of wall with wood panelling cut
into the shape of tree trunks, a graphic that anticipates the actual
garden a few metres away, on the other side of a large, sliding
glass door. When the door is opened completely, indoors literally
becomes outdoors. 'I imagined the garden as a continuation of
the retail space. My idea was to display clothes in the branches
of the trees,' says Meyrieux. If the proprietor of the shop is smart
enough to follow her suggestion, the apparel so displayed will add
a final touch of magical realism to a space which is already imbu-
ing shopping with the fantasy that fashion designers have been
giving to couture throughout history. About time, we say.

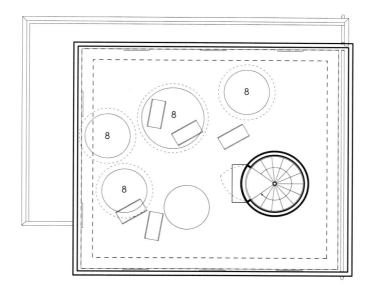

Third floor

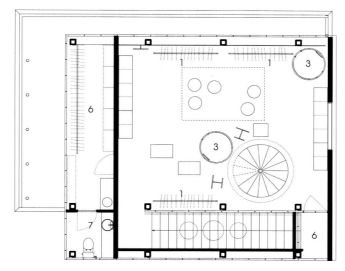

Second floor

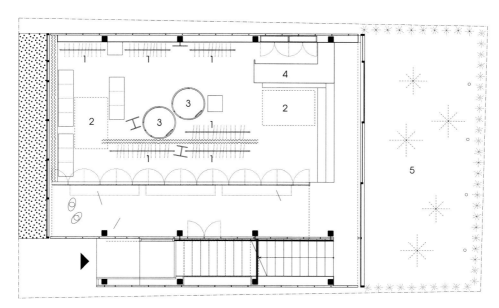

First floor

137

Below
At night, Le Ciel Bleu's two-storey, 140-square-metre outlet spreads a glow on the pavement outside the shop. The ground-level box is wrapped in tall glass panels and curtained in white.

A recessed façade above the display window features diamond-shaped mirrors that reflect the sky and animate the face of the shop.

Bottom
Like something out of a mid-20th-century Case Study House, a depression at the centre of the shop is hemmed by three shallow steps that partition the room and provide display surfaces.

This page
Pastel garments share the space with
distressed denim and bright white blouses.
Industrial pieces are paired with round
seating elements and Persian carpets.
Cylindrical white fitting rooms resemble
a modern fireplace.

This page and opposite
During the summer, Le Ciel Bleu's merchandise will hang from shrubbery in a garden at the rear of the shop. From the garden, a staircase leads to a parasol-crowned roof redolent of the Mediterranean. Simple shelves painted Bordeaux, orange or black add depth and warmth to the flawless white of the interior.

Le Ciel Bleu

Store
Stephane Dou & Changlee Yugin

Location
Taichung, Taiwan

Architect
CJ Studio

Shichieh Lu
'Ideas on shopping trends
are no longer as simple as they
once were.'

Text
Masaaki Takahashi

Photography
Kuomin Lee

CJ Studio visualized a free-flowing image of a fashion-show catwalk hung with clothes created by Taiwanese designers Stephane Dou and Changlee Yugin.

Featuring clothes by Taiwanese fashion designers Stephane Dou and Changlee Yugin, this project is the duo's second boutique in as many years, and their second joint venture with architect Shichieh Lu. The outlet is located in Taichung, Taiwan's third-largest city, which boasts a history that spans almost three centuries. Although the city's industrial areas have experienced significant growth in recent years, Taichung maintains its charmingly slow-paced, relaxed atmosphere. It was this atmosphere that attracted interest and initial plans for the construction of a Guggenheim Museum, to be designed by Zaha Hadid (a project eventually cancelled, unfortunately). By holding competitions for building projects such as the Taichung Metropolitan Opera House, however, the city demonstrates its continued desire to become an international hub and to play a larger role in the cultural life of Taiwan and the Far East. As many expensive homes, modern shopping complexes and new department stores rise in older parts of the city, which are now part of a large-scale redevelopment zone, there is a sense that public awareness of design is growing, with an even greater increase still to come.

Armed with a BA in architecture from Tung-Hai University, Shichieh Lu attended the Architectural Association School of Architecture in London, from which he graduated in 1993. Two years later he established his own office, CJ Studio, and he currently teaches at several universities. As a result of his design of the United Hotel and his subsequent association with an international chain called Design Hotels, Shichieh's involvement in the hospitality industry and in product design has expanded. He has also published a book. The range of projects in his portfolio extends far beyond interiors.

'Ideas on shopping trends are no longer as simple as they once were,' says Shichieh, who sees design and architecture not merely as expressions of artistic creation but also as social events. In his opinion, architecture is both an entrance to the world and an endless discovery. As part of this infinitely continuing process, each design project is a uniquely exciting experience, a constantly evolving adventure. His is a personal philosophy that prompts him to seize every opportunity to appreciate and understand the architecture of buildings and their interiors.

In designing the boutique, Shichieh reinterpreted the relationship between fashion and architecture. The result is a giant installation of eye-catching polished stainless steel, which also functions as a rack for hanging merchandise. The design hints at various influences – the spiral shape of DNA, carnival rides, aeroplane propellers – but perhaps the most interesting are those that refer to Shichieh's love of dance and art: among others, he mentions Marcel Duchamp's famous *Nude Descending a Staircase*; *Trace of Dance*, a book edited by Laurence Louppe; and Gilles Deleuze's *Cinema I* and *Cinema II*. 'What this installation expresses is frozen music,' he says. 'At the same time, it is a dancing form that's meant to symbolize the enjoyment of shopping.' Representing Shichieh's inspired fusion of fun shopping and playful dance steps is a doubled-railed, stainless-steel track or 'space ladder' that dips and swirls through the shop, at some places nearly skimming the floor and at others creating a canopy. Like a choreographed figure moving to the rhythm of soundless music, the graceful lines of the installation evoke the free-flowing image of a fashion-show catwalk.

Emerging from the designer's study of installation art, the project also helped to solidify his interest in the structures of music and modern dance. And to satisfy the brief, of course, the installation had to be a functional piece on which to display merchandise. As such, it is a dynamic intervention that can be configured and reconfigured on site in much the same way as a series of dance steps can be modified to meet new requirements. Aluminium-panelled walls and floor are another expression of the clients' views on fashion; although cool and aloof, the metallized surfaces give the space a crisp, clean look. Handbags and garments suspended from the stainless-steel roller coaster join display units and hangers in light-coloured wood to please the eye and soften the high-gloss metal interior. A retail space for the mind, it fulfils the designer's wish to create an environment in which customers can not only enjoy shopping but also appreciate the intricacies of the 'art installation'. Shichieh's shop design invites visitors into a gallery and sends them home with a prized item from the collection.

In spite of the accomplishments of Shichieh and others, Taiwan is not yet a country in which interior design has come into its own; many people are still confused by the differences between professional interior design, a discipline backed by forethought and purpose, and mere decoration. Shichieh does believe, however, that the general public often has a deeper interest in the interior of a building than in its façade. This type of thinking offers hope and possibilities for Taiwan's interior-design industry. Stay tuned for the latest developments.

Floor plan
1. Display table
2. Hanging display
3. Fitting room
4. Counter
5. Rear area

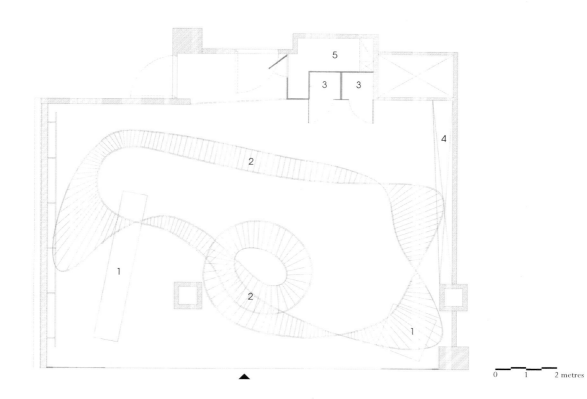

0   1   2 metres

143

Stephane Dou & Changlee Yugin

This spread
Hanging on metal cables from the ceiling, the stainless-steel installation is supported by 5-cm-high metal legs where it dips to meet the floor. 'Dancing Hangers' symbolizes the partnership of the fashion designers who commissioned it.

144

Clockwise from top left
To test his design, the architect constructed
a full-scale model. The installation comprises two curving stainless-steel rods (3 cm
in diameter), a vertical section (1.5 cm
in diameter) and straight rods spaced at
20-cm intervals.

Clockwise from top left
'Dancing Hangers' was built as a whole
at the factory, cut into six sections, trans-
ported to the shop, and reassembled
on site. Walls and sand-polished floor are
clad in 2-mm-thick aluminium sheet.
Two maple display tables form a striking
contrast to the metal surfaces.

Store
Uniqlo Ginza

Location
Tokyo, Japan

Architect
Klein Dytham architecture

Astrid Klein
'Whatever the quality of the product,
it's no good if customers feel as though
they're drowning in a sea of it. That's
what we had to change.'

Text
Masaaki Takahashi

Photography
Nacása & Partners

Low cost *can* equal high quality: six words that informed Klein Dytham architecture's retail design for casual-wear company Uniqlo in Tokyo.

Established in 1948, Uniqlo launched its first store in Tokyo's hip fashion quarter, Harajuku, 50 years later it went on to open outlets nationwide. Soon everyone had heard of it, and the brand became so popular that young people practically adopted Uniqlo as their national uniform. Despite making a bid to enter the global market, the company has been hard pressed to win out against the Gap, whose similar emphasis on clean design is bolstered by a more sophisticated image. Regardless of stiff competition abroad, however, Uniqlo remains a firm favourite in Japan. Recently, the company opened its flagship store in Ginza, Tokyo's most exclusive shopping district and the destination of those on the lookout for luxury. Opening a shop here reveals a new strategy for Uniqlo, one that places an emphasis on style and on an appeal to a class of clientele unlike its conventional target group. The store is located not far away from a famous intersection featuring many of Ginza's landmarks, such as Mitsukoshi and the Wako Building. It occupies the first five floors of the building, with womenswear housed on the ground floor and the first and second storeys, menswear on the top floor, and a mix of clothes for men and children sandwiched between them on the third floor.

According to Astrid Klein of Klein Dytham architecture (KDa), the firm responsible for the design, the store was created with several goals in mind: clearing up the misapprehension that low cost equals poor quality; reinforcing the idea that, although Uniqlo is cheap, it sells high-quality items; highlighting the fact that you can dress fashionably without spending lots of money; and creating a look that would give people the urge to shop, enticing in even passersby who had previously never considered buying Uniqlo.

In Japan, the name Uniqlo conjures up images of masses of clothing, each garment grouped with like items, as in a warehouse. As Klein observes, 'Even the most delicious spaghetti becomes unappetizing if a huge, overflowing plate of it is plunked down in front of you. In Japanese *kaiseki* cuisine, the elegant presentation of a small amount of food is what heightens its value. Equally, whatever the quality of the product, it's no good if customers feel as though they're drowning in a sea of it. That's what we had to change.'

Here, a pergola-like structure is combined with a series of frames, original carpeting and lighting that varies from area to area, producing a space that feels like a series of shops-in-a-shop. Along both side walls, Uniqlo's trademark method of displaying clothes ceiling high has been employed to create something of a tunnel. Visitors lured inside by the brightly glowing façade find themselves drawn along this tunnel to the heart of the store. KDa retained certain elements of the brand's already well-known identity by placing low, wooden tables throughout the interior for a relaxed domestic atmosphere; breaking up the overall sense of space; and displaying apparel for instant recognition of location, colour and style. 'To highlight the quality of the product, it was vital to have a hierarchical aspect to the display,' says Klein.

KDa wanted the façade to give customers familiar with Uniqlo's square logo a pleasant feeling of surprise upon spotting its Ginza incarnation and to prompt them to enter the store and buy. The choice of a square pattern in mirrored stainless steel is reminiscent of lighting louvres. Behind this lies an LED logo composed of computer-controlled lights that form a moving pattern. The subtlety of this lettering epitomizes the departure from Uniqlo's traditional look. The façade is a far cry from the huge screens that flash bright adverts on every Tokyo street corner. Instead, it captures the purity and elegance associated with the Ginza name and is in keeping with the desired image of a shop stocking a range of quality products.

Klein feels there are countless cases of Japanese companies misreading the consumer and coming up with disruptive advertising and design. Of this venture she says, 'We've conveyed the relaxed and honest nature of Uniqlo. Nowadays, stores have become more like galleries; if you just want to buy something, you can do it online.' On the same subject, partner Mark Dytham says, 'If you take a look at brand shops, you see that they have become a kind of stage. People stepping out of a store clutching lots of large bags covered in logos need an audience for their performance. So it's natural for super-brands not to have a virtual store. You have to keep this in mind in shop design too.' Tokyo stores that have caught Dytham's eye are Herzog and de Meuron's cutting-edge Prada boutique in Aoyama and a traditional, wood-framed sake shop near his home, a combination that matches the pair's flexible approach to design. This reflection of today's hybridization of fashion in their creations helps to explain KDa's current popularity.

Uniqlo Ginza

Preceding page
Uniqlo Ginza at night: the 24-x-15-metre façade features a programmable LED-and-fluorescent electronic screen with super-low-resolution (0.001 megapixel) images announcing the name of the shop.

Below
The menswear floor is an environment of masculine browns. Merchandise in this simple, open-plan space is presented in a variety of modular display units.

Opposite top and bottom
Cubic frames ('pergolas') and carpeting define domestically scaled sub-zones, while providing flexible support for displays.

Uniqlo Ginza

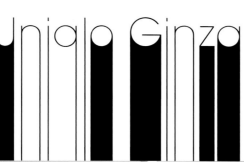

Uniqlo Ginza

Below
The women's department has a softer palette. Here the pergola frame provides a variety of display possibilities.

52

Uniqlo Ginza

Below
KDa designed the street-level 'Gallery'
as a showroom for the promotion of new
products, trends and thematic displays.
The glossy white space resembles the
interior of a museum of modern art.

Store
Tiberius

Location
Vienna, Austria

Architect
BEHF Architects

Stephan Ferenczy
'Lucid lines are vital to fashion retail, and
uncluttered architecture is the key to the
corporate identity of a fetish shop.'

Text
Edwin van Onna

Photography
Rupert Steiner

BEHF Architects created a minimalist shop in Vienna with a touch of the masquerade: a theatrical black and white space that distinguishes itself from the familiar sleazy leather-and-latex outlet.

In terms of architecture, Vienna is invariably coupled to the Secessionist movement. What would Vienna be, after all, without all those elegant lines and colourful *fin-de-siècle* interiors? Today, however, a different side of Vienna appears in the form of Tiberius, a shop that specializes in leather, latex and PVC apparel for fetishists. Interior-design honours go to BEHF Architects, which conceived and realized the low-budget project.

This small shop – not far from Mariahilferstrasse, Austria's premiere shopping street – features a 100-square-metre space in which an extravagant collection of garments, accessories and sex toys is on display. According to architect Stephan Ferenczy, part of the job was to reposition a store that had already been doing good business in Vienna for ten years. The goal was a well-organized space based on transparency *and* privacy. Simple, lucid lines, he says, are vital to fashion retail, and particularly to this style of clothing, in which uncluttered architecture is the key to 'supreme corporate identity'. BEHF had a prime example in Boutique Bizarre, which opened in 2000 on Hamburg's infamous Reeperbahn: a fetish megastore with 14 times more floor space than Tiberius.

Ferenczy points out that fetishists are not looking for architecture that emerges from a certain aesthetic perspective. This target group is more interested in the basics. The ordinary fetish shop has no distinctive frontage. 'On the contrary, those that aren't hidden away tend to have a low-budget look.' At Tiberius, therefore, the new conceptual focus was on no-fuss architecture, with open areas for spotlighting the product. The 19th-century Biedermeier-style building needed to be adapted to this concept. The two small shops that had formerly occupied the building were to become a single efficient space. A sizable wall divided the premises in two, and existing arched components clearly influenced the feel of the space. BEHF's solution was to paint the ceiling and walls completely black, which made the existing architecture dissolve into the background. Even the light fixtures are black. The eye is now drawn to low display units in the retail space towards the front of the shop. These wardrobe-like pieces, with their gleaming white surfaces, provide a stark contrast to the rest of the interior. Why black and white rather than a palette of lurid colours? Are BEHF's non-shades a foretaste of the fetish collection? Ferenczy says it had more to do with approaching the design from an experiential angle. 'Most of the merchandise consists of solid-colour items, as colour is often part of the fetish. Such products need to be viewed against a white background.' Dark-grey could have been substituted for black, he adds, but black better supports the 'stage effect'.

The white display units, which are small enough to see over, do not prevent customers from experiencing the shop as an entity. At the same time, their presence allows for a certain sense of intimacy. 'The larger pieces of furniture are positioned discreetly to ensure privacy, while also creating interest and variety,' explains Ferenczy. Apparel displayed in the central island, in particular, cannot be seen by everyone in the shop. Customers have to make their way through the display units to view the merchandise. The resulting sense of confinement is in sync with the mind-set of the clientele. One room has even been transformed into a cosy cabin, complete with white sofa. It's obvious that images of bawdy bedroom capers are encouraged here. The Tiberius slogan is not for nothing 'Fashion Is Passion'. The idea that other shoppers may be looking in only increases the excitement, as voyeurism is a fetish in itself.

Accessories – masks, high-heeled shoes, whips, belts, caps, sex toys and so forth – are more prominently displayed, perhaps because such extraordinarily designed objects seem made to be shown off. Products beckon from illuminated showcases and display units integrated into the black partition wall, whose inner surface is finished in white. Since many of the accessories are black, a white backdrop is ideal. Even passers-by have a good view of the upper showcases.

Farther along, behind the partition wall, are several spacious fitting rooms. Sober, austere and completely black on all sides, they cater to a preference for SM: heavy chains hang down, and a white seating element forms the only light relief. Here, too, the enclosure seems to invite a bit of hanky-panky. 'The "chain-chamber" is a VIP dressing room,' says the architect. 'Imagine how much money – and time – you can spend in such a shop. Certain customers would rather not be seen naked or dressed in extravagant outfits. Others, especially if they're well known, may not want to be recognized.'

Without a disguise, one cannot be totally incognito at Tiberius, however. Large 'window boxes' dominate the façade. Display windows and entrance are newly placed, and, thanks to the depth of the façade, two-part display windows feature frosted-glass dividing doors that can be opened to create a single, deeper space. When not used as such, the space can be halved by shutting the door, leaving the outer half as a display window facing the street and the inner half as a showcase facing the interior. Tiberius represents efficiency right down to the last centimetre.

Tiberius

Preceding page
A deep façade creates spacious display windows that can be halved by shutting a frosted glass door, leaving the inner section as a showcase that faces the shop interior.

This page
Heavy chains provide the atmosphere inside a discreet fitting room for VIPs.

Opposite
A black wall displaying accessories separates retail area from fitting rooms.

Floor plan and section
1. Entrance
2. Shop-window display
3. Display unit
4. Hanging display
5. Fitting room
6. Stockroom

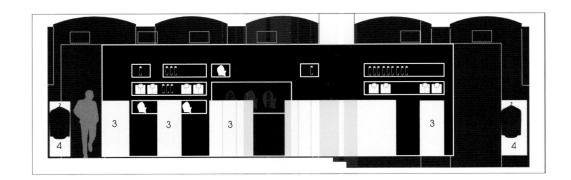

Store
Bethsabee

Location
Hasselt, Belgium

Architect
Creneau International

An Moors of Creneau International
'We call ourselves "atmosphere architects",
and we try to create the appropriate
ambience for every target group.'

Text
Brigitte van Mechelen

Photography
Filip van Loock

Feminine seduction culled from the ambience and palette of a 17th-century painting is at the heart of Bethsabee, a shoe shop in Hasselt created by 'atmosphere architects' Creneau International.

Imagine yourself a woman 'very beautiful to look upon', so beautiful that an enamoured king impregnates you, has your husband killed and brings you into his household. One man obviously fascinated by the story was Rembrandt van Rijn (creator of *The Night Watch*, a favourite work of visitors to the Rijksmuseum in Amsterdam), who in 1654 painted *Bethsabee au Bain* (*Bathsheba at Her Bath*), from which Anja Mulleners took the name of her shop, Bethsabee, with its exclusive collection of shoes, handbags, belts and wallets. How does Rembrandt's biblical Bethsabee relate to shoes? Perhaps the servant drying the toes of the plump beauty can be compared to the employee who holds the customer's foot as it slides into the selected shoe.

The shop, located in Hasselt, Belgium, needed a new look. In renovating the interior, Creneau International drew inspiration from the ambience and palette of the 17th-century painting. The firm's interpretation of Rembrandt's setting for King David's muse responded to Mulleners' request for a comfortable space for lovers of elegant footwear. Bathsheba does symbolize, after all, the woman who puts her best foot (among other things) forward to seduce her man. And most of Bethsabee's clientele are of the female persuasion.

Also based in Hasselt, Creneau International is an architecture firm with a staff of 35 whose clients include O'Neill, Lee, D.E.P.T. and Dr. Martens. 'The interiors, retail concepts and display systems that we design for these manufacturers are totally different from the luxurious, frothy, sophisticated atmosphere needed at Bethsabee,' says Creneau's spokesperson, An Moors. 'But we call ourselves "atmosphere architects", and we try to create the appropriate ambience for every target group. We have spotters between the ages of 16 and 26 in more than 50 cities to help us; they keep us informed of new trends – from politics and social issues to fashion and food – by means of digital photos, videos and email. This intelligence and research network, which is called "Mutation Spotting", cannot be compared to traditional market research. The online contact is vital. The trends I'm talking about come and go at a surprising pace.'

Shoes are made to be loved, especially those in this price bracket. The existing premises were not large enough for Bethsabee's seductive wiles; the display window was little more than a door. Creneau was forced to relinquish a bit of retail space to carve out the bay at the front, but the vast display window created in turn was well worth the sacrifice. Each shoe, bag and belt poses proudly on an elegant tier of grey laminated glass. Suspended above one glass platform occupied by a single shoe is an eye-catching crystal chandelier, which adds to the impression of an altar of worship.

The architects attempted to give an interior of modest dimensions (120 square metres) the feel of a spacious salon. Two mirrored walls allow customers to scrutinize themselves (and one another) from top to toe. Purpose-designed leather sofas in a rich mocha-brown line three sides of the space provided as a fitting area. Accompanying them are three matching hassocks on which employees can sit or kneel while helping customers try on shoes. All were made in Creneau's own manufacturing facility. Adorning the rear wall of the fitting area is stencilled wallpaper bearing a repeat pattern of Bathsheba having her feet washed, as painted by Rembrandt – another highlight designed and made by Creneau's graphic-design team. Located at the firm's headquarters in Hasselt is a large atelier equipped with much of the machinery needed for its projects, including in-house upholstering. These facilities make financial sense, while also contributing to a desire for originality. Two shades of chocolate brown were used for the wallpaper, but even though the adjacent seating is also clad in brown leather, this part of the store is anything but a dark hollow. Commanding the ceiling is a 3-x-6-metre elliptical chandelier sparkling with light reflected off hundreds of dangling Swarovski crystals.

Purchases are made at a 10-metre-long counter that takes its interesting relief from a combination of cornice mouldings. Thanks to a glass top, the counter doubles as a treasure chest, openly displaying a range of accessories. A 'shrine' at the centre of the counter features a smaller chandelier, which illuminates yet another item demanding special attention.

Ernst van de Weetering (chairman of the Rembrandt Research Project, which ascertains the authenticity of paintings attributed to the artist) praises the master's inimitable ability to convey illusion through a play of light and shadow. It is precisely this type of illusion that Creneau International has used to craft an aura for Bethsabee that suits a sumptuous shoe salon.

Floor plan
1. Lounge
2. Retail area
3. Cask desk
4. Rear area

Bottom
A rendering of the façade shows the
dual effect of the new display window: this
drastic enlargement of the existing window
has a magnetic impact on passers-by.

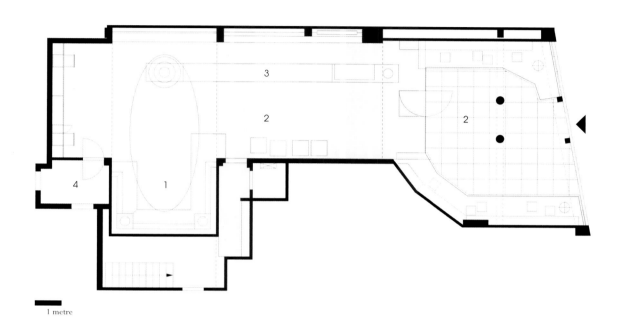

1 metre

Bethsabee

Bottom
The 10-metre-long counter – an imposing,
glass-topped structure painted a dark
chocolate brown – is clad in ornamental
moulding. The layered look of horizontal
lines accentuates the length of the counter.

Bethsabee

Bethsabee

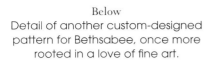

Below
Detail of another custom-designed
pattern for Bethsabee, once more
rooted in a love of fine art.

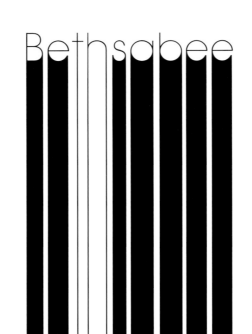

This page
In the fitting area, a long sofa occupies half the wall space. Hovering above the counter in this part of the shop is a 3-x-6-metre Swarovski-crystal chandelier. One wall is covered in stencilled wallpaper designed especially for the shop and inspired by Rembrandt's *Bathsheba at Her Bath*.

Store
Miss Sixty Boutiques

Location
Divers

Architect
Studio 63

Massimo Dei
'We aimed for a balance between
architecture and merchandise.'

Text
Shonquis Moreno

Photography
Yael Pincus

Around the world, Studio 63 is creating a series of individualized Miss Sixty boutiques that make shopping an act of nostalgia and a theatre for make-believe.

One by one, Studio 63 Architecture and Design (with branches in Florence, New York and Hong Kong) is realizing 60 boutiques and showrooms worldwide for Miss Sixty, trebling designer Wichy Hassan's global presence. Although part of a chain, each shop takes its distinctive character from the structure of the existing space and the context of its location.

Sharing a fascination with the glamorous 1970s, all Miss Sixty shops are studded with icons from that era. The boutiques revolve around graphic design, television and cinema from the '70s; old wallpaper and textile patterns; Verner Panton creations and Andy Warhol prints; and performances by David Bowie, alias Ziggy Stardust. Massimo Dei, one of two principals at Studio 63 (the other is Piero Angelo Orecchioni) believes the ambience created by such additions to the retail spaces – things 'woven into the culture' – are more important than giving shoppers something they have experienced directly or even something they consciously recognize. It's all about creating atmosphere. The shops also share an organic composition: curved shelving that creates an embroidery against the walls, edgeless benches, sculpted counters, drop ceilings with amorphous cutouts, wasp-waisted columns, vivid colours and sensuous materials. Such elements express the function of shops that invite customers to reinvent themselves, to revel in surface as a luxurious fiction, to make believe. Shopping here is not banal. Sixty fashions target playfully sexy women with the con-fidence to express themselves as individuals. The boutique is a receding backdrop for clothes: garments that are irreverently colourful, heavily layered and textured, brazenly tight-fitting, asymmetrical. 'We aimed for a balance between architecture and merchandise,' says Studio 63's Dei. 'Clothes are the protag-onist in each shop's narrative, until the shopper slips them on and becomes the protagonist herself.'

The contrast of materials – coarse and smooth, flushed and icy, hard and soft – drives the eye, stirs the senses and directs the traffic. Viscerally accomplishing these tasks are pink walls, lemon floors, white surfaces with orange accents, black-and-white rooms highlighted in red-and-yellow. Varied textures – deep shag carpeting, vinyl benches, a froth of white feathers under a girlish pink light, velvet drapery, shiny plastic walls, glossy floors – pull passers-by inside, where clothing transforms them into shoppers and a children's theatre of sweetly nostalgic fitting rooms turns them into buyers.

Underlying the glamour is a sense of irony. Feathers, vinyl and shag – often frivolous and kitschy – show that no one at Miss Sixty or Studio 63 is too much in earnest. Aware of the irony involved in play-acting, the designers give it full rein. 'It's a very theatrical element,' says architect Dei. And it communicates an identity of place.

For all the threads that run through this series of shops, the degree to which each store tells the story of its location is remarkable. The Los Angeles shop pays homage to the sprawling city and the industry that shapes it, taking its character from Hollywood and old sci-fi movies (*Barbarella*, *The Blob*, *The Day the Earth Stood Still*). Invading the Melrose Avenue outlet is a huge drop that pours from the ceiling, floods the space, and washes floor and counters in a pool of shiny yellow. Equally tied to its context is the Milanese shop, located amidst Via Montenapoleone's high-end boutiques. Fashioned in the image of its neighbours, the intimate, luxurious boutique has walls carpeted in beige shag interrupted by ceramic tiles and white-plastic bubble displays. Rounded beehive partitions mix with a clear-plastic Saarinen tulip table, slender zinc-wrapped columns, and layers of translucency achieved using clear plastic, aluminium, neutral colours and glass.

The SoHo boutique In New York has all the brilliant white modernism of a Stanley Kubrick film. At first glance the shop, with its radiused walls, references something organic, but the materials used are wholly synthetic. At the rear of the shop, a vivid orange, deep-pile moquette 'evolves' from the floor to form a bench, a wall and, finally, the ceiling. Like its cousins, the SoHo store has the alternately chilly and sensuous, worldly yet shallow, glamour of the '70s. It has the same cool seduction – slightly melodramatic and icy when experienced from afar – of a vain woman. Conscious of its own irony and vanity, however, the larger-than-life boudoir beckons the young-at-heart and the little girls they once were, traipsing around in Mama's clothes. Fitting rooms, in particular, are designed to recall the imaginative days of dressing up, dreaming of debutante balls, of being endlessly inventible and beloved: rooms that are part atelier – reserved for one's personal fitting – and part theatre. Dei calls the fitting room 'an intimate space' and 'a kind of stage where you are the main character'. He says that many SoHo shops 'try to convey the same feeling that Gothic churches conveyed centuries ago. They invite you to enter a space so great that it's almost divine: an elite, prestigious club that would never accept an ordinary person like you. In this sense, Miss Sixty is very different. It's a space with human proportions.'

Preceding page top
Although Miss Sixty is a chain, each shop reflects the existing space and its location. Shared features are references to the glamorous 1970s and interiors with anorganic composition: from softly curved shelving and furniture to drop ceilings.

Preceding page bottom
Contrasting materials and colour schemes – coarse and smooth, flushed and icy, hard and soft – drive the eye and the senses, while directing shoppers through the retail space.

Below
A departure from other outlets in the chain, the Miss Sixty/Energie retail emporium in Palermo, at the centre of the historical capital of Sicily, features hard materials and rich colours.

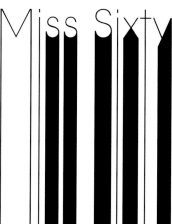

Miss Sixty

Below
Dark and angular, with rectangular shelving, the shop, like the city, has a multifaceted character.

The New York store has the alternately chilly and sensuous, worldly yet shallow, glamour of the '70s. Cool and white, the shop displays an organic air – with its radiused walls, columns and furniture – without shunning synthetic materials.

At the rear (top), an orange, deep-pile moquette rises from the floor to form a bench, a wall and, finally, the ceiling. Glossy white benches (bottom) are lit with warm lights and moated with feathers.

On a tony boulevard in Milan, the Sixty-boutique fits right in. The space features floral wallpaper (bottom), shag rugs (top), mid-20th-century modernist furniture and slender zinc-wrapped columns.

Store
Jacob & Co

Location
New York, USA

Architect
Arnell Group

The displays are intended
to allow clients to 'mine'
the merchandise

Text
Shonquis Moreno

Photography
Svend Lindbaek

A jewellery shop designed by the Arnell Group allows Jacob Arabo's clientele to mine a midtown Manhattan showroom for gems.

Russian-born jeweller Jacob Arabo, who started out as an immigrant in New York, is currently living the American dream. From a rough stall in the Diamond District, Arabo made his name (today they call him 'Jacob the Jeweler': no kidding) by designing opulent accoutrements for the celebrity elite – rapper 50 Cent, actress Angela Bassett and model Gisele Bundchen wear his watches – and by carrying on the centuries-old tradition of creating precious objects for royalty. Arabo banks on the fact that gems remain one of the greatest symbols of success in a country that adores its symbols. To represent Arabo's accomplishments and to highlight the sumptuousness of his designs, the New York-based Arnell Group Innovation Lab used the diamond mine as the central metaphor for the Jacob & Company New York flagship store.

In geology, a stratum is a bed or layer of sedimentary rock having approximately the same composition throughout; in society, a stratum is a level of people with a similar social, cultural or economic status. The horizontal organization (both physical and financial) of the mine lent itself tidily to the demands of a jewellery shop and to the social conventions to which such a shop must cater. The sleekly beautiful translation of the mine, with its veins and layers, into a retail environment was assisted by Arnell Group's clever use of Corian and computer-controlled milling to create three types of strata in the showroom for storage, display and lighting. To fabricate the skin of the shop, the designers first made sketches by hand. After diagramming the concept in both Illustrator and Photoshop and doing spatial studies in Maya and 3D Max, they moved on to AutoCAD. The architects sheathed the 111-square-metre interior in striated panels that wrap the shop from the façade inwards. All horizontal surfaces are made from weatherproof half-inch (1.27 cm) Corian bonded onto three-quarter-inch (1.90 cm) sheets of plywood and supported by metal frames. The glacier-white Corian resembles, but slightly clashes with, the stucco façade of the larger building that it foots (and which was simultaneously renovated by the Arnell Group). The clash occurs because the refined texture and horizontal articulation of the exterior Corian dressing upstages the less refined, vertically orientated, faux-stone blocks of its turn-of-the-century host. Nonetheless, the façade is unusual, beautiful and consonant with its function, and it benefits from the fact that the rough structure above it recedes graciously in the broad canyon of 57th Street, where it is difficult to take in the entire face of a building from the pavement.

The single flaw in the façade – which can't help but please the jeweller's fans – is a large doorknob marked with garish colours that mimics the face of the signature, oversized Arabo watch and interrupts the transparency of the glass entry door. Moving inwards (the stripes evoke the blur of a panning camera), the wall pattern flows through the diamantine facets and creases of the shop in a single continuous surface. Reveals between panels imply mineral veins or the spaces between them. Six sets of three panels - 167 square metres in linear surface – exhibit slight variations in the breadth and depth of the striations. 'The varying widths of the striations were achieved by distorting a photo of light penetrating a diamond and translating its prismatic effect into three-dimensions, thus creating variations in the depth and width of each line,' says Arnell senior designer Peter Arnell.

Glass shadow boxes hem the long walls from the front to the rear of the space, and display cases are canted diagonally from the walls like jutting boulders or uncut rock. The veins of display cases inset into the walls broaden and narrow in height in the manner of mineral veins, but these have the hard edges and flawless lines of a cut stone. Although displays invite visitors to 'mine' the merchandise, a card reader embedded discreetly in the surface of each display allows only clerks to access the pieces of jewellery. The cases also contain quasi-camouflaged drawers that interrupt the Corian pattern only minimally. Walls, however, are punctuated by 50 flat-panel screens scattered around the room, displaying custom-made animation and advertising themselves as an enhancement in the otherwise minimally seamed surfaces. By contrast, a strong, albeit simple, detail is the irregular, nearly arrow-shaped drop ceiling that features recessed lighting and vaguely echoes the geometries at work in the room below it. Arguably, the flagship is a finer gem than the sparklers designed to woo the glitterati.

Floor plan
1. Retail area
2. Hallway
3. Office
4. Lounge
5. Presentation room
6. Rear area

Bottom
The façade is sheathed in horizontally striated panels that penetrate inwards. The refined texture and horizontal articulation of the Corian dressing upstages the less refined, vertically orientated, faux-stone blocks of the turn-of-the-century building that accommodates the shop.

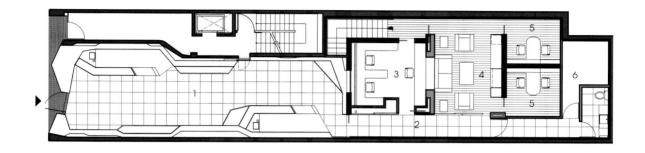

Jacob & Co

This spread
The Arnell Group Innovation Lab
transformed Jacob & Company's
Manhattan flagship into a diamond
mine. Irregularly thickened walls boast
1.27-cm-thick Corian bonded onto
1.90-cm-thick sheets of plywood and
supported by metal frames. The result
is a very grown-up Aladdin's cave.

Below
Using computer-controlled mills to cut the Corian, the Arnell Group created three types of 'strata' for storage, display and lighting.

Opposite top
Vitrines cant from the walls and run in horizontal veins like gems emerging from the ground, already cut and polished. They allow clients to 'mine' the merchandise with their eyes.

Opposite bottom
Office space and viewing lounges with huge aquaria are located at the rear of showroom, where a plainer look allows the jewellery to dominate visitors' attention.

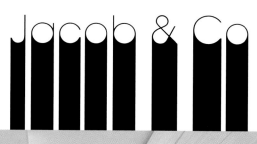

Jacob & Co

Store
Harvey Nichols

Location
Hong Kong, China

Architect
Christian Biecher & Associes

Christian Biecher
'One should experience it as if walking into
a film, where one moves around, discovers,
and goes from one scene to the next.'

Text
Chris Scott

Photography
William Furniss

Harvey Nichols in Hong Kong is Christian Biecher's on English heritage and magic as seen from abroad.

In 1828 Benjamin Harvey and Colonel Nichols opened their first department store in Knightsbridge, London. Today's Harvey Nichols, which boasts an ultra-stylish reputation, has stores not only in London, but also in Manchester, Leeds, Birmingham, Edinburgh, Riyadh, Moscow, Dubai and, more recently, Dublin and Hong Kong, two new stores that bear the signature of French designer and architect Christian Biecher.

Biecher initially met the present owner of Harvey Nichols, Dickson Pune, several years ago in conjunction with another project. After a brief introduction, Pune asked whether the architect would be interested in designing a Harvey Nichols store in Hong Kong. Six months later, Biecher and three big-name candidates for the job received a brief. When the smaller French studio was ultimately selected, the news came as a surprise to Christian Biecher & Associes (CBA), which was now confronted with an exciting, challenging prospect. Already with several shops to his credit, however, Biecher was no stranger to retail design. He approaches this sort of work by looking at the origins of a company or brand, and in the case of Harvey Nichols he found a strong heritage and a clear-cut vision: to create a sense of luxury that is not necessarily based on tradition. The management is open to fresh ideas and is keen to experiment, which is good news for a designer.

Biecher particularly wanted to weave the identity of the London store into his design, as he believes that Harvey Nichols 'could not exist were it not English' and that its special magic comes from its British background. He sees it as an exciting, fascinating fusion of punk, rock'n'roll, English country gardens and Liberty prints. He aimed for a mix of the unconventional and the classic: England as seen from abroad. 'As always, I wanted contrasts,' he says, 'but how was I to achieve a strong image that would link all areas of a 6000-square-metre surface spread over five floors?'

Work started with a palette of black and white, the colours that unite all five floors. To this he added various materials and colours, creating different looks and moods within the store: silver for men, bronze and gold for women, a colourful pop atmosphere for jeans and children, a luxurious modern ambience for accessories, and a sense of serenity for perfumes and cosmetics. Biecher and his team designed the space in its entirety, from shelf supports to graphics to lighting (including details like how light would fall on mannequins or hanging garments) to the design of menus for the deluxe top-floor restaurant. The large lobby of the building, erected in the 70s, had a certain warmth and homeliness that Biecher took pains to preserve.

On each floor, he combined long perspectives with the intimacy of the more compartmentalized spaces, while creating uniformity with the use of the same type of ceiling and flooring throughout. Light troughs in the chalk-white plaster ceilings provide direct and indirect light. Black and white tiling with golden chips, a composite-stone product made by Stonitalia, covers the floors. Used to great effect are patterned carpets and wall panels decorated with a variety of graphic and countryside motifs – birds, flowers, horses – as well as with Biecher's sketch of a female face, signifying creation.

The magnificent façade, a lovely reflection of the 'English contradiction' concept, was unveiled the evening before the official opening. Inspired by a piece of 19th-century lace found at a London flea market, Biecher created the lacy effect on his computer. The result was a honeycomb pattern whose proportions and thicknesses were etched onto the glass of the façade using a high-pressure water-jet technique. Although inspired by old English lace, the frontage has an undeniably modern, sexy translucence. At the centre of this patterned surface is the large display window. A black backdrop featuring fluorescent lights that re-create the Union Jack in acid colours is perfect for the presentation of the suspended mannequins. 'I didn't want shoppers to be distracted by the interior décor,' says Biecher. But he did want to instil a sense of pride in the Britishness of the experience, a feeling of walking into what is possibly the world's most stylish department store.

He insisted on designing the wonderfully simple, legible store directory, which offers basic information in bold Perspex letters. As no extra information is needed, Biecher is hoping the store will not become polluted by posters and the like. He compares the design process to editing a movie: 'One should experience it as if walking into a film, where one moves around, discovers, and goes from one scene to the next.' Harvey Nichols Hong Kong has caused quite an enthusiastic stir among the local population. 'It's more than just a store,' says Biecher. 'It's an experience – and one that ultimately makes you want to buy, to have something of all this to take home at the end of the day.'

Harvey Nichols

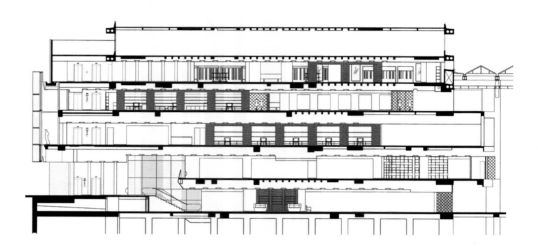

0 1 2   5 metres

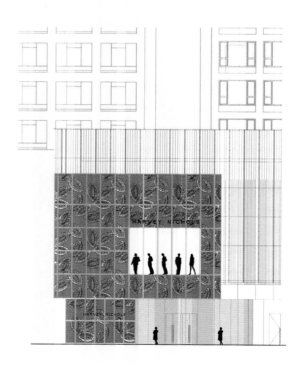

Opposite top
Primary colours and graphic lines give the restaurant an edgy, English cosiness. The space features a floor covering of composite stone and a painted plaster ceiling.

Opposite bottom
A touch of England emerges in the third-floor women's department, where a patterned carpet of royal blue and gold underpins a boldly graphic interior of black, white, and red. An extravagant black-and-gold chair clad in python leather is visible through lace-like honeycomb shelving.

Below
Offsetting the busy palette of colours and patterns found throughout the store are the cool, sharp lines of this display area for *haute couture*; as a whole, the store exudes a feeling of luxury, indulgence and fun.

Store
Julie Sohn

Location
Barcelona, Spain

Architect
CCT Arquitectos
(Conrado Carrasco and
Carlos Tejada)

Key roles were assigned to theatrical
imagery and to the poetic fantasy
involved in the world of fashion

Text
Sarah Martín Pearson

Photography
Eugeni Pons

Natural elegance with a faintly oriental undertone defines Korean fashion designer Julie Sohn's new Barcelona shop, showroom and studio: a project by CCT Arquitectos.

After years of collaboration in New York and Paris with Anne Klein and Peclers, Korean fashion designer Julie Sohn relocated to Spain where, after working with both Purificación García and David Valls, she went into business for herself in Barcelona. Sohn's distinctive fuss-free style combines an urban touch with comfort, simplicity and a faintly oriental undertone. These are the same qualities that CCT Arquitectos injected into her Barcelona boutique, which includes a showroom and the designer's studio. Led by Conrado Carrasco and Carlos Tejada, CCT aimed for a space free of artifice, in which bare surfaces portray the naturalness of Sohn's creative spirit and express her search for the essence of apparel. Key roles were assigned to theatrical imagery and to the poetic fantasy involved in the world of fashion. CCT's efforts are reflected in an almost surreal shop window that is more akin to a stage set than to conventional retail display. Customers entering the shop walk on a 'runway' bordered on both sides by walls of water. Rivulets continuously streaming down these vertical surfaces reflect light and shadow and murmur a quiet welcome. A security gate made of stainless-steel mesh framed in metal tubing turns on its axis, opens, and guides the visitor into the shop through sliding glass doors – all automatically.

Carrasco and Tejada selected a warehouse-like space to house Julie Sohn's collections, studio, showroom and storeroom. They achieved the desired effect by stripping the interior to reveal rough brick walls, high ceilings and concrete-tiled floors, all of which have been preserved. The result is a neutral, homogenous backdrop for the new retail and studio complex. An eye-catching element and a vital factor in determining the aesthetic of the boutique is the ceiling covering, which consists of inverted pyramidal shapes made from white-painted MDF. This origami-inspired ceiling not only defines the shop's circulation areas but also serves as a gigantic lamp that reflects and diffuses light in all directions, catching beams from surrounding light sources and spreading a glow of its own. Separated from perimeter walls, the suspended ceiling hides all mechanical systems while unifying the space to form an artful whole.

Greeting visitors and flanking the first part of the shop are mannequins wearing Julie Sohn creations. This area is the beginning of a corridor divided by rusty steel tables that separate the space into two parallel paths for browsing through the current collection. Garments hang from stainless-steel bars mounted on white-painted wooden panels, which serve as a neutral backdrop. Set into recesses in the brick walls and lit from behind, these panels seem to be suspended in midair, which gives them a sense of weightlessness. At the end of the corridor, the space broadens into an open area conceived as 'a square of reunion', an idea based on the traditional Spanish plaza. Here elegantly illuminated fashions and accessories line the walls, and tables topped with inlaid showcases display jewellery and smaller accessories. A table with a view of the corridor incorporates the cash desk and allows shop assistants to keep an eye on passers-by and customers entering the boutique. At the rear, 'floating' fitting rooms, also clad in oxidized steel, open towards an interior courtyard from which the shop draws natural light, always helpful to customers who want to view garments in daylight. The plaza, which encourages contact between customers and shop assistants, is the main sales and fitting area. Two king-size mirrors with stainless-steel frames lean against walls on opposite sides of the space. Other amenities accessible from the central square are toilets, kitchen, a basement storeroom and Sohn's studio, located upstairs.

Parallel to the shop and independently accessible via a staircase in the main building is the showroom in which Sohn receives retailers and VIP clients. Here, too, bare brick walls and a high vaulted ceiling reveal the original structure of the building. Casually displayed garments hang from floor-mounted, stainless-steel display units. A large mirrored wall conceals the shop window, prevents passers-by from looking into the room, and visually duplicates the space.

As Julie Sohn embarks on a new stage in her career, she can gather confidence from a location in a city generally considered to be the design capital of Spain. The space radiates the presence of a more mature designer, a trendsetter on a par with the top names in Spanish fashion design.

This page
An entirely made entirely of glass
offers a grand view of the interior,
with its origami-inspired ceiling, brick
walls and concrete floor.

julie sohn

This page
Although they are large and solid, panels
of white-painted wood lit from behind
convey a sense of weightlessness.

Julie Sohn

This page
Pyramidal white shapes across the
ceiling distribute and reflect light in
various ways.

Bottom
Elegantly illuminated fashions and
accessories line the walls, while tables
topped with inlaid showcases display
jewellery and smaller items.

Floor plan and section
1. Entrance
2. Retail area
3. The 'plaza'
4. Cash desk
5. Fitting room
6. Rear area

Opposite
At the rear of the space, 'floating' fitting
rooms clad in oxidized steel open towards
an interior courtyard – an element based
on the traditional Spanish plaza – which
offers natural light to shoppers who want
to see how garments look outdoors.

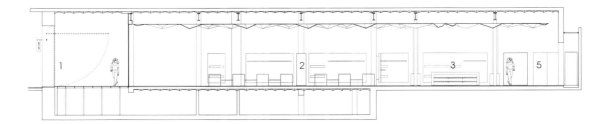

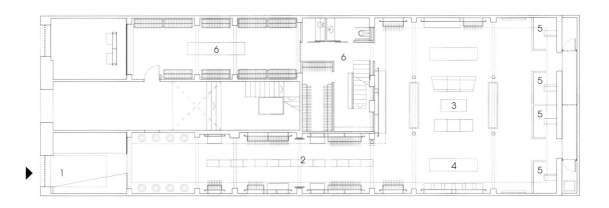

0   1   5   10 metres

Store
Fornarina

Location
Las Vegas, USA

Architect
Giorgio Borruso Design

Giorgio Borruso
'It was important to feel those shapes,
to try to understand what the person
walking inside the shop would feel.'

Text
Matthew Stewart

Photography
Benny Chan / Fotoworks

The work of Giorgio Borruso Design, Fornarina suggests a different world: a dreamlike space in over-the-top Las Vegas.

Making an architectural splash in Las Vegas is a tall order, even for the most visionary designer. In a city where over-the-top is the order of the day, the boldest statement can be easily lost amidst the visual clutter. In other words, it is the perfect laboratory for a gutsy experiment, which is exactly what apparel and footwear manufacturer Fornarina was looking to undertake in developing its new location. In true Italian fashion (no pun intended), the label mixes a well-established history – parent company Fornari dates back to 1947 – with a sharp, futuristic eye for street trends. Always the pacesetter, Fornarina's recent explosion in overseas, and especially American, markets had made the company keenly aware of the void, and thus the opportunity, in its direct-retail channels. Giorgio Borruso – the award-winning architect behind the Miss Sixty and Paul Frank shops in Southern California, Florida and Washington D.C. – was brought aboard to help the company fill that void with a strong design language that could be applied to all Fornarina retail outlets, beginning with the Vegas store.

'When we're kids, we don't have as much of a filter,' says Borruso, speaking of the bold and gestural moves that he applies to all his projects, which were seen as exactly what the doctor ordered for Fornarina. 'This project was perfect for that kind of exploration.' It was the kind of assignment most designers would kill for: Borruso was given carte blanche and, in true Vegas style, encouraged to think big. After an immersion with the company's designers and leadership, Borruso developed a strong, sculptural vernacular, much of which emerged from the designer's own hands: 'We started with software, but I also went back to working with my hands. I sculpted without being afraid . . . it was important to feel those shapes, to try to understand what the person walking inside the shop would feel.'

If past experience is any indicator, that person would feel dazzled by the unusual forms alone. The entry doors on the solid-glass façade, which faces a bustling shopping concourse in the ritzy Mandalay Bay Resort and Casino, are indicated only by mirror-polished stainless-steel handles. Their intriguing ovoid shape, which becomes a strong motif within the shop, suggests something between a Möbius strip and a cell undergoing mitosis. Before even setting foot within, the customer is treated to the major formal 'characters' that make up this space, the most arresting of which are 'tentacles' that descend, through a central void in the lowered

ceiling, from the uppermost reaches of the 9-metre-high space. Each tentacle is clad in a stretch-fabric skin pulled taut over a bulbous polymer frame; each terminates in a cluster of lights that read like multiple alien eyes.

Surrounding the overhead void and the tentacles are a series of suspended cast-resin panels patterned in a wavy relief. Display windows set into the panels are ringed by the same distorted motif that appears on the entrance handles. Here the ovoids are crafted in fibreglass; Borruso and his team achieved the effect with several moulds, which they alternately flipped and rotated to make each ring seem unique. Most are pearlescent white, with a few accent rings in a chrome-silver finish.

Along the perimeter are panels (each approximately 4.8 by 1.8 metres) of rolling and writhing fibreglass making up what Borruso refers to as 'eyelids'. Beginning at the ceiling, the sinuous panels curve outward to house lighting that illuminates the clothing below. These seemingly random forms are again the result of alternating moulds, in this case three, in varying combinations.

Fitting rooms and custom benches round out the rich language of form. Fitting rooms fall into one of three 'typologies', as Borruso refers to them. The first is a lightweight tubular aluminium frame covered with a stretch-fabric skin. The joints of the frame are painted rhodamine red, Fornarina's trademark colour; shoppers outside the cubicle see a faint rosy hue where joints exert pressure on the white skin. A resin 'egg', again rendered in rhodamine, is the second typology. The third is a simple drywall room construction. Pearlescent benches in wood and vinyl seem to rise from the floor; embedded in each is a clear cast-resin orb displaying a swirl of red pentals.

Apart from these few exceptions, colours have been used sparingly by a man who views colour in retail design as a dangerous commitment. 'You cannot anticipate the colours of the client's collections,' he says. 'You need something that can survive different seasons and different colours.' While the formal language is incredibly complex, the palette is virtually neutral. In addition to the static forms, Borruso worked rhodamine into a multitude of LED lights embedded in the tentacles, which pulse colourful heartbeats and can bathe the space on command in a sunset of colour. Both space-age and organic, the Fornarina shop suggests a different world, a dreamlike space where familiar rules no longer apply and where shoppers can browse freely, suspended of disbelief.

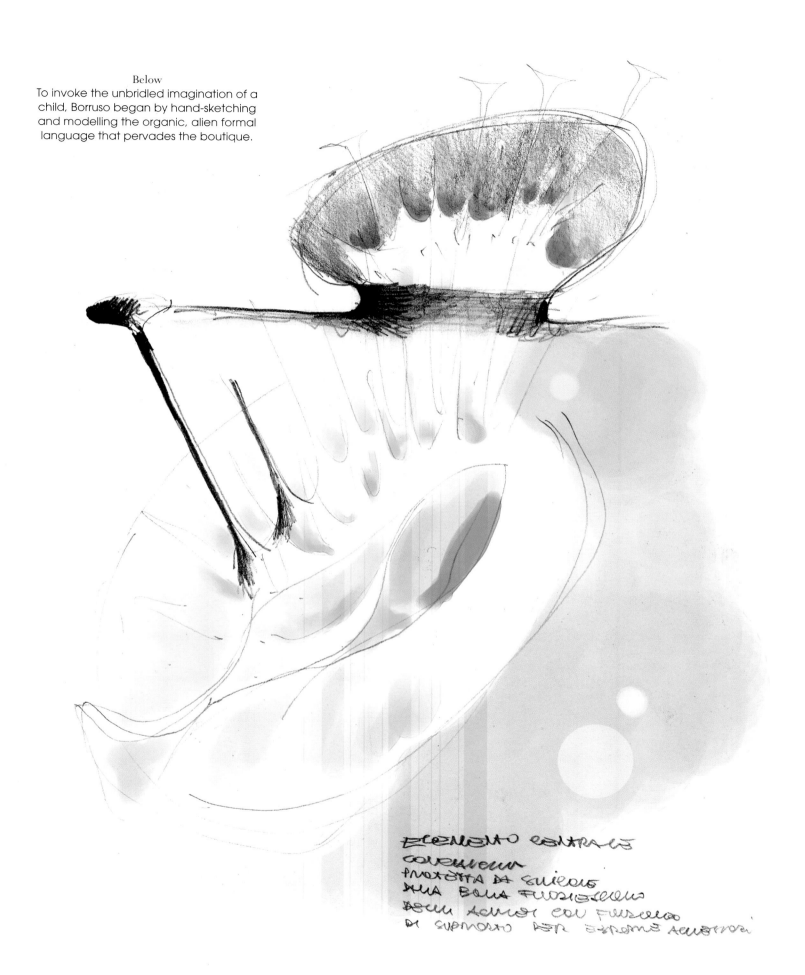

Below
To invoke the unbridled imagination of a child, Borruso began by hand-sketching and modelling the organic, alien formal language that pervades the boutique.

Floor plan and sections
1. Seating
2. Hanging display (eyelids)
3. Cascade panels (rings)
4. Tentacles
5. Cash desk
6. Fitting room
7. Office

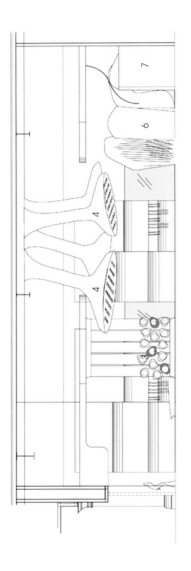

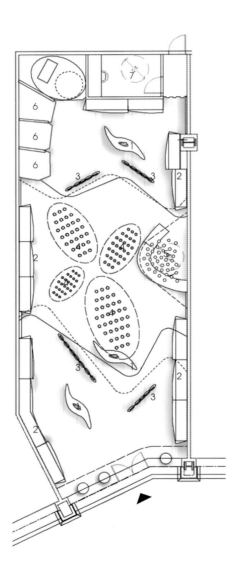

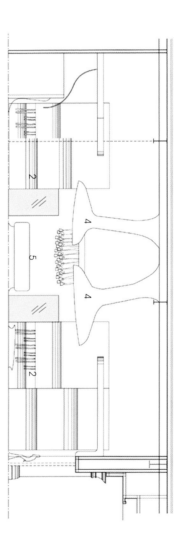

Preceding page
Wavy cast-resin panels are studded with display windows, each ringed with an O-shaped, moulded-fibreglass frame.

Below
The undulating 'eyelid wall' was crafted from moulded-fibreglass panels (each about 4.8 by 1.8 m). The wall bulges over the clothing racks; fluorescent lighting is tucked into the wall above the displays.

Opposite
Borruso's stretch-fabric-covered 'tentacles' descend from a central void in the ceiling, pulsating with colour from embedded LED lighting.

Store
Custo Barcelona

Location
Tokyo, Japan

Architect
OUT.DeSIGN

Tsutomu Kurokawa
'The well-designed shop is stocked
with merchandise, is equipped to handle
customers and still looks amazing day
in and day out. That's the type of store
I want to create.'

Text
Masaaki Takahashi

Enter OUT.DeSIGN, the firm chosen to transform Custo Barcelona's Tokyo branch from failure into success.

Certain urban locations seem doomed to failure. Whether the site accommodates a shop, a restaurant or a bar apparently makes no difference. Nothing works. Taking a scientific approach or relying on market research are two ways to tackle the problem, but the ultimate success of such locations often depends on the architect or interior designer selected to realize a given project – on his or her good instincts and cumulative experience. The Japanese company with exclusive import rights to Spanish clothing brand Custo Barcelona (fashions reflecting the Californian surfing culture) opted for a two-storey shop in Tokyo, at the corner of Aoyama-dori and Gaien-Nishi-dori, a location with a history of short-lived commercial fiascos. The property was clearly visible to pedestrians, as well as to motorists waiting for traffic lights to change at the intersection, and the interior was not very deep.

An important facet of boutique design is how to present the inside of the shop to those outside the shop. How much of the interior should be seen from the street? How much merchandise should be revealed? The answer has a huge impact on the future of the store. And it has a huge impact on the shopping experience itself. In making the façade, Kurokawa gave a new twist to a device he had used previously. For Custo Barcelona, he handcrafted four types of curved, 8-mm-thick glass panels. His composition of undulating panels functions as a semi-transparent drapery, lending privacy to those inside the shop, while distorting but not obliterating the view of the interior from outside the shop. Suspended from the ceiling is a display system of inverted T-shaped components featuring yellow acrylic batons (35 mm in diameter; 65 cm long) as rails for holding clothes on hangers. Kurokawa chose yellow, his favourite colour, for its association with Spain. Dashes of yellow punctuate the air, demanding attention. The batons were manufactured by Waazwiz.

Apparel with the Custo Barcelona label is characterized by bright colours, bold motifs and a blend of materials. These are fashions designed to make a splash. Kurokawa wanted to show off the already showy merchandise against a restrained background designed to bring out the unique features of the clothing. In addition to garments hanging from yellow batons, certain fashions are arranged like works of art in narrow niches along the wall, each of which contains a single item of clothing. The view from halfway up the stairs is that of a space that resembles an art gallery. As part of his design for the new interior, Kurokawa repositioned the original stairway to facilitate in-store traffic, which now flows smoothly. Upstairs, storage is provided by four rotatable units at the rear of the space, each 59 cm wide and 220 cm high; these are affixed to the ceiling by steel rods. The upper floor is also used as a presentation room.

Sadly, in July 2005, about two years after completing the Custo Barcelona project, Kurokawa died. He was only 43 years old. A man who liked to oversee all aspects of whatever job he was working on, Kurokawa had looked forward to his involvement in many more interior-design projects in Japan. His writings are few, but in addition to the thoughts he put on paper, we have the memories of his wife, Tomomi Kurokawa, his friends and his colleagues. Mrs Kurokawa: 'He was always saying, "Of course the shops that are completed but are not stocked with merchandise are said to look good. In reality, however, an empty store does nothing but boost the designer's self-satisfaction. The truly well-designed shop is stocked with merchandise, is equipped to handle customers and still looks amazing day in and day out. That's the type of store I want to create."' Having finished a project, Kurokawa never sat back and said, 'That's perfect. That's really cool.' He was never satisfied. During the period that retail design was all about white boxes and minimalism, Kurokawa voiced his objections in no uncertain terms. Colleague Satoko Onda: 'Kurokawa-san didn't like cold design. His designs were a combination of various points of view.' Because he didn't want to be categorized in terms of style, Kurokawa was open to innovation, to new technologies and to teamwork. The result was invariably a retail space that was easy to use for both customers and staff – and a space that tried to express beauty in a new way. Kurokawa found solutions in both the visible and the invisible. He may not have been born with the innate ability to be a designer, but he attained his goal, and distinguished himself along the way, through experience and a passion for his work. Engineer, craftsman and designer: he embodied all three.

Floor plans
1. Entrance
2. Main façade
3. Hanging display
4. Display shelving
5. Fitting room

6. Cash desk
7. Mirror
8. Stairs to first floor
9. Table
10. Chair
11. Stockroom

Bottom
A composition of undulating glass panes covers the main façade. Looking through this translucent 'drapery', passers-by get a distorted view of the retail interior.

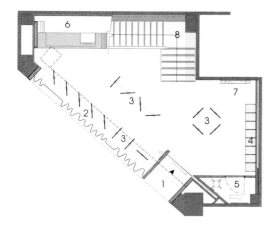

Ground floor

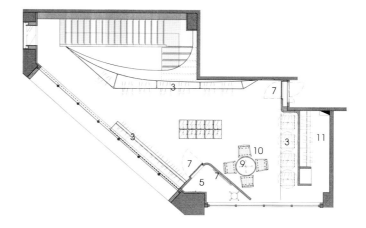

First floor

Custo Barcelona

Opposite
Seen as a whole, the 8mm-
thick glass tiles could almost
be mistaken for curtains.

Preceding page
The repositioned stairway, designed in
part to fill a void in the existing space,
keeps in-store traffic flowing smoothly.

Below
Suspended from the ceiling is a display
system of inverted T-shaped components
featuring yellow acrylic batons as rails for
holding clothes on hangers.

Opposite
Kurokawa used steel for the stair railing,
the stairwell wall and the cash desk on
the first floor.

Custo Barcelona

Store
Delicatessen
(Idit Barak and Sharon Gurel)

Location
Tel Aviv, Israel

Architect
Z-A

Guy Zucker
'Fashion design is a creative field that
has managed to completely merge
with contemporary life.'

Text
Shonquis Moreno

Photography
Nomi Yogev

In Tel Aviv, Z-A elevates the humblest of materials to make a statement – architects everywhere would do well to listen.

Guy Zucker has redeemed linoleum. This could not have been an easy task, but he made it look simple. With Tel Aviv's Delicatessen – not a corned-beef-on-rye joint but a clothing shop – Zucker has created an interior of unsurpassed resourcefulness and crisp good looks. Using only linoleum and cardboard tubes, the designer sheathed the 84-square-metre space in a thin 'garment' that forms the store's furniture: display racks, fitting room, cash desk and display window. With a change of season, change of mode or change of the owner's heart, this garment can be easily removed and replaced, permitting the interior architecture to keep pace with the mercurial fashion industry. Any repeat customer used to the turnover of merchandise will be pleased to encounter an occasional immersive shift in the space itself. (Indeed, we've learned that spaces made to be reconfigured aren't necessarily reconfigured by management; nonetheless, convertibility of retail space, especially fashion retail, is to be lauded and encouraged.) Not least, the entire project cost a mere US$3000: US$2000 for labour and US$1000 for materials.

Zucker cut, folded, rolled, stacked and wrapped his selection of pedestrian, ephemeral, ready-made materials, transforming them into something fine. He used fleeting materials to house fleeting fashions. Of course, unlike fashion, which is conspicuously overvalued, cardboard and linoleum have long been undervalued; labelling them 'design resources' elevates their status considerably. Zucker laid the furniture garment very lightly over the raw space of the interior and contrasted it sharply, in terms of both colour and form, with the outer envelope. Instead of blending the two, he applied the grey and yellow pieces to the envelope with a perceptible 'cut and paste' technique. The use of only two materials and two colours allowed him to maintain the sharp, clean, refined lines of the interior, an effect usually accomplished with classier materials, details and finishes. When compared with this tailored and finely garbed design, the use of expensive elements elsewhere seems like cheating.

The interior flows from the display window through a doorway and ends at the fashion designer's workshop at the rear of the boutique. To emphasize the symbiotic relationship (both physical and commercial) between spaces, Zucker stretched three linoleum strips from the back all the way into the window display. These strips climb, roll, wrap and curl around the tubes (which are bunched in a softened beehive form to create display surfaces) and across

the floor. They resemble assembly-line conveyor belts and recall for visitors an antiseptic version of the factory. These grey belts both hold the merchandise and serve as a backdrop that accentuates the clothing to keen effect.

Zucker's ongoing investigations into the boundaries between the permanent and the ephemeral in architecture make him a fine choice to design a fashion boutique. As Zucker sees it, every shopper is aware of the fact that she is paying, usually through the nose, for design and brand rather than for material. She's also aware that she stops wearing a garment when the current trend changes and not when and because the article of clothing wears out. In the field of architecture, this situation is reversed; the cost of building materials far exceeds the cost of the design. QED. Fashion design = 80% design + 20% material. Architectural design = 20% design + 80% material. Thus, instead of following the laws of architecture, Zucker flouts them quite prettily. By elevating inexpensive, lowbrow materials and by dressing the shop in a garment that can be easily discarded, he has made Delicatessen a shop that inverts the logic of architectural valuation and follows the logic of the fashion industry.

In another inversion of architectural convention, the designer chose his materials – yellow and grey double-sided linoleum and painted cardboard tubes – at the beginning of the design process instead of applying them to a full-blown concept. At Delicatessen, materials dictate the forms and the functional potential of the space. Zucker made the display furniture, for instance, by following the structure of the cardboard tubes. Display 'fins', much like poster racks, take advantage of the flexible qualities of linoleum. The fitting room, also made of linoleum, folds outwards to open and inwards when not in use, disappearing into the wall. As this folding and unfolding occurs, the dual colour of the linoleum accentuates a ritual that is peculiar to shopping for clothing.

'Fashion design is a creative field that has managed to completely merge with contemporary life,' says Zucker. 'The entire industry is based on global realities and constant transformation. Architecture has to confront the same realities of ever-changing programmes, budgets and building uses. If we want to learn from fashion design, we have to change our expectations. If we don't expect all architectural products to become monuments, if we can invest less in "high-end" materials, we might be able to give more importance to the manipulation of material and the quality of design rather than to the cost of material – and to give more importance to the designer than to the contractor.'

Preceding page
Guy Zucker crafted the interior of Tel Aviv's
Delicatessen boutique for a mere US$3000,
design and labour included. A ribbon
of grey linoleum links production space
at the rear with the crisply sartorial retail
area, emphasizing the physically and
commercially symbiotic relationship
between the two.

Floor plan
1. Retail area
2. Display shelves
3. Fitting room
4. Display table
5. Cash desk
6. Hanging display
7. Display fins
8. Rear area

Opposite
Using only linoleum and cardboard
tubes, the designer sheathed the tiny
shop in a thin 'garment' that forms display
racks, fitting room, cash desk and retail
space. Zucker's design elevates materials
normally considered quite humble.

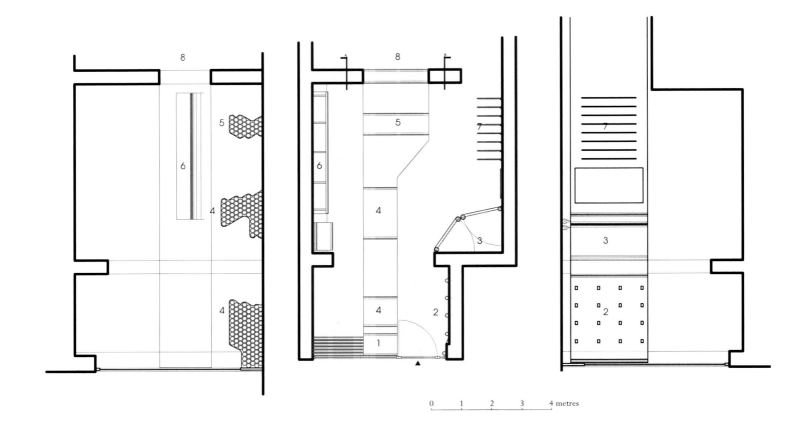

0   1   2   3   4 metres

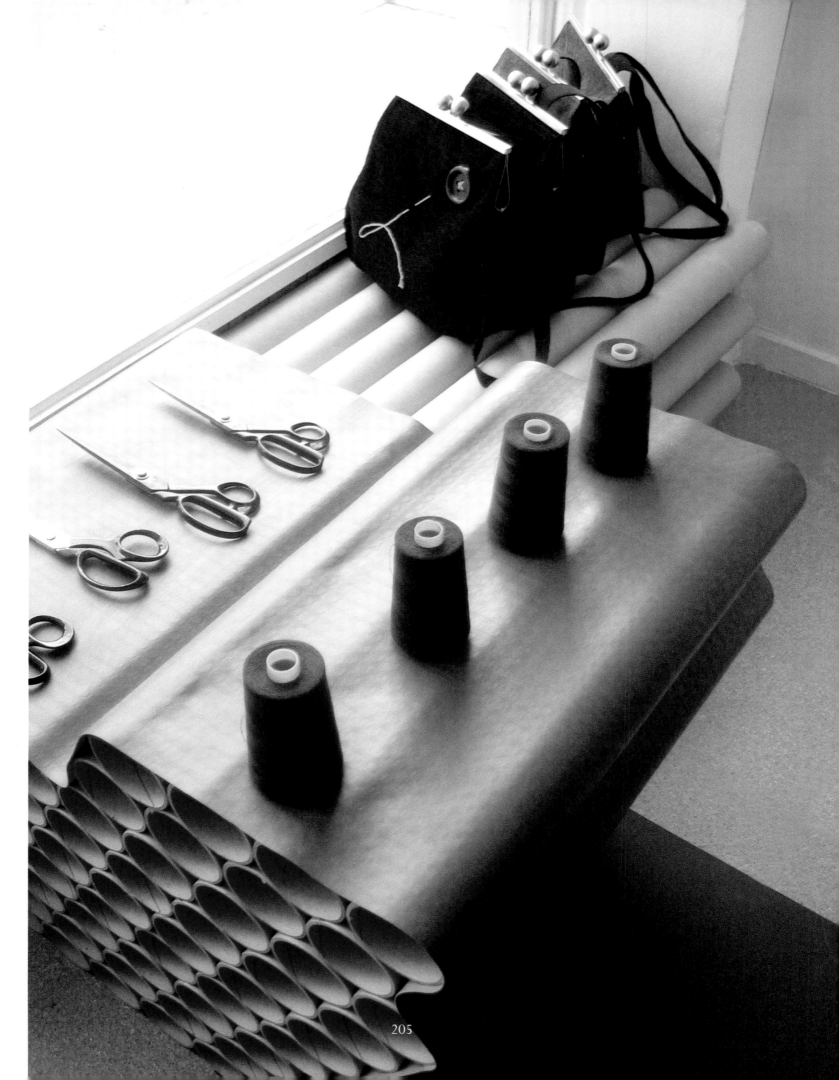

Delicatessen

Below, bottom and opposite
Zucker laid the furniture 'garment' very lightly over the envelope of the interior. To underscore contrasts in colour and form, he 'cut and pasted' the grey and yellow pieces over the envelope.

By using only two materials and two colours, he maintained the sharp, refined lines of the interior, something usually accomplished with much finer materials, details and finishes.

Store
Loveless

Location
Tokyo, Japan

Architect
Jamo Associates

Norito Takahashi and Chinatsu Kambayashi
'We wanted to give people the surreal
feeling of stepping into a huge,
unusual place.'

Text
Masaaki Takahashi

Photography
Kozo Takayama

The contrast between heaven and hell inspired Jamo to create an interior of opposites for Loveless, a magnet for fashionistas in Tokyo's trendy Aoyama district.

Loveless lies behind the severe grey walls of the building directly across from Comme des Garçon's Aoyama store, brainchild of designer Rei Kawakubo and Future Systems. This rarefied locale is also home to a host of other works by high-flying architects; topping the list is Herzog & de Meuron's Prada boutique. In a neighbourhood of such prime real estate, it's essential for anyone developing a new, large-scale store to come up with an extremely well-thought-out strategy.

Passers-by who look no further than the street-level display of exquisite luggage by Goyard are liable to miss the new addition to the coterie. Occupying the entire ground floor of the building, Goyard splits Loveless – housed in a pair of underground levels and on the first floor of the building – in two. Targeting the well-developed sensibilities of Japanese fashionistas, the boutique is stocked with exclusive, high-priced items, and the interior was obviously masterminded by someone in the know. In a move to transcend conventional shop design, the client handed over supervision of the project to a creative director from outside the company, who came up with a bold proposal.

Although Jamo Associates was commissioned to develop a design for all four floors, including Goyard, the brief for the luggage-maker's shop contained various constraints and conditions imposed by the brand image. The designers had more freedom when it came to Loveless, however, for whom they crafted an interior of contrasts based on 'heaven and hell'.

Ascending the elegantly curved staircase from Goyard, visitors catch sight of a colourful Venetian-glass chandelier, suspended in the stairwell like a visiting angel. Similar ornaments of vividly hued glass decorate the airy space on the first floor. Here, natural light illuminates white ceiling and floor, as well as walls that have been treated to give them an aged effect. Four white tables, whose height can be adjusted at the touch of a button, march in a straight line through the room. They are used to display merchandise that includes brands such as Chloe and Libertine.

Lending access to the basement floors is a narrow passageway that is tucked behind a nondescript glass door to the left of the entrance to the building. The door is guarded by the statue of a colossal eagle in mid-flight, which gives it the unexpected feel of

a nightclub. Crossing over the threshold into the dark stone-clad corridor adds the sensation of stepping into a disused mineshaft. Illumination is sparse, coming only from a few round bulbs dotting the arched ceiling.

Given the low ceiling and dim lighting from scattered spotlights at the next level, you'd be forgiven for thinking that this isn't a boutique at all. The first feature that greets the eye is a dark-countered bar with a 10-metre span. Next to this is a corner where neat piles of CDs and books offer the first suggestion of a retail space. Turning around, you realize that a huge chamber lies beyond the balustrade and that your vantage point offers a view down and across the entire floor below. It's a space that might have been modelled on the dungeon of a medieval castle. In keeping with this mood, much of the merchandise has a punk-rock edge; brands include South Paradiso Leather and Mastermind Japan.

Sharing their initial thoughts on the project, interior director Norito Takahashi and Chinatsu Kambayashi of Jamo Associates says, 'One of the first things we noticed about the space was that even though the interior was vast, the entrance and passage leading into the basement were narrow. We wanted to give people coming through the corridor the surreal feeling of stepping into a huge, unusual place. The first thing that came to mind was a ruined building.' With a bold, fresh look as his objective – something with an extreme edge that no one would dare imitate – as well as an amusing contrast between the interior and the goods on display, creative director Mr Yoshii and Jamo Associates spent six months working on plans. The details that would go into expressing Takahashi and Kambayashi's ideas were left up to the designer, and both this team and hordes of fashion-lovers seem to be very happy with the result. The concept revolves around a bright, plant-filled upper level and, in the subterranean space, the antithesis of brightness: a dark, oppressive atmosphere seemingly created by the weight of the surrounding strata of earth. Production costs totalled £200,000, but luckily the venture has experienced none of the management problems that have apparently plagued affiliated labels. One story making the rounds is of a customer who splashed out on £24,000 worth of merchandise in a single day.

Loveless was named after a 1991 album by Dublin rock band My Bloody Valentine. A sister boutique located in Daikanyama – Colour by Numbers – bears the name of the second album released by Culture Club. Both music-referenced outlets have Jamo to thank for their uniquely styled retail interiors, and both are featured in this book.

Loveless

This page
Stepping into Loveless is more like entering a club than a shop. Visitors find themselves in a dark stairwell that leads to a basement area, complete with a bar and the first sign of merchandise: CDs and magazines. Descending another flight reveals the main shop floor.

Opposite top
The ground floor of the building is dedicated to Goyard, which has a conventional retail interior devoted to leather goods.

Opposite bottom
On the first floor, display tables are raised and lowered electronically.

Below
The white interior of the first floor at Loveless has been treated to produce an aged effect. Flooring is made from pine.

Opposite top
Basement walls at Loveless
– suitable for projecting images –
have been faced in fake brick
to resemble the walls of a
ruined building.

Floor plans
(for all floors, including the
two underground levels)
1. Entrance
2. Shelving display
3. Hanging display
4. Display table
5. Cask desk
6. Fitting room
7. Stockroom
8. Toilets
9. Office
10. DJ table
11. Bar

Opposite bottom
Loveless stocks apparel, boos and CDs.
The bar at the back of the space is for customers. They can have drinks and snacks
for free, while waiting for their goods to be
wrapped. Every Friday night a DJ is invited
to play at the 'Loveless Night'.

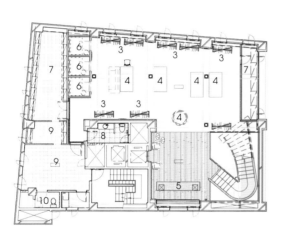

First floor

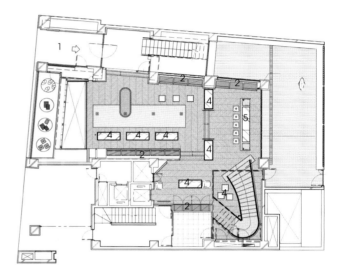

Ground floor

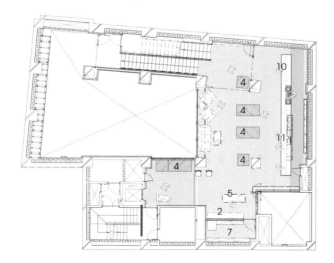

Basement

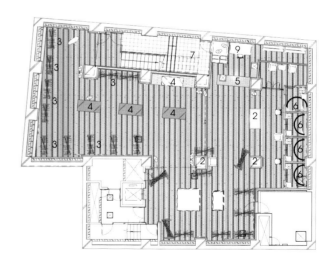

Lower basement

Store
Sigrun Woehr

Location
Stuttgart, Germany

Architect
Ippolito Fleitz Group

Peter Ippolito
'She's a fancy, playful woman,
and the store is very much a product
of the atmosphere in the initial
discussions we had together.'

Text
Matthew Stewart

Photography
Zooey Braun

Referring to themselves as 'identity architects', Ippolito Fleitz Group create a fancy and playful atmosphere for Sigrun Woehr's shoe boutique in Stuttgart.

Shoe retailer Sigrun Woehr's eponymous boutiques have taken southern Germany by quiet storm over the past two decades, with their accessible presentation of high-end designer shoes interspersed with sportswear and streetwear brands. It's the type of store where every woman can find something she likes. Woehr's success can be attributed to a good eye and good instincts; her stores have been inseparably influenced by her own identity and personality since their inception. Thus hiring Ippolito Fleitz Group to develop her sixth and final store makes perfect sense, for though the projects that make up the architecture firm's portfolio are diverse in nature (ranging from landscapes to graphic design), the common denominator running through all of them is a deep engagement with the identity of the client. Developing the crown jewel in Woehr's miniature empire was not simply a problem of interior design, says principal designer Peter Ippolito. 'We wanted to position her very well on the market,' explains the architect. 'She's a fancy, playful woman, and the store is very much a product of the atmosphere in the initial discussions we had together.' The store, located on a prime bit of luxury-shopping real estate in Stuttgart, opens on the street with a deep display window. 'We used the depth of the entry to build up tension, to create a space that invites the visitor to go through the door and into a complete new world,' says Ippolito. A narrow slot allows a highly restricted glimpse of what lies beyond.

Inside, a floor-to-ceiling landscape of crisp white display surfaces and powerful accent colours, developed as part of a new corporate-identity package, greets the eye. The interplay of the actual ceiling, painted a deep petroleum blue, and a bright white suspended ceiling sets up the logic of the arrangement. The suspended ceiling, edged in warm yellow, features several cutaway slots over special display areas. 'The slots are guidelines,' continues Ippolito, who says they draw the eye back through the store and past the display stands to a field of green behind the counter, where the new logo adorns the wall. Opposite the counter, the ceiling curves down to form a display wall, also petroleum blue, inset with white powder-coated steel shelves.

The store ends in a curved wall of white display steps. Shelving for shoes also lines the perimeter walls. At the centre of the space, two special display stands offer featured products. Each appears to be a continuous floor-to-ceiling shape with a horizontal section missing from its centre, creating an illuminated table beneath a curve-edged volume that directs light down on the footwear selected for ephemeral stardom. Slots in the suspended ceiling emphasize the stands, which, like the white counter, were created out of a soft foam material. The team liked the material for several reasons, says Ippolito. 'It has a fashion connotation. It's feminine. On the other hand, it's kind of disturbing. It supports the whole system of tension in the shop – between soft and hard, glossy and matte.'

Ippolito and the design team developed their spatial solution around the corporate identity they were creating. The use of new brand-identity colours was highly calculated – applied only to the ceiling, the suspended ceiling, a band a few centimetres above the floor and one accent wall – proving that less can indeed be more. 'Only focal points far away from the product have colour,' explains Ippolito. Shoes can be notoriously difficult to display: they are small and detailed, and, furthermore, summer shoes (delicate and colourful) vary greatly from winter shoes (larger and often brown or black). The team compensated for these discrepancies with white display shelving throughout, as well as with sensitively precise product lighting.

Apart from logo and colour scheme, the design team also introduced a signature dotted line into the corporate identity, which weaves ingeniously throughout the store, tracing a three-dimensional route along walls and ceiling. 'It's part of the narration, and something people memorize,' says Ippolito. 'It's a different way of combining the elements. It turns the architecture into a bodily experience; sometimes it's far away, and sometimes it's close. It adds a different perspective to the experience.' By turning graphic touches like the line and the fields of colour into living, engaging spaces, Ippolito Fleitz Group bridges the gap between branding and customer experience. The firm refers to itself as 'identity architects', and the retail space for Sigrun Woehr is a fine example of the potential strength of this approach.

Sigrun Woehr

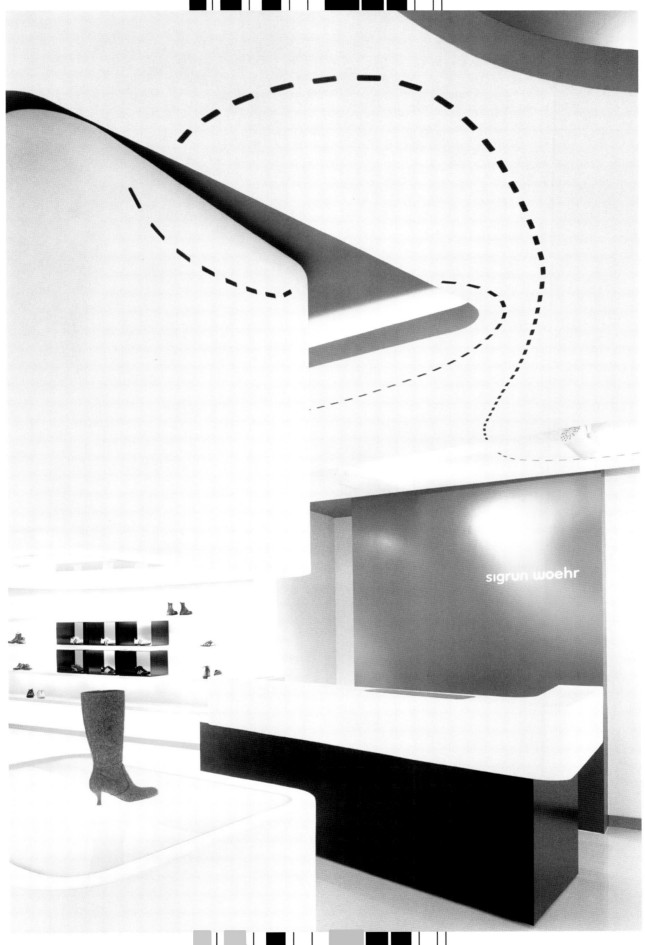

Preceding page
Ippolito Fleitz Group created a comprehensive design for shoe retailer Sigrun Woehr, implementing a completely new identity. The results are seen in meandering dotted lines reminiscent of sewing, and in a colour scheme applied both to patches of true ceiling visible behind the floating ceiling and to the accent wall behind the cash desk.

Sigrun Woehr

This spread
The eye drifts to the back of the
store and comes to rest on curving
tiered display shelves created by
Ippolito Fleitz Group as a 'panoramic
horizontal ribbon to end the view'.

A panel of Sigrun Woehr's signature blue
curves seamlessly down from the true
ceiling to accommodate accent shelves
for featured product display.

Central display tables, with forms
housing downlights descending from
slots in the ceiling, serve as dramatic
pedestals for footwear.

Floor plan
1. Shop-window area
2. Retail area
3. Cash desk
4. Fitting room
5. Rear of area
6. Stairs to storage

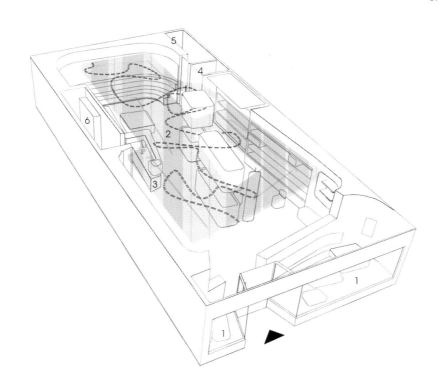

Store
Yoshie Inaba

Location
Divers

Architect
Studio Power with
Horse Bone Brothers

Tim Power
'The idea of the horizon is important.
We used it to expand the sense of space
and to bring it back to the ocean and
the plains.'

Text
Matthew Stewart

Elements from the sea and nature formed the starting point for Studio Power to design a new retail lexicon for Japanese fashion label Yoshie Inaba.

Those unfamiliar with the name Yoshie Inaba may still be familiar with the fashion designer's work. Already a highly celebrated Japanese fashion designer in the 1980s, Inaba is the head of a company that currently runs over 30 fashion brands. She has been designing uniforms for the cabin crew and employees of Japan Airlines since the early '90s to rave reviews from press and employees alike. Designer Tim Power, who was contracted to redevelop her retail concept in Japan, calls the woman known for her impeccably tailored, simple and sophisticated pieces 'a Japanese Armani or Max Mara'. Like the Italian giants, she has a core group that comprises, for the most part, older women who love her vision of the subtle and sublime.

But relying too heavily on a particular target group, especially an ageing one, can be a trap in retail. Keenly aware of the need for new inspiration in her store presence, Inaba asked Studio Power to inject some fresh energy into the label. Power recalls her saying, 'Now that we've locked ourselves into high-end retailing, how can we bring our products to a more fashionable clientele?' Inaba, no stranger to contemporary architecture – her early offices and atelier was designed by Pritzker Prize-winning architect Tadao Ando – furnished Studio Power with an open brief and ample room to develop its own ideas about the label and the spatial elements that would best serve it. 'We began with research into who Yoshie Inaba is and what she believes,' recounts Power. 'We discovered a commitment to ecological issues, and a longstanding relationship with the sea and nature, elements that allowed us to introduce and develop key elements in the design.'

Power crystallized Inaba's relationship with nature and the ocean in the form of an origami-like tortoise, which was conceived after researching the original logo of the Yoshie Inaba brand. The team then took the tortoise motif and abstracted the shell into a hexagon pattern that could be applied in various ways to create adornment or semi-opaque screens. When she saw the pattern, Inaba was thrilled; not only did it reflect her beliefs, but in Japan the symbol is an auspicious one for economic returns, making it doubly significant to the designer. 'She loved both parts of that story,' says Power, 'and insisted on putting it in all the shops.'

At the Osaka location, Power's first for Inaba, a hexagon screen forms the backdrop that separates the window display from the retail interior, curving in at the entryway to draw customers inside. To the right of the doorway the pattern is acid-etched onto white glass and, to the left, onto black glass. 'The pattern becomes obsessive,' says Power, stressing its strong visual impact from the exterior and the quieter interior landscape that surrounds shoppers who enter the premises.

Having passed the screens of the exterior, the visitor enters a serene environment featuring display elements crafted of many of the materials introduced at the entrance and large planes unbroken by vertical lines. 'The idea of the horizon is really important. We used it to expand the sense of space and to bring it back to the ocean and the plains,' says Power. Thus, glowing wood-veneered walls reach down from the ceiling halfway to the floor; below them are display racks backed by the hexagon pattern. The bleached wood, which references Japanese lanterns, is the type found in the traditional bathhouse, another connection to the water element. Fitting rooms were developed from white and black acid-etched glass, while large rectangular volumes along the walls, inset with colourful glass display boxes, utilize the advantages of acid-etched mirror. 'We played with reflective and non-reflective materials, and introduced the strangely coloured backlit boxes. We really tried to push the sense of infinity,' says Power.

Given that Studio Power was not designing a single store but reinventing a retail lexicon for an entire chain of stores, the question wasn't simply what the solution should look like, but what should be included in it at all. Power and his team based their answer in part on Inaba's environmental commitment. 'The idea was not to be stylistically minimal per se, but to convey the message that we don't have much time or material in the world to waste, so we should waste as little as possible and design as few things as possible to serve as many needs as possible.' Apart from the shell, therefore, the only piece of display furniture created was a simple, oversized square trunk that can be used for a range of purposes. During subsequent iterations, the clients have asked for other furniture – chairs, different displays and more – but Studio Power has stuck to its guns in an attempt to keep the unified simplicity of its concept intact. 'With lots of smaller pieces of functional furniture, this would look like every other shop on the street,' says the designer. But with Power's spare, naturalistic interior, Yoshie Inaba is in a league of her own.

Yoshie Inaba

Preceding page
Volumes carved from dark, acid-etched
mirrors to form display cases reveal bright
colours, the only presence of non-neutral
tones in Inaba's Osaka boutique.

Below
Designer Tim Power built on Inaba's con-
cern for the environment by creating a
strong sense of the horizon in the Osaka
store. He divided the display walls near
the midpoint between floor and ceiling
and minimized vertical lines.

Opposite
Backlit shelving units in the Yoshie Inaba
shop in Gifu are suspended from the ceiling, giving them the appearance of lightness as they hover above the floor.

Below
Shop furniture is restricted to multi-
purpose wood-and-glass display cases
and complementary benches.

Below
Power derived the shop's signature trian-
gle-and-hexagon pattern from Inaba's
tortoiseshell logo. The pattern recurs in
varying degrees of translucence.

Store
Colour by Numbers

Location
Tokyo, Japan

Architect
Jamo Associates

Colour by Numbers
demonstrates the vanguard of
fashion sense in the industry

Text
Masaaki Takahashi

Photography
Kozo Takayama

By mixing pop-music elements and stuffed animals, Jamo Associates transformed Daikanyama's Colour by Numbers into a dazzlingly sophisticated landmark.

Furry, frozen-featured stuffed animals and forbidding railings topped by spiky, cartoon-like shapes are just some of the objects cleverly positioned inside Colour by Numbers, a Tokyo boutique. Whereas some shoppers find the scene cute and kitsch, others are left feeling slightly uncomfortable. It's precisely this semiotic ambiguity that interests the team that devised this retail interior. Mounted specimens – fawn and baby rabbit – perched on a display table might seem a bit over the top to those concerned with nature conservation and animal welfare. A question to the stylist, however, reveals that such issues were taken into careful consideration. She explains that none of the animals were hunting trophies; stillborn young were used instead.

Even in the anything-goes atmosphere of Tokyo shop interiors, the presence of stuffed animals in a boutique targeting young customers is something of a rarity. The visitor who walks deeper into the space finds even more subtle twists of propriety, such as iron railings and draped lengths of chain conceived by British-based German designer Matthias Megyeri. His intriguing relationship with security devices – from padlocks, fencing and barbed wire to surveillance cameras – has led to an innovative collection that represents a radical departure from conventional equipment designed to protect humanity from harm. Railings demarcating the space are tipped with sharp-eared bunnies and razor-beaked penguins whose dangerous edges contrast starkly with their cutesy shapes, while closer inspection of the links in Megyeri's heavy iron chains reveals them to be heart-shaped. For sale in the boutique are his adorable 'Billy B' padlocks, which are smiling brass-and-steel teddy bears.

Given that fair is foul and foul is fair in the design world, overtly cool objects are not always fashionable, while something distinctly 'uncool' can quickly become a must-have item. The coolest stuff is always borderline, sending out a coded message to be understood only by those in the know. Design that transgresses boundaries by incorporating ambiguity has a strong impact on the viewer through its simultaneous appeal to polar values. Seen in this light, the interior of Colour by Numbers demonstrates the vanguard of fashion sense in the industry and is arguably the coolest shop around. The boutique is the sister store of Loveless, which opened in Tokyo's fashionable Aoyama district a year to the day before Colour by Numbers threw open its doors in chic Daikanyama. Created collaboratively by the same team, Yuichi Yoshii and Jamo Associates, it targets a female clientele and stocks selected fashion-freak labels. In order to elaborate the concept for the Daikanyama project, Yoshii flew to Los Angeles with the design team to scout the creative treasures of West Hollywood. After looking over hundreds of residences and boutiques, taking several thousand photos, and shooting large amounts of video footage, they finally found their ideal model in a café encircled by trees and flowers. Because a simple reproduction of what they had stumbled across would have been boring, they gave the Tokyo interior a completely different treatment. A huge fan of pop music, Yoshii looked to pop for inspiration, even though the mood at Colour by Numbers bears little relation to the Culture Club album from which it took its name.

Jamo Associates' Norito Takahashi worked in his spare time in the music industry as a DJ and party-event organizer before becoming a full-time interior designer. He sees clear parallels between the two jobs. 'Deejaying is about mixing music. Our generation is good at mixing, and if I were to tell you which designer I liked, it wouldn't be one of today's avant-garde figures, but a completely orthodox designer like Shiro Kuramata.' He believes the eclectic approach works equally well in music and design. His partner, Chinatsu Kambayashi, who took the plunge from editor to stylist, was responsible for pulling together an outline of the concept. She demonstrated cutting-edge styling in her choice and arrangement of the fittings and details that adorn the space.

Shoppers entering the store are dazzled by lighting of the type that illuminates modern factory floors. A blinding level of brightness is exactly what Takahashi and Kambayashi wanted their daring lighting design to provide. They also wanted a space that would allow them to explore a fusion of various textures with white objects and surfaces, and to introduce the element of fakery. Steel-legged tables topped with white slabs of Greek marble stretch across the space. Clothes and accessories arrayed across these tables form flexible displays that can be reorganized and updated in minutes. Behind the cash register, digital clocks flash a multitude of red LED numbers, only one set of which indicates the correct time. Artificial flowers flashing their petals throughout the space are beautifully crafted French-made blooms.

The recent tendency in Japanese boutiques towards displaying goods in tightly partitioned spaces is disregarded at Colour by Numbers, whose designers made the bold decision to go against the flow and, consequently, to lengthen lines of 'commercial traffic' wherever possible.

Colour by Numbers

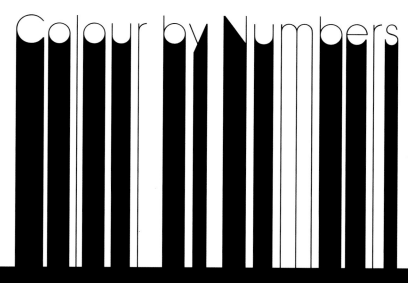

Below
During the day, the façade indicates nothing special, but after dark dazzling fluorescent light spills out into the night.

Opposite
Jamo Associates imported iron railings
created by Matthias Megyeri, a designer
whose teddy-bear padlocks are also for
sale in the shop.

Floor plan
1. Entrance
2. Display tables
3. Hanging display
4. Fitting room
5. Cash desk
6. Shop-window area
7. Office
8. Stockroom

Bottom
Behind the cash register, digital clocks
flash a multitude of red LED numbers,
only one set of which indicates the
correct time.

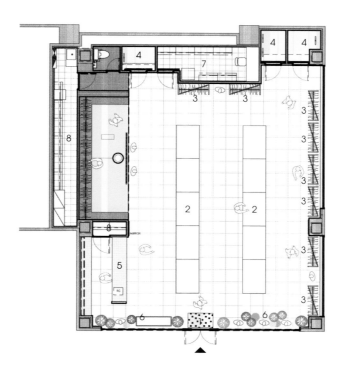

This page
Heart-shaped chains – another product
from Matthias Megyeri's company, Dream
Security – replace conventional hooks in
the fitting rooms.

Opposite
Descriptions as varied as 'a temporary
exhibition space' and 'a fashion-designer's
atelier' testify to the fresh...
Colour by Num...

Colour by Numbers

Store
Celux

Location
Tokyo, Japan

Architect
Studio Power with Eric Carlson
and David McNulty

Tim Power
'We blended traditional expensive
materials, like hand-cut marble, with
cheaper stuff, like linoleum and the
acoustic ceiling you'd find in a 1950s
American elementary school.'

Text
Matthew Stewart

Photography
Daichi Ano

Studio Power made Celux in Tokyo a luxury retail experience by using a surprising mixture of materials and combining high fashion with street culture.

When every 'office girl' totes a Louis Vuitton Murakami bag to work every day, where can the fashion-focused Tokyo woman with exclusive tastes, and the budget to back them, go to accessorize? It was precisely this question that led the brains behind LVMH Japan to develop Celux, a membership-only concept boutique stocking unique, limited-edition works from the labels in the LVMH – parent company to Louis Vuitton, Christian Dior, Fendi, Givenchy and Pucci – portfolio as well as exquisitely selected vintage goods, art, furniture and house wares. Would-be members undergo an interview and pay a one-time fee as well as annual dues. In exchange, they receive a Louis Vuitton monogram keyboard that folds to resemble a clutch purse and includes a special button for one-click access to the store's website, not to mention the privilege of shopping in the sumptuous boutique.

Celux is quite possibly the world's pre-eminent luxury retail experience. A special lift whisks card-carrying members to the store's nest in the top two floors of the Louis Vuitton Omotesando building, where they are greeted by uniformed assistants with glasses of champagne and invited to relax in a chic lounge surrounded by stunning views of the megalopolis. Milan-based designer Tim Power, who had previously collaborated with Louis Vuitton's Paris headquarters on retail projects, was tasked with creating the environment. The result – Power worked in collaboration with Eric Carlson and David McNulty – spread over two double-height floors, looks to the clothes themselves for an indication of what luxury means today, says Power. 'Our idea was to mix high fashion with street culture, not only in what is sold there, but in the way that we conceived of the project.'

Power's contrast is most notable in the material applications. 'We blended traditional expensive materials, like hand-cut marble, with cheaper stuff, like linoleum and the acoustic ceiling you'd find in a 1950s American elementary school.' By avoiding the archetypal applications, he made the materials appear mysterious rather than inexpensive. Here, the aforementioned ceiling material stands in as a wall. Built-in lighting elements, typical of this type of system ceiling, form a seemingly irregular pattern that is calculated, in fact, to optimally illuminate various highlights throughout the shop.

Another pedestrian material, felt, makes several appearances in Celux. The toilet's exterior is clad in white felt with different coloured strips as insets; each strip corresponds to a function or aspect of the toilet: sink, taps, paper-towel dispenser, and so on. White felt also lines the sweeping spiral staircase, where the sheer impracticality of the material as flooring itself becomes a statement on luxury. 'Tokyo is a very clean city, and our reasoning was that by the time people got up to the eighth floor, their shoes would be clean. But it also has to do with their idea of luxury, that changing out the felt from time to time would be no problem,' says Power. The staircase is the most striking permanent freestanding element of the interior. Each step features different proportions between riser and tread, with steps towards the top growing steeper. The team had to have the stairway classified as a work of art to avoid having landings.

Luxurious materials were given similarly unorthodox treatments. Each floor of the Louis Vuitton building features a signature material. Celux, being no exception, has walnut flooring throughout. Power not only used walnut for the floor; he also wrapped it like a continuous ribbon from ceiling to wall to floor on the eight floor before carrying it down to the sixth to form one wall and the floor.

Other than the staircase, Power's interior work focuses on the shell of the shop, to allow for seasonally rotating displays of clothing and furniture. Following the mould of a true concept shop, Celux offers for sale any object contained within the space fashioned by four walls, floor and ceiling, while rotating exhibitions introduce a cultural aspect to the retail environment, expanding its boundaries beyond the realm of consumerism. 'Knowing that the fashion world is not stable or consistent,' says Power, 'we spent a lot of time finding materials that would accept changes and developing a strong character that would allow other players to be involved.' As a result, members of Celux can return season after season, not knowing what to expect beyond a smiling hostess, chic furniture to lounge upon (and possibly purchase), and stunning surrounding views of the city that is their oyster.

Celux

Preceding page
Customers reach the sales floor by descending a sweeping spiral staircase.
Designed by Tim Power and constructed
by a well-known Japanese fabricator of
sculptural work, the staircase features risers
and treads that change proportions, growing narrower and steeper towards the top.

Floor plans and axonometric
1. Entrance
2. Stairs to eighth floor
3. Display shelving
4. Lift
5. Rear area
6. Terrace

Opposite
Power's concept for Celux mixes luxurious
materials with more pedestrian ones in unusual applications. Standard acoustic ceiling
panelling looks fresh when used as a wall
material, while the standard built-in lighting,
placed to highlight key areas, appears
strange and arbitrary.

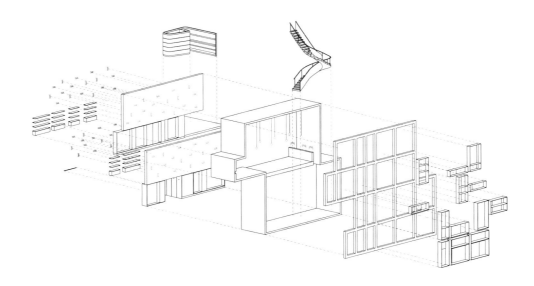

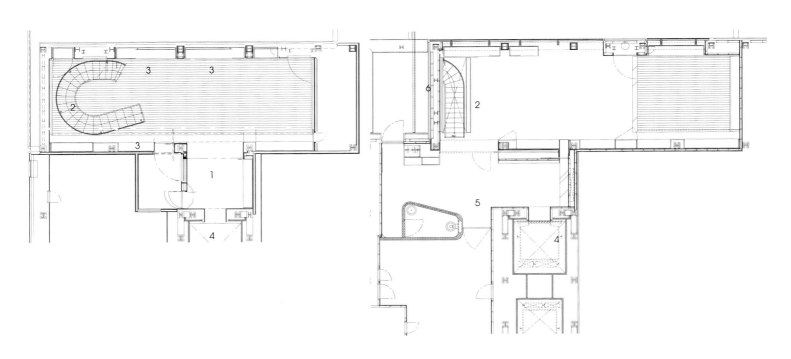

Sixth floor

Eight floor

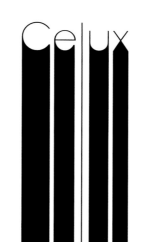

Celux

Celux

Below
Celux's entry floor features luxurious lounge
furniture – all for sale – and a walnut-strip
ceiling that wraps down the wall and onto
the floor of the lower-level boutique area.

Celux

Celux

Below
Having been served champagne by uniformed shop assistants, members of Celux can lounge and enjoy unparalleled views of downtown Tokyo while casually shopping for exclusive, one-of-a-kind designer items and accessories.

Store
Thurner Womenswear

Location
Eisenstadt, Austria

Architect
Martin Mostböck

With its dynamic movement and rich surface, the wave wall is a 'vertical landscape', which handsomely offsets the clothing displayed against it.

Text
Matthew Stewart

Photography
Udo Titz

To attract not only the mature woman, but also her daughter, Martin Mostböck redesigned Thurner Womenswear from the bottom up, dressing the Austrian boutique as if it were a shopper donning new clothes.

A loyal group of female patrons have long known about Thurner Womenswear, a high-end boutique located on a quiet but up-scale block in a pedestrian shopping zone in Eisenstadt, some 30 kilometres outside Vienna. While shipment after shipment of chic Italian sportswear has introduced fresh doses of colour and contemporary shapes and styles to the shop, the space itself languished around these products, untouched since its conception in the 1980s. Having a solid grip on the upper-middle-age market, Thurner wanted to attract a younger generation – the daughters of the women who already shopped there – to remain relevant. And to do that, it needed a much fresher image. Architect Martin Mostböck was the man they asked to provide it.

'I tried to figure out how to make a design concept for the shop that not only represented the fashions, but also focused on cultivating comfort,' says Mostböck of his solution. While initial discussions revolved around piecemeal fixes to the shop, both designer and client quickly realized that a more fundamental approach – a rethink of the space from the bottom up – was what it would take to accomplish the type of sweeping changes required to realize the retailer's goal.

Mostböck's biggest intervention was his repetition of a prefabricated form (in this case a moulded plywood backrest for a chair of his own design) to create a textured surface along the walls. The designer believes the undulations elicit a sensual response: 'They make it very attractive and very feminine, like a second skin, like fabric touching a woman's body.'

The plywood was bleached white, not painted, which is an important distinction to Mostböck. 'You can still see the structure of the wood,' he explains. 'It's not a dead surface. It's a living surface. I tried not to cover anything . . . to show the real underlying elements.' With its dynamic movement and rich surface, the wave wall is, in Mostböck's terms, a 'vertical landscape', which handsomely offsets the clothing displayed against it.

The moulded plywood walls set the tone for the rest of the shop, says the designer, an interior that balances a simple sensuality with a consistent approach to materials – namely, softly folded hard materials. Bent and folded aluminium presentation tables are

similarly simple, artifice-free. Mostböck created accompanying leather pads to lend a sense of luxury to these objects and to make them easier to customize. Nestled close together or set perpendicular to one another, the tables form an extremely flexible system for merchandise display. The racks and shelving on the wall, custom made from a sandwiched aluminium material, are also easily reconfigured, allowing for an even greater variety of display options.

Shoppers pass through a full-height glass façade, attracted to the inner depths of the space by the mysteriously undulating wall within. Coconut mat flooring in the entryway cleans shoes and offers a transition from the pavement to the harder marble flooring of the retail interior. Paired with the more mundane aluminium and plywood surfaces, the marble adds a much-needed sense of gravity and luxury to the space. Imported from Turkey, the marble is grey and white with vibrant dashes of pink, red and yellow. It provides a striking contrast to the neutral finishes that characterize the rest of the shop. Mostböck used the material for this very reason. 'It gives the shop a rather rough and rakish appearance,' he says of the Turkish marble, which he deliberately set against 'the other slick surfaces'. Then, too, the sense of weight inherent in marble anchors the shop. And in terms of function, marble can withstand the wear of delivery carts, racks and other elements in the high-traffic areas of this retail interior. Fitting rooms at the rear of the shop are cubes bordered by hanging curtains, which are anchored into channels in the ceiling bearing recessed neon tubing to illuminate the fabric. 'I tried to give them a soft appearance,' says Mostböck. Lighting was calibrated to approximate full daylight. 'That way,' says the designer, 'you don't have to step outside to check the colours of your clothes.'

Mostböck might have known his design would be successful when, while showing a friend around the soon-too-be-opened shop, still free of merchandise, she exclaimed, 'Where are the clothes? I want to buy clothes!' But numerical proof soon followed: with scores of young women flowing into the shop, Thurner Womenswear experienced its highest-grossing weekend a month after introducing the redesign. With such success on the ground, official recognition – in the form of being a prize winner for the Austrian Adolf Loos State Prize for retail design – can only be considered icing on the cake.

Preceding page
Fitting rooms are surrounded by
double-layered curtains that hang from
tracks in the ceiling. Neon tubing inside
the tracks illuminates the fabric, lending
definition and life to the cubicles.

Floor plan and section
1. Entrance
2. Hanging display
3. Display table
4. Display shelving
5. Cash desk
6. Fitting room
7. Stairs to first floor

Opposite
Mostböck chose marble flooring to
give the shop a 'rough and rakish
appearance' and to enhance the
interior with a highly durable surface.
Display tables of bent and folded
aluminium are easy to reconfigure.

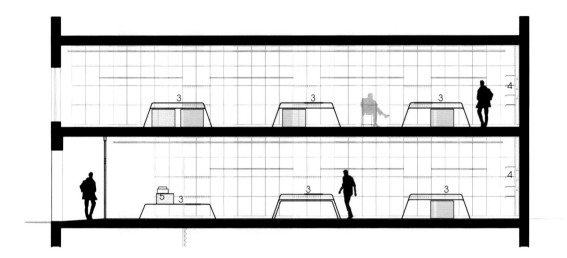

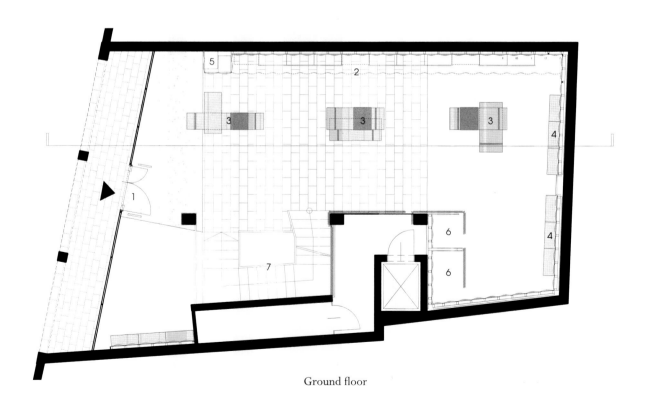

Ground floor

This page
Designer Martin Mostböck created a
striking 'vertical landscape' by layering
moulded forms of bleached plywood on
the walls of the boutique. The resulting
texture is a soft and sensuous backdrop
befitting the feminine image of the shop.

Opposite top and bottom
Fitting rooms feature illuminated mirrors and
special lighting that approximates daylight.
'You don't have to step outside to check
the colours of your clothes,' says Mostböck.

243

Store
Verso

Location
Antwerp, Belgium

Architect
Glenn Sestig Architects

Glenn Sestig
'Displaying clothing in the right way is
essential, and the use of colour should support that objective as well as possible.'

Text
Edwin van Onna

Photography
Jean-Pierre Gabriel

Once a bank and now an aristocratic shopping Shangri-la: Antwerp boutique Verso is royal allure cloaked in the sober simplicity so characteristic of work by Glenn Sestig Architects.

Verso wanted an exclusive and extraordinary location for its latest Antwerp shop. Not far from the city's Fashion Museum, a unique 2000-square-metre space that once began as side-by-side 16th-century hotels had been housing the Deutsche Bank for decades. Glenn Sestig Architects (GSA) of Ghent was called in to renovate the building and to transform it into a shop. GSA had previously done the interior of the former Verso boutique on Huidevetterstraat, also in Antwerp. 'Because we'd already designed the former Verso shop, the client had a lot of faith in us,' says Glenn Sestig.

The new venture resulted in far more than 'just another boutique'. The stately tone of GSA's cosmopolitan fashion palace perfectly exemplifies the tradition of Antwerp's better retail establishments. Behind the distinguished façade is an aristocratic shopping Shangri-la. But even visitors without blue blood will be impressed by an interior with such classic allure – a space enhanced by black accents. Nonetheless, says Sestig, this is not a minimalist design. 'I can't deny that sober, simple lines define our architecture. But in terms of material and colour, our aim was an air of grandeur. The basic composition of the building is clearly symmetrical, and we carried that symmetry into our design. The shop is divided into two zones: one for menswear and the other for women's fashions.'

A glamorous interior style not only reveals GSA's signature, but also mirrors the look of Verso's high-end collections. 'It's all about luxury items that deserve to be displayed in an opulent environment,' says Sestig. 'That explains our choice of chic materials, such as wood and lacquer, and the use of darker shades, which underline an aura of grandeur.'

A determining factor was Verso's decision to broaden its retail concept with the addition of Verso Cosmetics and Verso Lifestyle, the first a selection of quality cosmetics and the second a line of designer products. The new facilities fill an enormous central island with U-shaped counters which are made from furniture that originally lined the periphery of the space. The old mahogany pieces were sandblasted to bring out the texture of the wood and then stained black. Accessories, cosmetics and perfumes are presented in glass display units on the counters.

Contemporary interventions are few and subtle. Out of respect for the existing architecture, Sestig left the majority of architectonically valuable elements intact. 'Verso didn't make the request in so many words, but both parties implicitly realized the importance of preserving the classical character of the building.' Little change has been made in the layout: a central hall flanked by rooms with a somewhat private nature. A newly gleaming marble floor – fit for the arrival of royalty – is complemented by oak flooring polished to a sheen. Wood panelling installed in the 18th-century covers walls beneath a lead-glass dome 12 metres in diameter. The round skylight draws an abundance of natural light into the corridor. On the floor, a large white circular rug echoes the shape of the dome and the light it provides.

To accentuate the splendour of the building, GSA inserted five heavy columns into the central hall. These dark wood volumes define the openness of the corridor and underpin the contrasting privacy offered by rooms used to display clothing. The columns have a practical function, too, as they contain mechanical systems such as heating. Another addition consists of a number of blocky fitting-room volumes. Individual shops for Dolce & Gabana and Armani lie in the extension of the hall. Dark walls and black furniture give these retail spaces to the rear a regal and mysterious appearance.

Less deliberately designed perhaps, but just as important to the perception of the hall is the contrast between light and dark. Counterbalancing the dark columns and black counter are a light-coloured floor and walls and ceilings in pale tints. 'Working with contrasts is typical of our architecture,' Sestig affirms. 'And the calculated use of colour allows us to push certain elements into the foreground and to neutralize others to one degree or another. Displaying clothing in the right way is essential, and the use of colour should support that objective as well as possible.' Verso's new shop features something else that its predecessor lacked: the Verso Café, a stylish space that occupies a former 19th-century conference room at the front of the building. Here the contrasts between light and dark and between materials and textures are even more noticeable. Dark colours, smoked-glass mirrors, warm orange light and posh table-and-chair ensembles create an elegant sensory experience and make the contours of the original architecture even more pronounced. A classical fireplace adorned with caryatids completes the sense of sheltered intimacy. If Verso were a Belgian bonbon, it would have a pale creamy centre covered in dark chocolate.

This page
A conference room belonging
to the former bank has been
transformed into a chic yet cosy
café with a sensuous atmosphere
of glamour.

This spread
The building is the consolidation of two aristocratic hotels that gained a stately classical façade in 1927, which now lends access to a shopping Shangri-la. A reminder of the bank that also occupied these premises for decades is a floor plan whose central corridor is flanked by rooms with a private character.

Floor plan and façade
1. Entrance
2. Accessories area
3. Cosmetics area
4. Armani corner
5. Dolce & Gabbana corner
6. Fitting rooms
7. Stockroom
8. Patio
9. Café
10. Bar
11. Cask desk

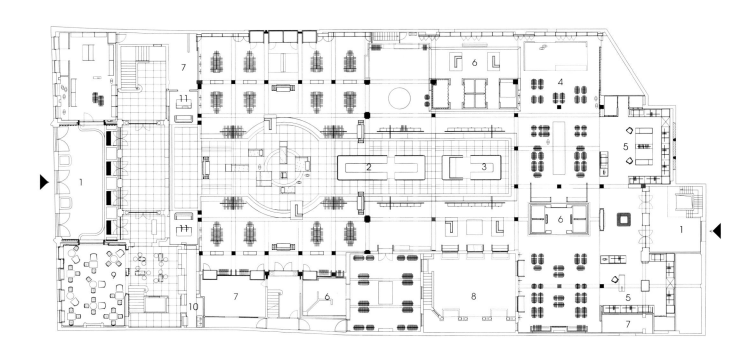

Verso

This page
Exclusive accessories are displayed
in a setting marked by the contrast
between light and dark colours.

Store
Mayke

Location
Oisterwijk, Netherlands

Architect
Peter Robben 3D Projecten

Peter Robben
'What's essential is to create a shopping
environment that reflects the retailer's
authenticity and individuality.'

Text
Edwin van Onna

Photography
Tineke Schuurmans

Peter Robben 3D Projecten redesigned Mayke, an exquisite shop in Oisterwijk with a feminine face and macho overtones.

Minimalism and the baroque: at first glance a *contradictio in terminis*. But in Oisterwijk, in the southern part of the Netherlands, minimalism has indeed managed to reach a dramatic apotheosis. Mayke, a shop specializing in shoes and bags, experienced a makeover that reflects this dualistic idea. The firm responsible for the new design had already implemented a large-scale renovation of Mayke in 1998, when an adjacent property had been integrated into the existing premises. The results of that project had increased Mayke's reputation to such an extent that the shop was soon able to offer its customers big-name brands such as Prada, Dior, Dolce & Gabbana, Girbaud, Miu Miu, Gucci, JP, Tod's, Hogan and Burberry. Things went so quickly that a follow-up was required in 2004. The brief was 'more space for more products'. Architect Peter Robben of 3D Projecten was given carte blanche. A vital part of his job was to maintain the exclusive feel of the interior without eliminating its welcome air of accessibility.

Retail design is a mainstay of 3D Projecten's portfolio. 'What's essential is to create a shopping environment that reflects the retailer's authenticity and individuality,' says Robben. 'At the moment, too many shops are being redesigned – in musical terms, it's all about covering and remixing. Fortunately, there are also examples that radiate a more distinctive identity.'

Mayke's face-lift, with its strong two-fold concept, underlines Robben's standpoint. Upon entering the shop, one is struck by the serenity and the spacious layout. Showcase, wall-mounted shelving and rectangular display units are grouped around a central island where table-like displays compose an oasis for the presentation of select items. Vitrines displaying the pricey collection of bags rise from display surfaces like glass towers. Each product is given the attention it deserves. Browsing in the maze of displays, the customer has the opportunity to view the collection undisturbed, as employees have been trained to keep their distance unless approached. The light, airy ambience is reinforced by a palette of pale shades and the prominence of white artificial light. Display units have translucent bases of frosted glass that seem to lift the display surface and make the tabular form appear virtually weightless. The use of frosted glass also contributes to the contemporary look of the interior.

Perceptually inconspicuous and thus all the more sophisticated are black ceiling elements suspended above the central area of the interior. 'Because the shop looked rather low, partly owing to the large floor area, we used fields of black against the ceiling to generate a sense of height,' says the architect. 'They also spice up the space as a whole and underpin the allure of the shop.' Robben's preliminary consultations with the owner had made clear that the project would not be a functional renovation but a redesign of the 'Mayke concept'. His task was to express that concept through the desired atmosphere and the way in which it is perceived. The solution assumes almost religious proportions. In Robben's words: 'At the rear of the shop, I wanted an altar with a very rich image that would become more abstract as it moved towards the entrance.' Breaking the space breadthways is a large showcase with niches for accessories. Thanks to the elongated form, it functions as a physical termination of the space. Visual culmination is a reproduction of *Titus Besieging the Temple of Jerusalem*, a painting by French classicist Poussin, an impressive picture that fills the rear wall in the form of full-scale fragments, creating a kind of altarpiece. Robben sees the picture as the soul of the shop. The baroque painting injects drama and movement into the otherwise austerely designed interior. It almost seems as though the Roman emperor and his rearing horse are storming the retail space. Like a powerful magnet, the image pulls people into the shop. 'We selected the painting as a complement to the feminine feel of the interior and the merchandise,' says Robben. 'The image is strong and bold. It has an erotic effect that appeals to women shoppers.

Abstract reminders at the front of the shop preview Poussin's 'grand finale'. Graphic shapes and details adorn the ends of wall racks, as well as the bases of display units in the shop window. This decorative imagery lends the shop an extraordinary layered effect. Poussin's painting also determined the palette: gradations of taupe for carpeting, bases and showcase; warmer tints for long, centrally positioned sofas and the more exclusive corner seating. The use of imagery responds to current trends in retail design. 'Ten years ago, a shop had to create a lucid environment for the product,' says Robben. 'Nowadays, product and environment may reinforce each other. The shop itself is a form of visual merchandising. At Mayke, imagery is used to support the shopping experience. It gives the store a certain air of distinction and luxury. If there's one thing I don't like it's stylists, but retail design is leaning more and more in that direction. There's no avoiding it. The trick is to find the right balance.'

Mayke

Preceding page
Illuminated bases of frosted glass support display surfaces that appear virtually weightless. Black ceiling sections above the central island generate a sense of height.

Below
The team from 3D Projecten lent form to the 'Mayke concept' by breaking the retail space with a broad showcase – the 'altar' – and highlighting the shop with the reproduction of a baroque painting by French artist Poussin.

Opposite
The idea that led to the illuminated table-like displays is echoed in the shop window, where the collection is presented on display units of a uniform height.

This spread
Browsing in the central island, customers
can view the cream of the collection
undisturbed and subsequently try on
shoes while seated on a handsome sofa.

Store
Offspring

Location
London, England

Architect
Jump Studios

Simon Jordan
'Most shop windows are static.
Nothing really happens.'

Text
Matthew Stewart

Opting for a mix of faux-natural elements and intelligent display systems, Jump Studios met the challenge of creating a new image for Offspring's three London outlets.

Exposed raw brick, galvanized steel counters and fittings, graffiti on the walls, a head-bobbing DJ in the corner on the decks, and a disaffected young staff ambling about and occasionally bothering to acknowledge the customers: these have become a by-the-numbers formula for the urban-hip boutique. Anyone remotely engaged with today's consumer culture can rattle off scores of examples of retail environments fitting this description, without pausing to think. Offspring, the British trainer retailer, was a trailblazer of this type of establishment. When its flagship Covent Garden location opened in 1995, Offspring was among the first to wed a hard-edged street look (which originated in the shoe culture they were promoting) to a slick retail outlet. Ten years and two additional locations later, the savvy brains behind the outfit knew that the street-smart look, which at this point is more appropriate to teen sections in suburban department stores, would no longer pass muster with sophisticated shoppers. But replacing imagery so central to the trainer culture associated with the image of this chain would be difficult.

Offspring tapped Jump Studios of London to undertake the transition, a choice based on the strength of the creative team's vision for the future of this market. Jump's proposal went far beyond an updated version of Offspring's 'street' look to an interior design that asked the retailer to turn its gaze inward. 'Rather than reflect the culture of their customers, we decided to reflect the culture of Offspring itself, their passion for the technology inherent in the product, their passion for the beauty of sneakers,' says Jump principal Simon Jordan. 'Nature mediated through technology' is Jordan's description of the main elements currently pumping new character into Offspring's three locations: Covent Garden, Camden and Old Compton Street. Perhaps the most striking additions are the ghostly cast-resin trees that thrust from floor to ceiling in each of these retail interiors. The back walls are lined with images of a forest. These same tree graphics appear on Perspex cubes that function as stools. Together, says Jordan, these faux-natural elements 'explicitly take the concept away from the urban idea. For us,' he adds, 'nature is the antithesis of urban.'

Of course, footwear is the heart of the matter at Offspring, and creating a memorable and effective display system for shoes was a key component of Jump's design challenge. The team's elegant solution uses clear polycarbonate blades which slot into channels running along curved panels that line the walls of the shop. The unusual shape of the panels not only follows the lead of the organic imagery, but also serves an ingenious purpose: it keeps shoes at the bottom and the top of the display the same distance from the prospective buyer as those set at eye level. The blades are small enough to allow the shoes to float in midair, or so it seems. Atop each section of the curved panelling is a small LED display. Programmable displays give Offspring an element of control over an otherwise tricky-to-manage inventory of quickly shifting products and greatly varying numbers of products within multiple brands.

The shoe-display system is complemented by a very different, and equally engaging, display system for clothing and other merchandise. Inspired by the 'collectability' of trainers, the team referenced another collectable item from their childhoods: plastic models and, specifically, the frames from which the builder snaps out the separate parts of the model. In a playful interpretation of these frames, Jump designed display systems of white tubular steel, which seem to hover against the walls of the shops. These are emphasized by lighting concealed in the painted metal ceiling, as well as in channels carved out of muted-grey floors made from poured resin.

Yet a third display element was installed in the front windows of the stores, where a system of rotating, mirror-polished, stainless-steel louvres makes building and changing window installations a breeze. 'Most shop windows are static. Nothing really happens,' says Jordan. 'Here was an opportunity to do something more dynamic. They can actually be moved; they can be shut and have graphics put on top of them.' He explains that whenever necessary, the staff can open two or more louvres and add more trainers to the window display, allowing for an almost real-time promotion of various products and for the ability to emphasize certain brands, events or themes within the store. Just inside the door, a similar LED display creates an opportunity for instant, customizable, real-time communication with shoppers.

While Offspring's customers have applauded the new design, it has benefited the footwear firm's contacts with other groups as well. According to Jordan, in its bid to carry an even more exclusive line of products, Offspring needed to prove to suppliers that it had the proper concept and environment. Since the redesign, the chain has done exactly that, landing a couple of important new contracts. Once again it's evident that, even beyond keeping the customer base engaged, design truly matters.

Offspring

Right
Mirror-polished stainless-steel louvres
featured in the display windows create
a dynamic façade that can be quickly
altered to promote products or
accommodate sales themes.

Offspring

Below
Polycarbonate blades slot into curved display walls to create a floating wall of shoes for sale. Programmable LED screens at the top of each panel allow for customizable and flexible product organization.

Opposite
Shop-window louvres can be opened or closed. Used as shelves or as the backing for various graphic applications, they give merchandisers total control of street-facing displays.

Store
Wayne Cooper

Location
Melbourne, Australia

Architect
Hecker Phelan & Guthrie

Hamish Guthrie
'The change room is dedicated entirely to
the theatre of dressing up and trying on.

Text
Edwin van Onna

Photography
Shannon McGrath

A contemporary interpretation of the Victorian drawing room houses the Wayne Cooper boutique in Melbourne, a design by Hecker Phelan & Guthrie, whose theatrical retail environment fuses past and present.

On the first storey of the GPO – the building that once housed Melbourne's General Post Office – fashion designer Wayne Cooper displays his latest collection. The building's 19th-century architecture is a perfect match for high-necked gowns and crinolines, but times have changed. This shop is a backdrop for foxy frocks and trim-fitting tops. Cooper's brief for Hecker Phelan & Guthrie (HP&G) requested a contemporary Victorian drawing room for an exclusive line of women's fashions.

The GPO complex consists of an atrium surrounded by stately, venerable arcades. The architecture clearly pays homage to the past: unique Victorian details adorn both exterior and interior. After suffering extensive damage from fire and enduring a period of disuse, the historical site recently underwent a major renovation. Former offices now accommodate over 60 posh retail establishments that add a whole new dimension to the Melbourne shopping experience.

Cultural and historical concerns linked to the preservation of important buildings affected the design of the interiors, says architect Hamish Guthrie. 'There were a number of strong and defining heritage constraints placed on the building, which to some extent dictated how tenants' designs could impact on the existing architecture.' HP&G's point of departure for the new retail space was, therefore, the existing 19th-century brick and plaster work. Out of respect for the past, the architects left intact, wherever possible, features of the original interior such as panelled doors and mouldings. Added to their preservation plans was a desire to reinforce existing elements with contemporary accents. The solution was to complement the old interior with new, movable elements: furniture, lighting and partitions. Within three months, the project had been completed, and Wayne Cooper had at his disposal two comfortable, predominantly white salons enlivened by stylized details.

Entering the shop, the visitor is greeted by a large, round sales counter supported by bulky turned legs. A glossy white finish gives the piece its light, feminine character. Expressing the desired Victorian aesthetic is a bronze, fern-filled vase on the counter. A circular mirror provides an opportunity for the shopper to check her make-up inconspicuously before entering the second room, where she can try on the garments of her choice. 'The change room is dedicated entirely to the theatre of dressing up and trying on,' says

the architect. Here a monumental three-part mirror dominates the space and screens off two fitting rooms. Like all mirrors at Wayne Cooper, this one has been purpose-designed for the shop. Here, too, a glossy white finish softens the bold baroque design language of the mirror frames.

In addition to chandeliers and spots, daylight is an essential source of illumination. High, vintage-style windows draw in a great deal of light which, thanks to the mirrors, is reflected throughout the space, bringing the outdoors inside. Accents from the 1960s and '70s offset the otherwise dominating Victorian character of the space. 'The classic furniture and lighting pieces temper the high Victorian decorative elements,' says Guthrie, 'and bring it back to a more contemporary interior.'

Determining the stylish atmosphere of the interior is the use of exotic plant motifs. Simple, freestanding clothing racks have been given a special accent thanks to their bamboo-inspired frameworks. The design refers to the cast-iron decorations of 19th-century greenhouses. The interior looks like an exotic echo of Australia's British-colonial past, but with an emphatically refreshing undertone. One example is a stylized floral pattern based on Japanese art, which marks the midpoint of the change room. 'This is a handmade carpet inlay,' says Guthrie. 'Carpet patterning is a fantastic and relatively inexpensive device for injecting texture and colour into a space. It appears quite often in our work.' The heart of the flower is the best vantage point for a customer who wants to see the effect of the outfit she's wearing. Surrounded by enormous mirrors, this is the place to pirouette prettily.

HP&G has created a tasteful and well-considered retail environment that corresponds to Wayne Cooper's crossover collections. Guthrie says that meeting each client's specific needs exemplifies HP&G's way of working. 'Our office has been commissioned to undertake a broad range of retail projects throughout Australia, from one-off boutiques to a number of fashion chains of various kinds. The approach is always inherently HP&G, but the look is unique to the brand. We try to instil all our projects with a sense of theatre, with strong patterning and texture, with classic and original furniture and lighting pieces – which together make for a unique interior approach. We always start by defining the brand and develop our design direction from there.'

This page
View from the first drawing room of the
second salon, a space with a monumental
tripartite mirror and a floral-patterned floor
covering that features a 'handmade
carpet inlay'.

This page
Exotic details, such as the bamboo-inspired
frameworks of the clothing racks, alternate
with examples of baroque ornament and
20th-century design.

Wayne Cooper

Preceding page
The focal point of the first drawing room
– HP&G's apt introduction to Wayne
Cooper's crossover collections – is a large,
glossy-white counter on bulky turned legs.

Floor plan and section
1. Entrance
2. Hanging rack
3. Fitting room
4. Stockroom
5. Cask desk

Opposite
The boutique takes its intimate character
from cosy drawing rooms with high ceilings,
authentic Victorian detailing and a stylized
interior design. Surrounded by enormous
mirrors, the floral motif at the centre of the
second room encourages customers to
pirouette prettily.

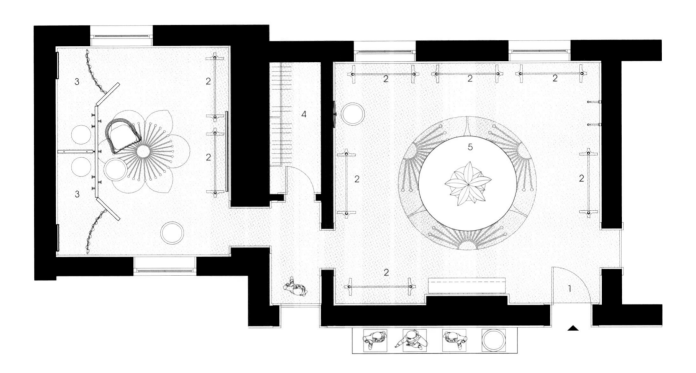

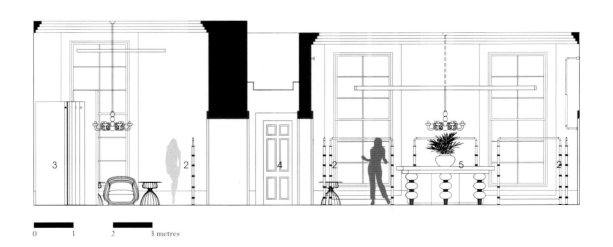

0   1   2   3 metres

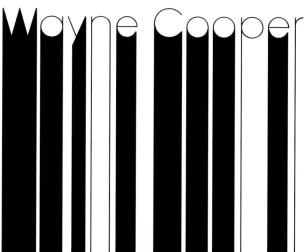

Store
B8 Couture

Location
New York, USA

Architect
Elmslie Osler Architect

Robin Elmslie Osler
'We were manipulating how you
see the space. Is that a wall or is it
a reflection?'

Text
Shonquis Moreno

Photography
Frank Oudeman

B8 Couture, a boutique located in New York City's Meatpacking District features the owner's eclectic, hand-picked collections of men's and women's European fashions, engendering exclusivity by selling only one garment in each size.

The project was restrained by a tight budget, an equally strict construction schedule and a brief that called for a uniquely Gothic palette of black and purple. 'Karine (proprietor Karine Bellil) wanted the space to be dark, so it would be like going into a jewellery box, with all these beautiful things in it,' says principal designer Robin Elmslie Osler of Elmslie Osler Architect (EOA). 'The darkness of the space helped augment the exclusivity. You're coming in off the street, and you feel as if you've entered a secret room. It's a little bit Alice in Wonderland.' Osler opted to draw purple into the space not by applying the colour to surfaces but by using it as the light that illuminates the store. Her goal was to obscure the edges of the room, create a box of crepuscular light and add a secondary layer to help define the edges of that light.

To do this, and to hang and hide lights, EOA layered vertical plywood and MDF panels of varying widths (but uniform thickness) against the black perimeter wall. This strategy created slots for holding fluorescent tubes. The result was an unusual way to incorporate purple while still allowing the colours of the garments to be read truly and, not least, generating a shallow, three-dimensional graphic against the wall in the form of a vast bar code that wraps the envelope of the room. 'Initially, we used the panels to create light and depth in a dark place, but the bar code this created was perfect,' says Osler, 'because this is a retail space and the bar code is a signifier of things being sold.' Across the panels, EOA anchored plywood and MDF shelves, which form a sandwich around a purple-laminated strip of glass filled with fluorescent lights, making the shelves an additional source of diffuse light. The shelves double as display racks, while simple secondary racks made from aluminium tubing reach from floor to ceiling and float away from the wall, allowing Bellil to raise garments out of reach during events held at the store and to hang especially long gowns.

In the rear, fitting rooms are two milky-white glass boxes that seem to glow out of the darkness. Once the door is opened, however, customers step into another dark box with black walls and carpet – a jewellery box within the jewellery box. 'Shopping is very personal,' says Osler. 'These rooms are like stepping into a special little light box. You open the door and step into this safe place that's dark and warm.' To maintain the customer's privacy, rather than putting mirrors only inside the boxes Osler placed a wall-sized mirror outside and between the two dressing rooms. When the door of each is opened, the new unit continues to function as a private space while extending the fitting room and providing a two-way mirror that reflects the customer's image, front and back.

By placing mirrors perpendicular to each other, lining the narrow edge of a wall with a mirrored strip and drawing the mirrors down to the floor instead of floating them, EOA layers reflections and light. 'In fashion, you're working with vanity and manipulation of perception, because that's all fashion is; it's a powerful tool you can use to manipulate how others see you,' says Osler, who was a fashion model for ten years before coming to architecture. 'When you use mirror, especially in a retail store, you can play with perception. There's a little bit of a perceptual challenge to the experience of B8. Is that a wall or is it a reflection?' The glass of the fitting rooms compounds the reflectivity of the mirrors, and the mirror dematerializes certain sections of wall. Through the mirror, the fitting-room box looks like either a light or an opening – you lose the edges of the space. Even in a small space, visitors feel pleasantly lost; even in an exclusive public space, they have a cosy sense of privacy.

'My take on shopping is different from a man's take on shopping,' says Osler. 'I think it has to do with a woman's self-perception, the body image thing, the way we women are still struggling to define ourselves. The darkness in the store creates a kind of warmth. This is important, because the dressing rooms are one of the most important spaces from a commercial point of view. This is the point of sale.'

In the centre of the room, EOA created two zones – one for men and the other for women, defined by the clothes themselves and separated by a shoe display-cum-sofa – that are basically the same but geared slightly towards the woman shopper, with a place for her bags and a place for her partner to sit while she tries on clothes. The irony is that in the autumn of 2005, Bellil reopened B8 as a men's shop. Will the same strategy and the same colours work just as well for big-city blokes?

Floor plan and sections
1. Shop-window display
2. Menswear
3. Womenswear
4. Mirror
5. Fitting room
6. Rear area

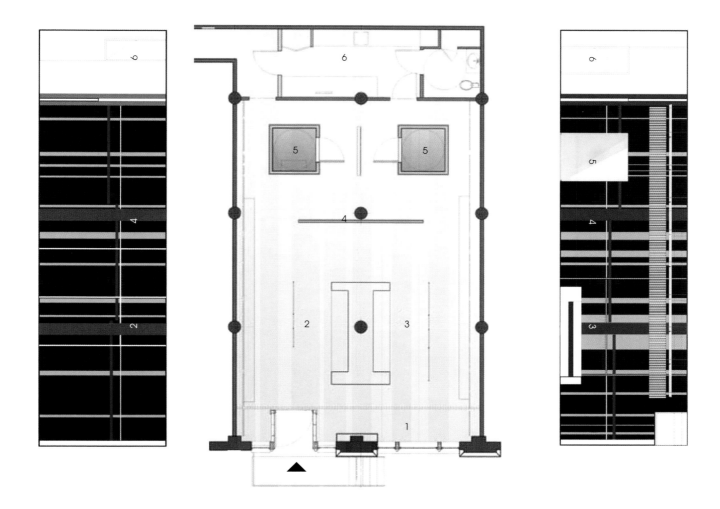

0 1   5   10 metres

This spread
The black and purple palette is meant to give shoppers the feeling of walking into a jewel box. Wall panels that form a bar code are a graphic symbol of the retail world.

Opposite and this page
Fitting rooms are translucent white boxes that float in, and seem to illuminate, the space like gems. Opening the door of the fitting room extends the user's private space and reveals a two-way mirror.

Store
GIBO

Location
Milan, Italy

Architect
Cherie Yeo

Cherie Yeo
'The boundaries between shopping,
exhibition, entertainment, refreshment
and socializing are blurred.'

Text
Shonquis Moreno

Photography
Mariacristina Vimercati

Blurring layers of history, architect Cherie Yeo and fashion designer Julie Verhoeven come up with a Milanese boutique that harbours a curious sense of wholeness.

Architect Cherie Yeo designs a second shop for friend and GIBO fashion designer Julie Verhoeven that is all about what could be. For three-year-old Italian fashion label GIBO, London-based architect Cherie Yeo designed a shop that opened fall 2003 in Milan. In this black-and-white and steel-framed shop, emptiness looks as interesting as abundance, and luxury mixes with banality. The Milan shop – a dedicated outlet for the clothing of fashion designer, artist and illustrator Julie Verhoeven – is GIBO's second location, following the completion of a flagship on Conduit Street in London that Yeo designed in 2003. Although the Milan boutique shares design elements with the London store, everything at the Italian venue has been altered to the size and character of the existing space. Yeo says that neither store is based on a preconceived notion of what a shop should be; her designs emerged from the same processes of invention and play that she wants to extend to GIBO's clientele.

To make the space greater than it appears to be, the architect played with perspectives and perceptions of space, using such devices as reflective surfaces, floor-to-ceiling mirrored wall sections, and eye-fretting wall and floor patterns. Visitors entering the shop step onto a black-and-white-chequered marble 'footpath' that guides them along an internal 'courtyard'; the chequered floor and modular furniture were inspired by 'pop art and Arte Povera' images that Verhoeven showed the architect, as well as by the courtyards of Italian Renaissance villas.

A series of metal frames – engineered to move freely but with predetermined 'resting positions' – serve as garment racks. These mobile rectangular tubes are space-defining forms, frames within frames that can nest together, retreat into form-fitting recesses in the wall or, when folded out, run at angles to each other to form various configurations. 'It's like a huge sculpture that you can walk into,' says Yeo, a fan of Alexander Calder's work. A pair of larger linear steel frames further defines the footpath by rotating into position on the main shop floor when the smaller frames are completely folded away. The furniture, designed specially for the Milan shop, is used in a modular way and has the schematic potential to turn the interior into a veritable art installation, as well as to enable practical display. Frames fold into walls to give the shop an 'empty' look (and are replaced by the larger 'courtyard' frames) or to make room for occasional evening events. The use of convertible frames

also creates a casual atmosphere in which shoppers have the sense of rummaging through clothing at a street fair. Frames also form a wall-drawing that comes to life in three dimensions: When 'closed' or folded into grooves in the concrete wall relief, they form a composition within the wall; when 'open', they become a huge sculpture that extends into the shop at all sorts of dynamic angles, giving the space a tangled, strident, engaging sense of activity. 'The boundaries between shopping, exhibition, entertainment, refreshment and socializing are blurred,' says Yeo. 'It makes for a very exciting time for both shoppers and designers. Shoppers are intelligent, demanding, well-informed and cultured. If they can get that something extra – be uplifted, informed, entertained, engaged, intrigued, well-served – they may just come back more often. The shop is all about shopping, and through playfulness, art installation, changeability and informality, we hope to reward the shopper with a bit more than an ordinary shopping experience.'

And so she does, with both the overall look and minute details. A floor-to-ceiling 'shoe wall' that could be an art installation provides a textured, perforated surface for displaying clothes and accessories. Yeo anchored the frames by fixing their feet into depressions in the floor made from round steel plates that are mirrored in the ceiling by a smattering of bespoke cylindrical glass lights. The apparently random pattern of lights complements the frames and counters the chequered floor. At night, LED lighting illuminates the footpath and, thanks to reflections on mirrored surfaces at either end of the footpath, generates a three-dimensional shape.

'The approach was to apply no decoration or patterning without an underlying function and discipline, and for the space to have an atmosphere of reserve and, at the same time, to be an invitation to play and change,' Yeo explains. Perhaps the only feature with no underlying function other than that of brand identity is a contemporary fresco of women's faces. Verhoeven's illustrations – drawings that mix dreamy doodling with the willowy distortions and seduction of Aubrey Beardsley or Alfred Mucha prints – were what first drew public attention to the fashion designer. Her direct application of art to fashion inspired Yeo, who is six years into running her own practice after working with David Adjaye and William Russell.

'The main ideas are about providing possibilities for display, for interpretation, for art and fashion, for the customer, for interaction, for GIBO to play with the space, for the space to change with different collections. It's important that the shop is never static. I cannot see a commercial space, even in an ideological sense, as a fixed space.'

Preceding page
View of the entrance of Gibo. On display
is the illustration of a mannequin's head
by Julie Verhoeven.

Floor plan
1. Entrance
2. 'Footpath'
3. Modular hanging
display
4. Cash desk
5. Rear area

Bottom
Part boutique and part gallery, Gibo
features a textured 'shoe wall' that, when
used for the display of merchandise, resembles an art installation.

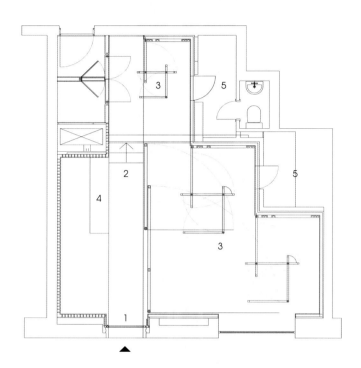

277

Below and opposite
Stainless-steel frames-within-frames are
multifunctional. Folded into the walls,
they empty the interior, form a sculptural
relief and define the space; unfolded and
extending at variable angles, they display
clothes, aid circulation and create a
Calder-like sculpture with endless configurations. The shop looks as beautiful empty
as it does full.

Store
Galaxie Lafayette

Location
Berlin, Germany

Architect
Plajer & Franz Studio

Alexander Plajer
'We didn't want to design something so
trendy that after six months you can't look
at it anymore.'

Text
Matthew Stewart

Photography
diephotodesigner.de

Circles and discs form the focal point of Plajer & Franz Studio's interior design Tendance Astrale in Galaxie Lafayette, an urban-hip addition to the galleries Lafayette, Berlin.

Jean Nouvel's glass building housing the Berlin outpost of the famed Galleries Lafayette department store, which began as a Parisian landmark, stands shimmering at the corner of Friedrichstrasse and Französischestrasse, the crystalline heart of the thriving Mitte District. Nouvel's 1995 design gestures towards the retailer's famed Boulevard Haussmann location, which boasts a full-height atrium ringed with sales floors, but updates it with bold and dynamic geometric additions. Most dramatically, Nouvel has introduced two monumental glass cones, one rising from street level to propel visitors to the upper reaches of the store, the other descending to cut through several sales floors. Building in such a well-known space, as Plajer & Franz Studio can attest first-hand, requires playing to the strengths of the architecture and masking the weaknesses, all while attempting to leave the concept intact.

Selected by the French department store from a pool of competition entrants to develop a new multi-brand retail department targeting young urban women, Plajer & Franz Studio embraced Nouvel's building and riffed on its geometry to create a strong identity for the new department. Galaxie Lafayette, as the department has come to be known, centres around the bottom tip of Nouvel's descending cone, which pierces the ceiling and hovers threateningly above the floor just slightly off the centre of the 500-square-metre space.

Plajer & Franz created a set of three interlocking discs that ring the tip of the cone, which serves as the centre point of the department. This area acts as a cross-promotional space for some of the clothing, whereas distinct brands have proprietary spots around the edges of the floor. The wooden discs, painted white, sandwich LED lights that illuminate the edges of the discs, each of which is enclosed within a removable diffusion cover of frosted plastic. The lights revolve around the edges of the discs, making the centre of the department a dynamic showcase area that draws the eye. An added bonus is the customizability, says principal designer Alexander Plajer. 'You can remove the plastic covers and put whatever printed images you want underneath, then put the covers back on top and the images are still visible, though in a frosted manner.' Adding images or key colours allows merchandisers to showcase certain collections or seasonal themes. Coloured LEDs were embedded in Nouvel's cone to tie the elements together. Suspended

discoid ceilings echo the forms of the display discs. Crafted of seamless Barrisol, these ceilings are strong enough to house downlighting for the display area. A contrasting white circle made of durable Hi-Mac has been set into the glittering black polyurethane floor covering, which Plajer compares to the shimmering concrete of pavements in New York City.

The theme of circles that originated with the design team's response to the tip of the cone was applied throughout the space, beginning with the entrance to the department from within the store. Customers arrive via a staircase of progressively smaller stacked concentric white discs. Set into these are smaller black discs that act as pedestals for mannequins. Another Barrisol disc hangs in a circular void overhead. This entry space, gleaming white, gives way to the darker, sultrier tones of the department. Walls and columns are painted white or black, with a contrasting dashed circle pattern (white on black, or anthracite on white for higher contrast value) throughout. Behind the cash desk, a wall with cut-out circles fronts a screen with images projected from the rear. In its default state, the screen displays ambient images of flowing liquids, for example, but it can also be connected to sync with music from a DJ. The wall in front of the screen can be removed to reveal the entire screen for special presentations, such as fashion shows.

Divvying up the rest of the space to the 15 brands was an exercise in equal representation. Plajer & Franz developed a modular system allocating 120 centimetres for branded imagery, as well as common elements for front- or side-hanging clothing display and additional surfaces for brand imagery and horizontal display. The system provides both maximum flexibility for products and equal parameters for each brand occupying a space in the department.

'There are so many shops where you can go to buy jeans that are shabby chic,' says Plajer, 'but that's not what we wanted in Lafayette.' Instead, unlike the ultra-trendy boutiques with which it may compete, the design of Galaxie Lafayette aims to be innovative but long-lasting and flexible. 'We didn't want to design something so trendy that after six months you can't look at it anymore.' Following in the footsteps of the parent store, Galaxie Lafayette is out to weather shifting trends with smart, responsive retailing.

Galaxie Lafayette

Floor plan
1. Entrance
2. Highlight area
3. Retail area
4. Jeans wall
5. Vertical displays
6. Cash desk
7. Fitting room
8. Tailoring room
9. Stockroom
10. Office
11. Escalator

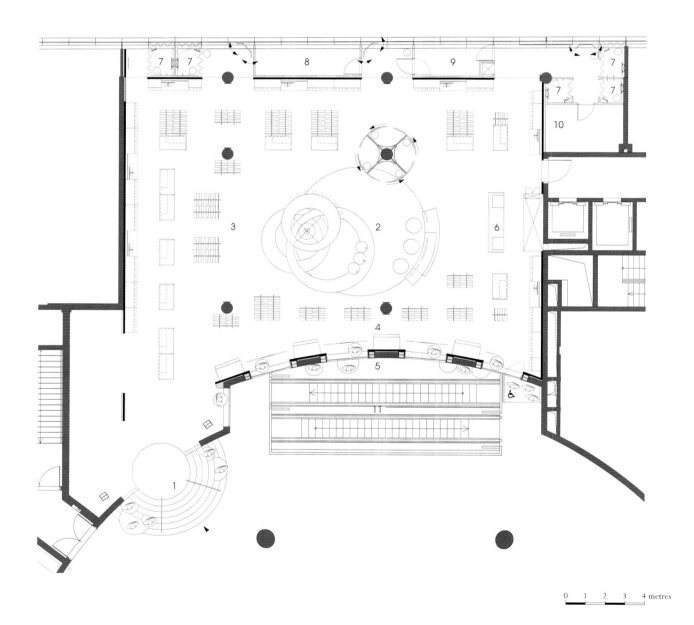

0   1   2   3   4 metres

Galaxie Lafayette

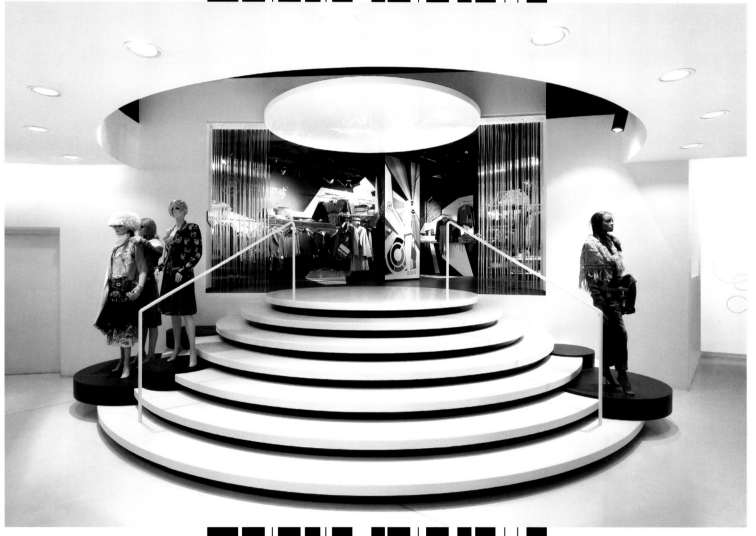

Engaging with Jean Nouvel's architecture for the department store, which features an enormous glass cone penetrating the floors above and terminating in the centre of Galaxie Lafayette, gave Plajer & Franz their organizational scheme, as well as the circular motif that defines the space.

Plajer & Franz Studio divided the space equally between 15 brands, using modular display systems for hanging and folded merchandise and additional surfaces for brand graphics.

Store
Addition

Location
Tokyo, Japan

Architect
Steve Lidbury Design

Combining modern materials with
a Japanese sensibility, Lidbury creates
a men's clothing shop that honours
the past and anticipates the future

Text
Shonquis Moreno

Photography
Hikaru Suzuki

Combining modern materials with a Japanese sensibility, Steve Lidbury creates a men's clothing shop in Tokyo that honours the past and anticipates the future.

The latest addition to the Addition clothing shop in Tokyo adds up to more than the sum of its parts. Architect Steve Lidbury of Steve Lidbury Design (SLD) was asked to design 'a shop that hasn't been seen in Tokyo before', and, without any bells and whistles, he did so. The one-room men's section opened in September 2004 at the rear of the original shop in the Omotesando area of Japan's capital city. Addition is an unexpected combination of cold, hard surfaces (steel and concrete) and diaphanous layers of glass, polyurethane and reflected light. Fitting for a country with an unparalleled textile tradition, Lidbury's addition feels like a fabric that simultaneously evokes history and the future, solid earthiness and the ephemerality of an insect's wings.

Still in his twenties, Lidbury is a man who takes the 'when in Rome' adage to heart. Born in London, he arrived in Japan via Italy, where he worked at Fabrica under creative director Oliviero Toscani. SLD took the Addition project from concept to construction in two months on a budget as small as the 30-square-metre space, making each feel more generous than it was. The Addition clothing label includes the high-end, high-concept couture of 40 ascendant designers who favour unusual manufacturing techniques and a surprising mix of materials. Lidbury made this sophisticated relationship of materials, textures and forms the touchstone of his own design.

The new space preserves the rough finishes and understated minimalism of the original shop. At the centre, multiplied by its reflection in a wall of mirrors and another of windows, a display unit made from acrylic and oak is suspended from the ceiling and anchored to the floor on one side with cables. Made by German fashion designers Bless, the unit resembles a mobile slung low to the ground and sways gently at every touch. Non-structural ceiling beams made from worn grey wood were once part of Canadian garden fences. Lidbury used the same timber to frame slimline ceiling lights, to back and separate mirrored wall panels (wood emerges at the edges of each wall) and to conceal electrical wiring. The scuffed and mottled concrete floor – coated with transparent clay urethane – is blurrily reflective. Lidbury had workers expose the room's original walls, ceiling and floor, revealing kanji characters that previous construction workers had scribbled with a felt-tip pen. Their notes are now displayed behind a glass pane

projecting from the wall, a piece of recent history preserved beneath a smooth, hypermodern finish.

The rawness of walls (painted with diluted polyurethane) and floor is complemented by the glossy faces and depths of glass and mirrors, and by a futuristic industrial look lent by five angular steel display elements (coated in white, burnt-melamine resin) which Lidbury refers to as 'trapeziums'. An overhanging lip at the top of each unit has a fine strip cut out along its width on which hangers can rest. When not displaying a profusion of clothes, the units have a sculptural quality that stands out against the grey walls on which they are mounted. These alcoves pop onto the eye, frame the clothing, and provide shelving at head and foot, as well as niches on the floor, for displaying accessories. Of varying shapes and widths, the trapeziums support the weight of large vertical glass panes, the edges of which are set three mm apart. Because the panes don't touch, they create gratuitous vertical seams along the wall ('not too much distraction,' says Lidbury, 'but just enough') and a pleasing syncopation. Taken together, the layered elements – ageing concrete beneath open white cupboards and seamed glass curtains and, as a surface finish, the bright reflections of T-bulbs – generate a sense of depth.

On one side of the room, overlapping mirrored panels cover the walls from floor to ceiling, with one almost imperceptibly canted panel strategically interrupting the reflection. The sliding mirrored door of the fitting room becomes a continuation of the reflective panels when closed and, when open, a continuation of the interior and a potential display area; the inside of the cubicle features grey wood and a mirrored surface. To indicate vacancy or occupancy and, not least, to titillate, a narrow radiused rectangle has been cut from the door at eye-level, an unusually risqué detail in Japanese retail culture. This cutout echoes the shape of wooden light frames on the ceiling and a vertical, wall-mounted bracket used for hanging clothes inside the fitting room. On the wall opposite, a picture window and sliding glass door leading to the concrete patio are dressed with a dark-brown, solar-protective film, giving a crepuscular hue to the world outside. The effect, like the design as a whole, is to pluck the shopper's imagination off the tony streets of Tokyo and anchor it firmly inside the shop. 'Together, the combination of raw and man-made materials and sharp-angled forms pushes the notion of observing and respecting the past whilst contemplating the future,' says Lidbury. 'These are the issues – tradition and stability versus futurism and uncertainty – that contemporary Japan is trying to deal with on a daily basis.'

286

Addition

Preceding page
Addition, with only 30 square metres of
floor space, feels much larger thanks to the
strategic juxtaposition of white display units,
mirrored walls and glass panels, which use
reflection to create depth. Windows are
coated with a dark film to keep all eyes
inside the shop.

This spread
German fashion designers Bless created
the display suspended at the centre of the
room. Around it, broad sheets of glass are
set clear of the wall. Reflections of T-bulbs
(2 cm in diameter) overhead resemble the
white lines on a motorway, creating a
deceptive sense of speed and depth
within a very small space.

Floor plan and sections
1. Entrance
2. Hanging display
   unit (trapezium)
3. Window
4. Mirror wall
5. Fitting room
6. Rear area

Opposite
Lidbury canted floor-to-ceiling mirrors
along one wall to break up reflections
that help shape the room.

Store
Le Ciel Bleu

Location
Sapporo, Japan

Architect
Noriyuki Otsuka

Noriyuki Otsuka
'Spatial design appeals most to one's
sense of sight, but an interior that
stimulates all five senses is crucial.'

Text
Masaaki Takahashi

Photography
Kozo Takayama

Taking inspiration from library shelves, Noriyuki Otsuka filled Japanese boutique Le Ciel Bleu with books, all entitled *Le Ciel Bleu*.

Interior designer Noriyuki Otsuka is intrigued by the number of excellent libraries that have been built in Japan in recent years. Cafés and internet access have made libraries interactive environments, thus encouraging public use of facilities once thought of as being silent spaces for study and research. 'The general image of a library is that of a place for intellectuals,' says Otsuka. 'With the new trend in libraries aiming more at design, the basic principles behind conveying traditions and cultural values are also changing. In designing the boutique, I've made an attempt to apply the same principles to fashion. When people go shopping for clothes, the sense of power that comes with the purchase of a new outfit is not always apparent. When they visit the library, the sense of power that comes with borrowing and reading books is far more evident.'

Le Ciel Bleu, a fashion label based in Kobe, has expanded rapidly throughout Japan since its inception in 1995. Otsuka has done the retail design for all the brand's outlets, including number eight, the one featured here. Located in Paseo – an underground shopping street in Sapporo, Hokkaido – this boutique surprises visitors with book shelves lined with nearly 2000 volumes. Although the covers and pages are completely white, on closer inspection each book bears the same embossed title: *Le Ciel Bleu*. Passers-by catching a glimpse of the book shelves may think they're looking at wallpaper, a decorative gimmick that Otsuka did consider before consulting a graphic designer who does bookbinding as well. The advice he received was that making books and placing them on the shelves was not only the less expensive option, but also an obvious way to heighten the sense of realism. Covered with a thin plastic film, the books are easy to maintain. They are uniform in height and width, but vary in thickness. Otsuka's lighting scheme gives the books a casual, inconspicuous presence.

The entrance is a scant 2.2 metres wide, but bronze-tinted mirrors inside the entrance, wall mounted to form a kind of gate, reflect the surroundings and make the entrance appear to be bigger and more open than it is. Otsuka realized that a larger entrance would provide easier access, but he elected to grab shoppers' attention with a design that would rouse their curiosity and lure them inside, where mirrored reflections continue to shape the ideal ambience. Display cases feature black-tinted glass of the same type often used in car windows.

As a contrast to the monochrome space, Otsuka chose lighting from Spanish company Metalarte in a shade of red, a warm colour that he believes fosters human interaction. Many photographs of the interior distort the colour, making it seem bolder than it is in reality; fluorescent lighting in the shop softens the red to a pinkish hue. (A good photographer himself, Otsuka designs lighting that can be adjusted to create the photographic image desired.) Because primary colours and subdued interiors highlight much of Otsuka's work, his spaces breathe an air of deceptive simplicity that fails to reveal all the effort leading up to the final solution. Otsuka nearly always begins with a rather more complex concept and with a number of elements that, as a result of trial and error, are either pared down or discarded along the way. 'It's easy to create a sense of fullness with lots of furnishings,' he explains. 'At first glance, an interior may look simple, but it's been carefully pruned to reveal a crisp design.' Attention to the detailing and knowledge of all the calculating that's gone into the design process will show, he says, that it's not easy at all. 'Spatial design appeals most to one's sense of sight, but an interior that stimulates all five senses is crucial. For example, even ceiling heights can affect the human psyche. An environment designed for comfort and relaxation stimulates the urge to buy. And a profusion of mirrors gives customers something to look at while also creating something tangible, something that can be felt.' When first commissioned to create Le Ciel Bleu's interiors, his thoughts went immediately to the relationship between spatial dimensions and light, a combination that led him to the design of comfortable retail interiors.

'As internet shopping continues to grow in popularity and sales, real shops can draw customers only by displaying fresh designs with a strong impact on the senses. People want a place where they feel in control, a place staffed by employees, who are becoming more and more important.' Europe has a long tradition of collecting art and cultural artefacts, and of passing such objects on to future generations. It's a tradition that may benefit design. Asian design, however, is heading in another direction, and Otsuka is an advocate of Japan's non-Western trend. 'I would like to see fashion as the focal point of our era. Although some designers ascribe to a neo-decorative style, there's still evidence of an increase in casual, trendy fashion. Why not a revival of the fashion-conscious shopper? One who cares about her appearance and wears the right outfit for every occasion?'

Le Ciel Bleu

Preceding page
Bronze mirrors are mounted on the wallsand ceiling of a rather narrow entrance area; passing through, the shopper is invited inside by the sight of fashions surrounded by shelves of white-covered books.

Floor plan and sections
1. Entrance
2. Shop-window display
3. Shelf display
4. Display table
5. Sofas and table
6. Counter
7. Hanging display

8. Book shelves
9. Mirror
10. Fitting room
11. Cash desk
12. Office
13. Machine room
14. LED display

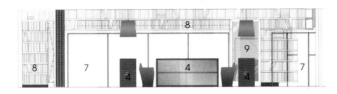

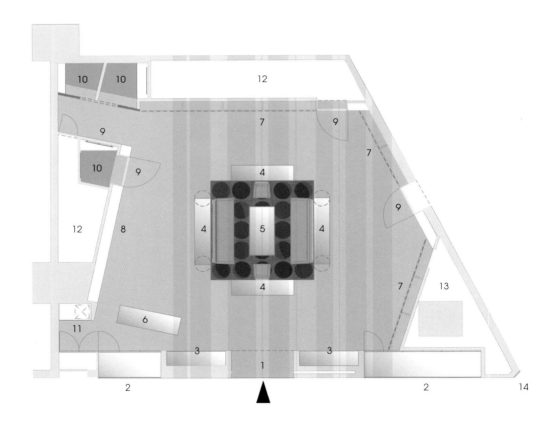

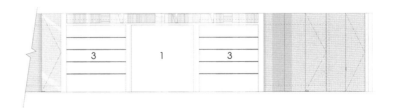

This page
The interior features about 2000 books
in three thicknesses; books are coated in
a plastic film for easy maintenance.

295

Below
Bathed in the rosy light of the interior,
customers can sit on centrally positioned
sofas and leaf through catalogues of
Le Ciel Bleu merchandise.

Bottom left
A wooden counter expresses the
library theme. A purpose-designed
carpet covers the concrete floor.

Le Ciel Bleu

Store
Custo Barcelona

Location
Madrid, Spain

Architect
Teresa Sapey

Teresa Sapey has compared today's
boutiques to medieval cathedrals
'in the sense that the temples of
cult in modern society now house
fashion gurus' creations, which
set the trends for each season'

Text
Sarah Martín Pearson

By simply portraying the imagery of Custo Barcelona, Teresa Sapey created a colourful, graphic addition to Madrid's Golden Mile.

Currently based in Madrid, Italian architect Teresa Sapey moved to Spain 12 years ago, where she has benefited from an economic, cultural and creative boom that nurtured her talent and allowed her to expand professionally. Known for her adventurous spirit and surrounded by a youthful and dynamic team, Sapey approaches architecture as an all-encompassing art that is not limited to one or more aspects of a particular project. She sees each commission as a laboratory for experimentation. Her unique style – a classically timeless fusion of surprise, irony, technology and innovation – has attracted clients such as Absolut Vodka, Fox Channel, Tandem DDB, Renault, Cartier and Delito & Castigo. Sapey aims for entertaining, eye-catching designs that nevertheless respond to the client's brief and serve the purpose for which they were built.

Sapey also applied her experimental methods to a retail concept for Custo Barcelona. In accordance with the client's desire to envelop the brand in an aura of sophistication, the location chosen for the shop was on Claudio Coello Street, also known as Madrid's Golden Mile, an exclusive strip lined with boutiques bearing the names of fashion royals like Louis Vuitton, Chanel, Dior, Fendi, Versace and Gucci. Young and enterprising, Custo Barcelona holds its own among such heavyweights, thanks in part to a distinctive graphic style. Portraying Custo's imagery was key to Sapey's plan for the new shop. For artistic inspiration, she looked not only to constructivism and cubism, but also to artists such as Delaunay and Varini. She wanted to achieve a plastic entity by blending form and colour in much the same way that Custo's designers are able to 'build' a single garment from different fabrics and prints. Based on Delaunay's art and bathing the space in colour is a vibrant, custom-designed carpet with sweeping lines and planes: an underlying palette that, together with the brightness of angular furnishings in white-painted MDF, enhances the display of colourful fashions. In stark contrast is the grey façade, the apparel-less shop window and the main entrance: a three-part overture to the main act. There's not a glimpse of tint or attire until the retail space unfolds and gradually reveals the intensity of its colours – and its contents. Diagonally overlapping clothes-hanging units open towards the interior, turning their backs on the entrance, so to speak. The mystery is all part of a strategy to lure passers-by inside – to whet their curiosity about a shop that seems so reluctant to share its secrets.

Inside the shop, lighting vies with colour for the position of most vital factor in shaping the personality of the space. Indirect fluorescent lighting built into the bases of display units casts a warm glow, while seemingly lifting these volumes from the floor and, at the same time, adding 'visual' height to the ceiling. The floating sensation is further emphasized by lighting built into the displays themselves. Another example of built-in lighting is at the far end of the shop, where a reticular shelving system positioned over a glass wall clad in layers of coloured vinyl radiates a warm pink hue. As usual, Sapey and her staff custom-designed all furnishings. Putting her signature on every detail in the shop was Sapey's way of responding fully to the client's needs and of giving the space the desired sense of exclusivity. A special feature is the freestanding display case with integrated seating covered in a white Alcantara fabric.

This shop exemplifies what might be called 'modular retail design'. Even the purpose-designed carpet boasts a geometric scheme of intersecting lines. And each bold white volume adds to a balanced composition that exudes a sense of harmony. Avoiding clashes and confrontation, lighting complements the colours and shapes of the retail design, as well as those of the clothing on display.

Teresa Sapey has compared today's boutiques to medieval cathedrals 'in the sense that the temples of cult in modern society now house fashion gurus' creations, which set the trends for each season'. The 'masters' to whom she refers are building commercial palaces that double as places of worship and as tourist attractions – modern monuments led by Prada's New York flagship, a Rem Koolhaas creation, and a more recent Prada showpiece in Tokyo, the work of Herzog & de Meuron. Sapey's philosophy, on the other hand, is to get to the essence of the matter, to focus on giving that little extra while tending to the wellbeing of those who inhabit her spaces. In the case of Custo Barcelona, giving that 'little extra' was all wrapped up in 'seduction' – in her attempt to entice pedestrians into the shop. It was a goal that allowed her to meet the needs of her client, while making life more enjoyable for the general public. The impact of Sapey's design was so effective that Custo Barcelona soon asked her to export the inventive concept to new outlets across the globe.

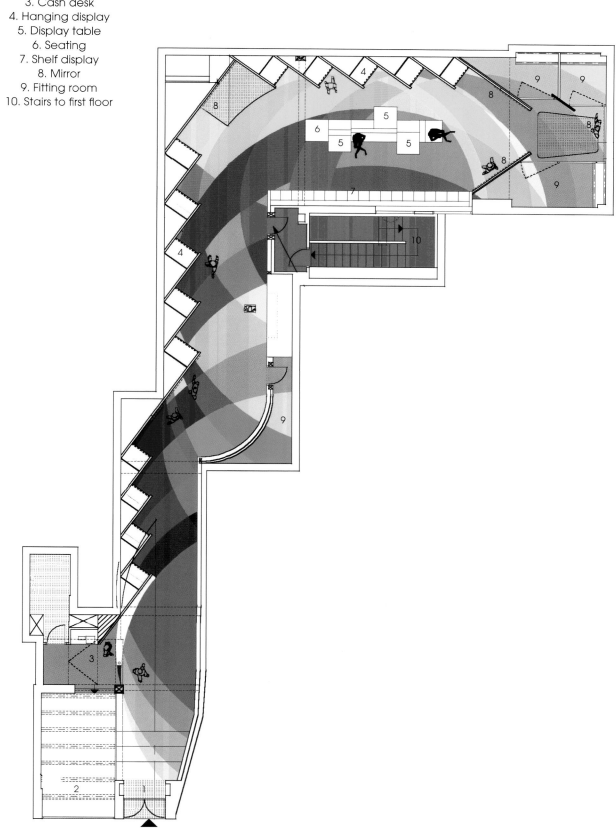

Floor plan
1. Entrance
2. Shop-window display
3. Cash desk
4. Hanging display
5. Display table
6. Seating
7. Shelf display
8. Mirror
9. Fitting room
10. Stairs to first floor

Custo Barcelona

Below
Built-in lighting behind
reticular shelving casts
a warm pink hue over
the whitesurfaces of
the interior.

Custo Barcelona

Below
Overlapping displays
reveal their contents along
the corridor in reverse, while
built-in lighting adds a
floating sensation to white
display units.

Opposite and below
The Delaunay-inspired carpet, in combination with white display units, blends
form and colour to achieve a plastic unity
enhanced by indirect lighting.

Store
Neil Barrett

Location
Osaka, Japan

Architect
Neil Barrett and Garde
(Yutaka Yamamoto)

Text
Masaaki Takahashi

Photography
Matsuoka Hirokazu

What do clothing and architecture have in common? Both protect us from rain, snow, heat and cold: from the harsh environment of the outside world.

British fashion designer Neil Barrett collaborated with Tokyo-based Garde in the design of his Osaka shop, which features an art installation based on the catchphrase 'clean and one extra thing'.

What do clothing and architecture have in common? Both protect us from rain, snow, heat and cold: from the harsh environment of the outside world. And equally important to garments and buildings are materials and the sense of comfort they provide. We might even conclude that apparel is a miniaturized form of architecture. What would be more natural, therefore, than a fashion designer – a man continually aware of sensations affecting the human body – who has a serious interest in interior design and architecture?

Currently a highly popular figure in Japan, British fashion designer Neil Barrett enjoys participating in the creation of his own shop interiors. Both fashion design and retail design allow him to interpret the world as he sees it. In Tokyo's Aoyama district, Neil Barrett's Japanese flagship store features six plasma televisions – still relatively rare in Japanese households – stacked one atop the other. Each screen displays an image of fluffy white clouds floating in a blue sky. Highlighting Barrett's new store in Osaka is a contemporary art installation, similar to the work of Joseph Beuys, which invites viewers to contemplate the phrase 'clean and one extra thing'.

The outfit that executed Barrett's design was Garde, a Tokyo-based firm with offices in Italy that specializes in the conception, planning and building of commercial facilities. Garde's portfolio includes major projects such as Tod's Omotesando store and Barneys New York Ginza. The firm's Italian branch conferred with Barrett before relaying his ideas, including a number of detailed drawings and floor plans, to Yutaka Yamamoto in Tokyo, who supervised the construction of the new shop.

Barrett's initial idea called for suspending shelves and hangers from the ceiling, but after taking the narrowness of the space into account, he decided to use industrial-style rails on the ceiling that are attached to pulleys. Rods suspended from these rails support mannequins, display cases, hangers, merchandise – the works! In imagining this retail interior, the fashion designer took a particular interest in the textures of objects and surfaces. Rapidly cooling the newly forged red-hot steel used to make rails and pulleys, for example, created an industrial effect; all oxidized areas resemble black suede. Juxtaposed with rough and rusted metal that evokes scenes of old warehouses and shipyard sheds are contrasting areas of pristine white. Against this backdrop, Barrett's fashions acquire a

sense of glamour. Referring to the catchphrase 'clean and one extra thing', Yamamoto solves the riddle by saying: 'The pure white space is Barrett's idea of "clean". The pulleys are "one extra thing".' According to Yamamoto, Barrett based his original concept for the Osaka shop on *Dogville*, the 2003 film directed by Lars von Trier. Drawn in white on a flat, dark stage, the barest of set designs featured not a house, but the outline of a house; not a church, but the outline of a church; not a road, but white lines indicating a road. Partial walls and sparse furnishings added a third dimension to the town of *Dogville*. Within this setting, players enacted an avant-garde thriller. Barrett sent Yamamoto stills from the movie and drew outlines on his floor plan – shirts here, knits there and so forth – creating clearly delineated areas of merchandise. Unfortunately, the premises were too small to carry out his plan in its entirety. What remains of it is a floor marked with lines inspired by the movie.

Barrett has compared a wide open retail interior that tells all at a single glance to merchandise tagged with prices visible from a distance: if a window-shopper can not only view the entire interior and everything in it from the pavement, but can also read the price tags on the garments on display, she will walk in only if she's spotted exactly what she wants. As others have obviously come to the same conclusion, we now see many shops with a rather enigmatic ambience that draws customers inside to explore the premises from front to back. 'In the case of this store, however,' says Yamamoto, 'which is a work of art in its own way, there was no need for that sort of secrecy.' Along with other retail interiors that have managed to achieve success without holding anything back, Barrett's Osaka enterprise is not exemplary of the come-in-and-snoop-around policy.

Yamamoto is critical of the recent trend that has seen many brands turn over the initiative for their retail design to outsiders. 'They just gather a bunch of people together and have them design a store, even though frequently those involved have no real understanding of the merchandise and how to display it.' And even those within the company – what he calls 'the brand's corporate hierarchy' – don't always grasp what it takes to create a design that works. 'That's why we've been trying to design stores that incorporate a wide range of plans and ideas,' he says, 'from those of the designer to those of the buyers and various members of the staff.'

Neil Barrett

This page:
Almost all merchandise in the shop is
presented on suspended displays.

Floor plan
1. Sliding display box
2. Hanging model
3. Hanging display system
4. Display table
5. Cash desk
6. Monitor
7. Fitting room
8. Shelving

Bottom
The contrast between a pure white space and rusty industrial equipment is the designers' interpretation of 'clean and one extra thing'.

Opposite
The original concept included antique armoires, doors removed, which were to hang on thick ropes from the ceiling. In the final version of the plan, however, the armoires were replaced by steel shelves suspended by means of a block-and-tackle system.

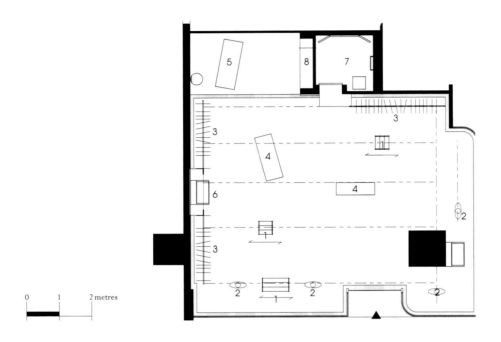

0   1   2 metres

Left
Oxidized Corten steel was used to
create the appearance of age.

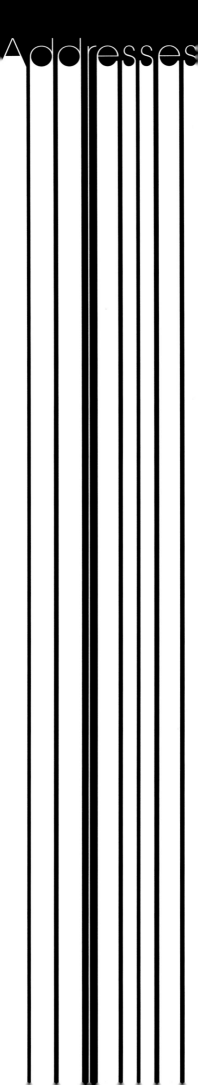

Addresses

AEDS
5, rue de l'Harmonie
75015 Paris
France
T +33 1 4842 4944
ammar@digit-all.net
www.digit-all.net

Arnell Group
130 Prince Street
New York, NY 10012
USA
T +1 212 219 8400
contact@arnellgroup.com
www.arnellgroup.com

B-architecten
Borgerhoutsestraat 22/01
2018 Antwerp
Belgium
T +32 3 2318 228
info@b-architecten.be
www.b-architecten.be

BEHF Architects
Kaiserstasse 41
1070 Vienna
Austria
T +43 1 5241 750-0
behf@behf.at
www.behf.at

Block Architecture
83a Geffrye Street
London E2 8HX
England
T +44 20 7729 9194
mail@blockarchitecture.com
www.blockarchitecture.com

Brinkworth
4/6 Ellsworth Street
London E2 0AX
England
T +44 20 7613 5341
info@brinkworth.co.uk
www. brinkworth.co.uk

CCT Arquitectos
C/ Puerto Príncipe
nº 26-40 1º 12ª
08027 Barcelona
Spain
T +34 93 4080 367
cct@coac.es
www.cctarquitectos.com

Christian Biecher &
Associes
14, rue Crespin du Gast
75011 Paris
France
T +33 1 4929 6939
info@biecher.com
www.biecher.com

CJ Studio
6F, #54 Lane 260
Kwang Fu South Road
106 Taipei
Taiwan
T +886 2 2773 8366
cj@shi-chieh-lu.com
www.shi-chieh-lu.com

Corneille
Uedingslohmann Architekten
Rossstrasse 12
50823 Cologne
Germany
T +49 221 5777 285
info@cue-architekten.de
www.cue-architekten.de

Creneau International
Hellebeemden 13
3500 Hasselt
Belgium
T +32 11 2479 20
info@creneau.com
www.creneau.com

D_raw associates
23b Goodge Place
London W1T 4SN
England
T +44 20 7636 0016
info@d-raw.com
www.d-raw.com

Atelier Jan De Cock
Auguste Gevaertstraat 15
1070 Brussels
Belgium
T +32 2 5208 975
atelier@jandecock.net
www.jandecock.net

Shuhei Endo
Domus A01
5F, 5-15-11 Nishitenma,
Kita-ku
Osaka 530-0047
Japan
T +81 6 6312 7455
endo@paramodern.com
www.paramodern.com

Elmslie Osler Architect
526 West 26th Street,
suite 514
New York, NY 10001
USA
T +1 212 989 0652
mail@eoarch.com
www.eoarch.com

Fumita Design Office
Fukuda Building 1F-B1F,
Minami Aoyama,
Minato-ku
Tokyo 107-0062
Japan
T +81 3 5414 2880
info@fumitadesign.com
www.fumitadesign.com

Garde
5-2-1 Minami-Aoyama,
Minato-ku
Tokyo 107-0062
Japan
T +81 3 3407 0007
info@garde.co.jp
www.garde.co.jp

Kristian Gavoille
and Valerie Garcia
16, rue Bellot
75019 Paris
France
T +33 1 4209 4242
contact@kristiangavoille.com
www.kristiangavoille.com

Giorgio Borruso Design
333 Washington Blvd #352
Marina Del Rey, CA 90292
USA
T +1 310 821 9224
info@borrusodesign.com
www.borrusodesign.com

Glenn Sestig Architects
Fortlaan 1
9000 Ghent
Belgium
T +32 9 2401 191
contact@glennsestig
architects.com
www.glennsestig
architects.com

Hecker Phelan & Guthrie
3c, 68 Oxford Street
Collingwood, Victoria 3066
Australia
T +61 3 9417 0466
hpg@hpg.net.au
www.hpg.net.au

ippolito fleitz group
Bismarckstrasse 67b
70197 Stuttgart
Germany
T +49 711 9933 92-330
info@ifgroup.org
www.ifgroup.org

Ito Masaru
Design Project / SEI
101 Mikawadai Heights,
4-3-6 Roppongi,
Minato-ku
Tokyo 106-0032
Japan
T +81 3 5785 3681
sei@itomasaru.com
www.itomasaru.com

Jamo Associates
Sunflat Ligura Building 1F,
1-6-9 Azabudai, Minato-Ku
Tokyo 106-0041
Japan
T +81 3 5545 3639
office@jamo.jp
http://jamo.jp

Jump Studios
35 Britannia Row
London N1 8QH
England
T +44 20 7688 0080
info@jump-studios.com
www.jump-studios.com

Klein Dytham architecture
AD Building 2F, 1-15-7 Hiroo,
Shibuya-ku
Tokyo 150-0012
Japan
T +81 3 3505 5330
kda@klein-dytham.com
www.klein-dytham.com

Lynch / Eisinger / Design
224 Centre Street, 5th floor
New York, NY 10013
USA
T +1 212 219 6377
studio@lyncheisinger
design.com
www.LynchEisinger
Design.com

Marmol Radziner
+ Associates
12210 Nebraska Avenue
Los Angeles, CA 90025
USA
T +1 310 826 6222
info@marmol-radziner.com
www.marmol-radziner.com

Maurice Mentjens
Martinusstraat 20
6123 BS Holtum
Netherlands
T +31 46 4811 405
info@mauricementjens.com
www.mauricementjens.com

Merkx + Girod
Gietersstraat 23
1015 HB Amsterdam
Netherlands
T +31 20 5230 052
arch@merkx-girod.nl
www.merkx-girod.nl

Laur Meyrieux
Shinkiso #201, 7 Sugacho,
Shinjuku-ku
Tokyo 160-0018
Japan
T +81 3 3341 3858
laur.lola@gmail.com

Martin Mostböck
Schönlaterngasse 5/4/3
1010 Vienna
Austria
T +43 1 5136 590
mail@martin.mostboeck.com
www.martin-mostboeck.com

Hiroshi Nakamura
Sanjou Building 3F,
2-3-18 Tamagawadai,
Setagaya-ku
Tokyo 158-0096
Japan
T +81 3 3709 7936
nakamura@nakam.info
www.nakam.info
www.nodo.jp

Noriyuki Otsuka
6-13-5-401 Minami Aoyama,
Minato-ku
Tokyo 107-0062
Japan
T +81 3 3406 6341
nodo@blue.ocn.ne.jp
www.nodo.jp

O.D.
(formerly OUT.DeSIGN)
#902, 1-7-5 Jiyugaoka,
Meguro-ku
Tokyo 152-0035
Japan
T +81 3 3723 5546
tomo@outdesign.com

Peter Robben 3D Projecten
Kooikerstraat 1
5042 XC Tilburg
Netherlands
T +31 13 5220 702
F +31 13 5220 375
info@3d.nl
www.3d.nl

William Russell
11 Needham Road
London W11 2RP
England
T +44 20 7229 3477
email@pentagram.com
www.pentagram.com

plajer & franz studio
Erkelenzdamm 59-61
10999 Berlin
Germany
T +49 30 6165 580
studio@plajer-franz.de
www.plajer-franz.de

PURPUR.ARCHITEKTUR
Brockmanngasse 5
8010 Graz
Austria
T +43 316 8373 230
studio@purpur.cc
www.purpur.cc

Steve Lidbury Design
Tuttle Building 5F,
2-6-5 Higashi Azabu,
Minato-ku
Tokyo 106-0044
Japan
T +81 3 5545 4834
sld@stevelidbury.com
www.stevelidbury.com

Studio 63
Architecture and Design
Via Santo Spirito 6
50125 Florence
Italy
T +39 055 2399 252
info@studio63.it
www.studio63.it
~
601 West 26th Street, #1510
New York, NY 10001
USA
info@studio63usa.com
www.studio63.it
~
12/F, Hilltop Plaza
49 Hollywood Road, Central
Hong Kong
China
info@studio63asia.com
www.studio63.it

Studio Power
Via Canonica 67
20154 Milan
Italy
T +39 02 3361 9062
info@tim-power.com
www.tim-power.com

Teresa Sapey
Architecture Studio
Francisco Campos 13
28015 Madrid
Spain
T +34 91 7450 876
estudio4@teresasapey.com
www.teresasapey.com

Keiko + Manaub Uchiyama
8-18-2 Kitami Setagaya
Tokyo 157-0067
Japan
T +81 3 3416 0714
alliekei@s3.ocv.ne.jp

Cherie Yeo
architecture + design
25c Frognal
London NW3 6AR
England
T +44 7940 5769 16
cherie.yeo@virgin.net

Z-A
11-27 47th Avenue
Long Island City, NY 11101
USA
T +1 917 922 6690
guy@guyzucker.com
www.guyzucker.com

Roos Aldershoff
T +31 20 6732 725
roosaldershoff@xs4all.nl
www.roosaldershoff.com

Daici Ano
T +81 3 3668 7722
daici@mac.com

Zooey Braun
T +49 711 6400 361
info@zooeybraun.de
www.zooeybraun.de

Benny Chan / fotoworks
T +1 323 730 0100
fotoworks@sbcglobal.net
www.fotoworks.cc

Leon Chew
T +44 958 4065 68
chewcon@gmx.net

diephotodesigner.de
T +49 30 2759 2380
ken@diephotodesigner.de
www.diephotodesigner.de

Jean-Pierre Gabriel
T +32 2 6404 818
jp@jpgl.be

Gareth Gardner
M +44 7950 7015 35
T +44 20 8747 8902
gareth@garethgardner.
demon.co.uk
www.garethgardner.com

William Furniss
T +852 9741 2787
wfurniss@mac.com
www.williamfurniss.com

Hertha Hurnaus
T +43 699 1044 1733
hehu@hurnaus.com
www.hurnaus.com

Eric Laignel
T +1 917 204 4338
ericlaignel@hotmail.com

Kuomin Lee
T +886 9363 4828 6

Svend Lindbaek
T +1 212 473 7750
svend@svendlindbaek.com

John Edward Linden
T +1 818 888 8544

Shannon McGrath
T +61 407 3307 67
F +61 3 9417 5810
shannon@shannonmc
grath.com
www.shannonmcgrath.com

Louise Melchoir and
Lara Gosling
T +44 7973 8236 20
lmp3@mac.com

Myr Muratet
T +33 1 4205 2225
myrmurate@free.fr
http//:myrmuratet.free.fr

Nacása & Partners
T +81 3 5722 7757
www.nacasa.co.jp

Nobuaki Nakagawa
T +81 422 7201 97
atsurei@aa.bb-east.ne.jp

Takeshi Nakasa
T +81 3 5722 7757
nasa@nacasa.co.jp

Kouji Okamoto
T +81 92 5331 150
technistaff@sunny.ocn.ne.jp

Frank Oudeman
T +1 646 298 8400
frankoudeman@hotmail.com

Yael Pincus
T +972 5444 8783 2
yae_l@netvision.net.il
www.yaelpincus.com

Eugeni Pons
T +34 972 3725 05
info@eugeni-pons.com
www.eugeni-pons.com

Christian Richters
T +49 251 277 447
chrichters@aol.com

Arjen Schmitz
T +31 43 3263 194
arjenschmitz@home.nl

Tineke Schuurmans
T +31 6 2916 6728
tinekeschuurmans@
wanadoo.nl
www.tinekeschuurmans.nl

Rupert Steiner
T +43 1 5819 520
office@rupertsteiner.com
www.rupertsteiner.com

Hikaru Suzuki
T +81 3 3965 8512
hikaru-office@m7.dion.ne.jp

Kozo Takayama
T +81 3 5724 5051
kozo@mxt.mesh.ne.jp

Udo Titz
T+ 43 1 4082 476
mail@udotitz.com
www.udotitz.com

Filip Van Loock
T +32 16 2605 92
filip.vanloock@pi.be
www.filipvanloock.be

Vercruysse & Dujardin
T +32 9 3244 855
frederik.vercruysse@
pandora.be

Mariacristina Vimercati
T +39 02 3655 3179
cri@mcristina.com

Joachim Wagner
T +49 30 4467 6956
post@joachimwagner.net

Nomi Yogev
T +972 52 8730 357
noomiyogev@yahoo.com

Paul Warchol
T +1 212 431 3461
requests@warchol
photography.com
www.warcholphotography.
com

Addition
Arrow Plaza 1F, 4-19-8
Jingumae, Shibuya-ku
Tokyo 150-0001
Japan
T +81 3 5786 0157
addition@proof.ocn.ne.jp
www.thewall.co.jp

Albrecht 7
Albrechtgasse 7
8010 Graz
Austria
T +43 720 3000 61
office@wolfensson.com
www.wolfensson.com

Alexander McQueen
www.alexandermcqueen.
com

B8 Couture
27 Little West 12th Street
New York, NY 10014
USA
T +1 212 924 2717
karinebellil@hotmail.com

Bethsabee
Kapelstraat 36
3500 Hasselt
Belgium
T +32 11 2339 45

Celux
Louis Vuitton Omotosando
Building, 5-7-5 Jinguemae,
Shibuya-ku
Tokyo 150-0002
Japan
www.celux.com
(Japanese only)

Colour by Numbers
20-23 Daikanyama-cho,
Shibuya-ku
Tokyo 150-0034
Japan
T +81 3 3770 1991

Costume National
8001 Melrose Avenue
Los Angeles, CA 90046
USA
T +1 323 655 8160
www.costumenational.com

Custo Barcelona
Claudio Coello 91
28006 Madrid
Spain
T +34 91 5751 414
custo-coello@custo-
barcelona.com
www.custo-barcelona.com

Custo Barcelona
AY Building 1F-2F, 3-2-2 Kita
Aoyama, Minato-ku
Tokyo 107-0061
Japan
T +81 3 5414 5870

De Bijenkorf
Achter het vleeshuis 26
6211 GS Maastricht
Netherlands
www.debijenkorf.nl

Delicatessen
4 Barzilai Street
Tel Aviv
Israel
T +972 3 4621 583
idit@delicatessen-
studio.com
www.delicatessen-
studio.com

Firetrap
21-23 Earlham Street
London WC2 9LL
England
T +44 20 8753 0200
firetrap@wdt.co.uk
www.firetrap.com

Fornarina
Mandalay Place 3930, Las
Vegas Boulevard South 105
Las Vegas, NV 89129
USA
T +1 702 215 9300
www.fornarina.com

Galaxie Fayette
Französische Strasse 23
10117 Berlin
Germany
T +49 30 2094 8 112
www.galerieslafayette.de

GIBO
Via Sant' Andrea 10a
20121 Milan
Italy
commerciale@gibo-co.com

Harvey Nichols
The Landmark, 15 Queen's
Road Central
Hong Kong
China
T +852 3695 3388
www.harveynichols.com

Hussein Chalayan
1-4-8 Aobadai, Meguro-ku
Tokyo 153-0042
Japan
T +81 3 5728 6022
info@viabusstop.com
www.viabusstop.com

Jacob & Co
48 East 57th Street
New York, NY 10022
USA
T +1 212 719 5887
jewelry@jacobandco.com
www.jacobandco.com

Jan Comme des Garçons
5-12-3 Minami-Aoyama,
Minato-ku
Tokyo 107-0062
Japan
T +81 3 5468 8301

Julie Sohn
C/ Diputación nº 299
08009 Barcelona
Spain
T +34 93 4875 796
tiendas@juliesohn.com
www.juliesohn.com

Karen Millen
247 Regent Street
London W1B 2EW
England
www.karenmillen.com

Lanvin
7-9-17 Ginza, Chuo-ku
Tokyo 104-0061
Japan
T +81 3 3289 2779
mtaniuchi@lanvin.co.jp

Le Ciel Bleu
2-9-7 Sannomiyacho,
Chuo-ku
Kobe, Hyogo 650-0021
Japan
T +81 78 3250 801
kobe@lcb.co.jp
www.lcb.co.jp

Le Ciel Bleu
Paseo B1F,
3-2-1 Kita-6jou, Kita-ku
Sapporo 060-0806
Japan
T +81 11 2135 803
sapporo@lcb.co.jp
www.lcb.co.jp

Le Ciel Bleu
1-275-1 Daimyou, Chuo-ku
Fukuoka 810-0041
Japan
T +81 92 7180 059
fukuoka@lcb.co.jp
www.lcb.co.jp

Little Red Riding Hood
Friedrichstrasse 148
10117 Berlin
Germany
T +49 221 2579 130
info@littleredridinghood.de
www.littleredridinghood.de

Loveless
3-17-11 Minami-Aoyama,
Minato-ku
Tokyo 107-0062
Japan
T +81 3 3401 2301
sato.nobuo@sanyo-
shokai.co.jp

m-i-d Press Room
4-13-16 Jingumae,
Shibuya-ku
Tokyo 150-0001
Japan
T +81 3 3405 4400
www.m-premier.jp

Marithé + François
Girbaud
Cherche-Midi
7, rue du Cherche-Midi
75006 Paris
France
T +33 1 5363 5363
b38.cherchemidi@mf
girbaud.com
www.girbaud.com

Marithé + François
Girbaud
Malher
20, Rue Malher
75004 Paris
France
T +33 1 4454 9901
b38.malher@mfgirbaud.com
www.girbaud.com

Marithé + François
Girbaud
Midosuji
Yodokou Daini Building 1F,
4-2-15 Bakuro-Machi, Cho-Ku
Osaka 541-0059
Japan
T +81 6 6121 7115
mfg-midosuji@fib.takaya.co.jp
www.girbaud.com

Marithé + François
Girbaud
New York
47 Wooster Street
New York, NY 10013
T +1 212 625 0066
F +1 212 625 0553
girbaudUS@aol.com
www.girbaud.com

Mayke
De Lind 31
5061 HS Oisterwijk
Netherlands
T +31 13 5288 330
info@mayke.nl
www.mayke.nl

Miss Sixty Milan
Via Montenapoleone 27
20121 Milan
Italy

Miss Sixty Palermo
Via Ruggero VII 17
90139 Palermo
Italy

Miss Sixty Los Angeles
8074-8080 Melrose Avenue
Los Angeles, CA 90046
USA

Miss Sixty New York
386 West Broadway
New York City, NY 10012
USA

Missoni
Moda e Modi
Frankrijklei 70
2000 Antwerp
Belgium
T +32 3 2341 778
info@modaemodi.be
www.modaemodi.be

Neil Barrett
Herbis Plaza,
2-5-25 Umeda, Kita-ku
Osaka
Japan

Nike iD Studio
255 Elizabeth Street
New York, NY 10012
USA
www.nikeid.com

Offspring
22 Camden High Street
London NW1 7BU
England
T +44 20 7267 9873

Pleats Please Issey Miyake
Galeries La Fayette
Friedrichtstrasse 76-78
10117 Berlin
Germany

Pleats Please Issey Miyake
28, rue des Trois Journees
66000 Perpignan
France

Reiss
387 West Broadway
New York, NY 10012
USA
T +1 212 925 5707
info@reiss.co.uk
www.reiss.co.uk

Restir
3-1-15 Kitanagasa-dori,
Chuo-ku
Kobe 650-0012
Japan
T +81 78 3216 611
restir-kobe@lcb.co.jp
www.restir.com

Rodenstock Galerie
du Brille Ginza
6-8-5 Ginza, Chuo-ku
Tokyo 104-0061
Japan
T +81 3 6274 5111
www.brille-ginza.com

Sigrun Woehr
Kirchstrasse 12
70173 Stuttgart
Germany
T +49 721 9203 984
info@sigrun-woehr.de
www.sigrun-woehr.de

Stash
Wyckerbrugstraat 45
6121 EB Maastricht
Netherlands
T +31 43 3253 576
info@s-t-a-s-h.com
www.s-t-a-s-h.com

Stephane Dou &
Changlee Yugin
Taiger City department
Taichung
Taiwan
stephanedou@yahoo.com.tw
www.stephanedou.com

Thurner Womenswear
Hauptstrasse 54
7000 Eisenstadt
Austria
T +43 2682 6216-0
office.thurner@aon.at
www.thurner-wm.at

Tiberius
Lindengasse 2a
1070 Vienna
Austria
T +43 1 5220 474
office@tiberius.at
www.tiberius.at

TroisO
5-46-12 Jingumae,
Shibuya-ku
Tokyo 150-0001
Japan
T +81 3 400 0550
ooo_03@troiso.jp
www.troiso.jp

Uniqlo Ginza
5-7-7 Ginza, Chuo-ku
Tokyo 104-0061
Japan
T +81 3 3569 6781
www.uniqlo.co.jp

Verso
Lange Gasthuisstraat 11
2000 Antwerp
Belgium
T +32 3 2269 292
info@verso.be
www.verso.be

Wayne Cooper
Shop F01 at GPO,
300 Bourke Street,
corner Elizabeth Street
Melbourne, Victoria 3000
Australia
T +61 3 9671 3963
www.waynecooper.com.au

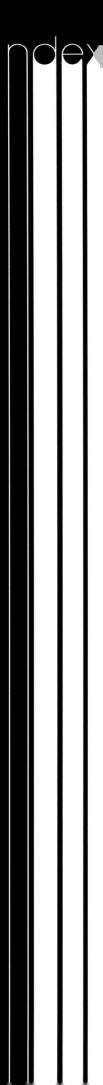

Addition
286
~
Architect
Steve Lidbury Design
Client
Addition Adelaide W. Links Y.K
General contractor
Ta Craft
Graphic film
Sign Club
Furniture
Swing
Total floor area
30 m²
Total cost (¥)
5,800,000
Duration of construction
6 weeks
Opening
9 September 2004

Albrecht 7
28
~
Architect
PURPUR.ARCHITEKTUR
Client
Albrecht 7
Engineer
Reinhard Pötsch
Manufacturers
Krobath Metallbau
Total floor area
70 m²
Total cost (€)
300,000
Duration of construction
12 weeks
Opening
April 2005

Alexander McQueen
16
~
Architect
William Russell
Client
Alexander McQueen

B8 couture
268
~
Architect
Elmslie Osler Architect
Client
Karine Bellil
General contractor
Downtown Domain
Total floor area
140.7 m²
Total cost (US$)
255,000
Duration of construction
7 weeks

Bethsabee
160
~
Architect
Creneau International
Client
Stivaletto

Furniture and fixture
Crenau International
Total floor area
120 m²
Duration of construction
3 weeks
Opening
5 August 2005

Celux
232
~
Architect
Studio Power
Client
LVMH Japan

Colour by Numbers
226
~
Architect
Jamo Associates
Client
Sanyo Shokai
Constructor
Tanseisha
Lighting
Toru Goto
Total floor area
178.06 m²
Total cost (¥)
35,000,000
Duration of construction
3 weeks
Opening
23 July 2005

Costume National
118
~
Architect
Marmol Radziner + Associates
Client
Costume National
Lighting
John Brubaker
Structural Engineer
Niver Engineering
Total floor area
240 m²
Duration of construction
12 weeks
Opening
2000

Custo Barcelona
298
~
Architect
Teresa Sapey
Client
Custo Barcelona
Consultants
Litecon
Total floor area
280 m²
Duration of construction
8 weeks
Opening
June 2004

Custo Barcelona
196
~
Architect
OUT.DeSIGN
Total floor area
140.4 m²
Duration of construction
4 weeks
Opening
3 October 2003

De Bijenkorf
70
~
Architect
Merkx+Girod
Client
De Bijenkorf
Total floor area
8000 m²
Duration of construction
16 months
Opening
2003

Delicatessen
202
~
Architect
Z-A
Client
Idit Barak and
Sharon Gurel
Total floor area
90 m²
Total cost (US$)
3000
Duration of construction
4 weeks
Opening
February 2005

Firetrap
46
~
Architect
Brinkworth
Client
WDT
Lighting
Modular Lighting
Engineers
Michael Baigent, Orla Kelly
Manufacturers
Etchells, Glass Deign, Syntec,
Bruce Tipper, Wren Industrial
Total floor area
235 m²
Duration of construction
10 weeks
Opening
September 2004

Fornarina
190
~
Architect
Giorgio Borruso Design
Client
Fornari USA
General contractor
Fineline Group

Lighting
NorthShore Consulting
Flooring
Lonseal
Furniture and fixtures
T. Alongi, BamBam Designs,
Eventscape, PRL Glass
Systems
Total floor area
218.3 m²
Opening
2004

Galaxie Lafayette
280
~
Architect
plajer & franz studio
Client
Galeries Lafayette
Deutschland
Graphics
xix
Engineers
AGP Architekten
Furniture and fixtures
Konrad Knoblauch
Lighting
Ansorg
Total floor area
502 m²
Duration of construction
10 weeks
Opening
29 September 2005

GIBO
274
~
Architect
Cherie Yeo
Client
GIBO / Onward Kashiyama
Italia
Structural Engineers
Alan Conisbee and
Associates
Executing Architect
Studio Pianon
Building Contractor
RGS Arredamenti
Lighting
Hoare Lee Lighting
Illustrator
Julie Verhoeven
Total floor area
62 m²
Total cost (€)
210,000
Duration of construction
17.5 weeks
Opening
September 2003

Harvey Nichols
178
~
Architect
Christian Biecher & Associes
Client
Harvey Nichols (Hong Kong)
General contractor
Ping Kee
Lighting
ACL

Total floor area
6,000 m²
Total cost (€)
9,000,000.00
Opening
September 2005

Hussein Chalayan
58
~
Architect
Block Architecture
Client
Via Bus Stop
Lighting
Dan Campbell Design
Graphics
Work in Progress
Engineer and manufacturer
Onward Creative Centre
Total floor area
340 m²
Total cost (£)
400,000
Duration of construction
8 weeks
Opening
April 2004

Jacob & Co
172
~
Architect
Arnell Group
Client
Jacob & Co
General Contractor
Americon Construction
Builder
FZAD Architecture
Engineers
Bayside Controls,
PST Design Group
Lighting
Martin Shaffer
AV/Media
Bayside Controls, Dimensional
Communications
Furniture
AEI, Alu, Arper, CK Pro Glass,
Erco Quadra, Gordon
International, Jeff Evans,
John Nguyen Woodworking,
Keilhauser, Lievore, New York
Oceanic Aquariums,
Peck's Office Plus, Sign Art,
SS Clean Trade, Wood
Flooring International
Total floor area
587.6 m² (only retail 111.5 m²)
Opening
1 December 2004

Jan Comme des Garçons
130
~
Artist
Jan De Cock
Client
Comme des Garçons
Opening
5 April 2005

Julie Sohn
184
~
Architect
CCT Arquitectos
Client
Julie Sohn
Constructor
d'PAC Construcciones
Total floor area
325 m²
Duration of construction
24 weeks
Opening
March 2005

Karen Millen
94
~
Architect
Brinkworth
Client
Karen Millen
Consultants
Brian Hart Shopfitting,
Birchalls
Engineers
Copper electrical,
Elliott Wood
Manufacturers
Glass Design, Oyster
Total floor area
300 m²
Duration of construction
12 weeks
Opening
July 2005

Lanvin Boutique Ginza
10
~
Architect
Hitoshi Nakamura
Client
Lanvin Japan K.K.
Constructor
Space Trust, Takenaka
Corporation
Manufacturers
Ikeya, Studio-kaya
Total floor area
825 m²
Duration of construction
24 weeks
Opening
February 2004

Le Ciel Bleu
34
~
Architect
Keiko + Manabu Uchiyama
Client
Le Ciel Bleu
Structural engineers
Akira Suzuki
Mechanical and Lighting
Eos Engineer, S Studio,
Shou Takahashi
Sound
Hibino Corporation
Exterior and interior
construction
D. Brain

Façade
Morikawa
Total floor area
275 m²
Duration of construction
16 weeks
Opening
1 July 2005

Le Ciel Bleu
136
~
Architect
Laur Meyrieux
Client
Le Ciel Bleu
Architectural development
Kenchiku Uchiyama
Structural ingeneer
for building
Suzuki Akira
Air conditioning and lighting
EOS Engineers Studio
Construction for building
Yasunari
Construction for interior
and furniture
D. Brain
Total floor area
140 m² (shop on two floors),
40 m² (garden), 59 m²
(terrace)
Duration of construction
3 months (building),
3 weeks (interior)
Opening
6 august 2005

Le Ciel Bleu
292
~
Architect
Noriyuki Otsuka
Client
Le Ciel Bleu
Lighting Plan
Ushio Spax
Book Production
Moon Crow Studio
Yoshinori Kikuchi
Engineers
Parco Space Systems
Furniture Design
Noriyuki Otsuka Design Office
Total floor area
125.61 m²
Total cost (¥)
25,000,000
Duration of construction
4 weeks
Opening
5 March 2005

Little Red Riding Hood
64
~
Architect
Corneille Uedingslohmann
Architekten
Client
Little Red Riding Hood
Manufacturers
Stork Ladenbau (furniture),
FVK Dessau (walls),
Bolidt Kunststoffvertrieb (floor)

Total floor area
366 m² on two floors
Duration of construction
16 weeks
Opening
April 2004

Loveless
208
~
Architect
Jamo Associates
Client
Sanyo Shokai
Lighting
Toru Gotoh
Contractor
Nomura
Total floor area
788.49 m²
Total cost (¥)
200,000,000
Duration of construction
4 weeks
Opening
23 July 2004

m-i-d Press Room
88
~
Architect
Fumita Design Office
Client
m-i-d Press Room
Lighting
Ushio Spax
Graphics
Names
Manufacturer
D. Brain
Total floor area
359.2 m²
Duration of construction
5.5 weeks
Opening
14 December 2004

Marithé + François Girbaud
106
~
Architect
Kristian Gavoille
Client
Marithé + François Girbaud

Mayke
250
~
Architect
Peter Robben
3D Projecten
Client
Mayke
Graphics
Tineke Schuurmans
Lighting
Delta Pro Lighting
Furniture
3D Projecten
Glass showcases
Roelants Glas
Total floor area
250 m²

Duration of construction
4 weeks
Opening
February 2005

Miss Sixty Los Angeles
166
~
Architect
Studio 63
Client
Sixty Group
Lighting
Nord Light
Furniture
Buzzoni Arredamenti
Total floor area
250 m²
Duration of construction
16 weeks
Opening
November 2003

Miss Sixty Milan
166
~
Architect
Studio 63
Client
Sixty Group
Lighting
Nord Light
Furniture
Buzzoni Arredamenti
Total floor area
180 m²
Duration of construction
12 weeks
Opening
September 2003

Miss Sixty New York
166
~
Architect
Studio 63
Client
Sixty Group
Lighting
Polverini Lampadari
Furniture
Buzzoni Arredamenti
Total floor area
270 m²
Duration of construction
20 weeks
Opening
October 2002

Miss Sixty Palermo
166
~
Architect
Studio 63
Client
Sixty Group
Lighting
Polverini Lampadari
Furniture
D&D
Total floor area
300 m²
Duration of construction
14 weeks

Opening
June 2003

Missoni
40
~
Architect
B-architecten
Client
Missoni (Moda E Modi)
Logo and graphics
Sjoerd Sies
Manufacturers
Karoo Interjeurs
Total floor area
100 m²
Total cost (€)
85.000
Duration of construction
9 weeks
Opening
15 September 2005

Neil Barrett
304
~
Architect
Garde
Client
Neil Barrett
Total floor area
77 m²
Duration of construction
13 days
Opening
26 April 2005

Nike iD Studio
124
~
Architect
Lynch / Eisinger / Design
Client
Nike
Exterior and metalwork
subcontractor
Material Process Systems
Interior subcontractor
Tangram
Lighting
Rambusch
Total floor area
102.2 m²
Opening
April 2005

Offspring
256
~
Architect
Jump Studios
Mnaufacturers
P2
Total floor area
1100 m²
Duration of construction
6 weeks
Opening
May 2005

Pleats Please
Issey Miyake
76
~
Architect
AEDS
Client
Issey Miyake
Engineers
Thornton Tomasetti Group
Chicago
Total floor area
25 m² (Berlin)
20 m² (Perpignan)
Total cost (€)
45,000 (Berlin)
35,000 (Perpignan)
Duration of construction
16 weeks
Opening
22 December 2004 (Berlin),
24 September 2005
(Perpignan)

Reiss
112
~
Architect
D_raw associates
Client
Reiss
Engineers
Team CIS
Manufacturers
Space Craft Projects UK
Lighting
Team CIS
Graphics
Made Thought
Total floor area
500 m²
Duration of construction
16 weeks
Opening
March 2005

Restir
52
~
Architect
Laur Meyrieux
Client
Restir
Graphic image and
wall paper
Laur Meyrieux
Manufacturer
D. Brain
Total floor area
950 m² on two floors
Duration of construction
5 weeks
Opening
27 August 2005

Rodenstock
100
~
Architect
Shuhei Endo
Client
Brille Japan
Opening
March 2005

Sigrun Woehr
214
~
Architect
Ippolito Fleitz Group
Client
Sigrun Woehr Schuhe
Colour consultant
Stefan Gabel
Total floor area
110 m²
(without storage space)
Duration of construction
8 weeks
Opening
December 2003

Stash
82
~
Architect
Maurice Mentjens
Client
Yves Vola & Joelle Bastin
Lighting
UTI-licht
Graphics
Rico Bastin
Floor
Atelier Winterink
Manufacturers
WS-Interieurs
Total floor area
34 m²
Total cost (€)
40,000
Duration of construction
4 weeks
Opening
1 August 2004

Stephane Dou &
Changlee Yugin
142
~
Architect
CJ Studio
Client
Stephane Dou and
Changlee Yugin
Total floor area
130 m²
Duration of construction
4 weeks
Opening
May 2005

Thurner Womenswear
238
~
Architect
Martin Mostböck
Client
Thurner Womenswear
Lighting
Siteco- Lighting Systems
Furniture
Braun-Lockenhaus
Carpets
Vorwerk
Stone works
Pauleschitz
Steel Constructions
Wibeba

Total floor area
252 m²
Total cost (€)
260,000
Duration of construction
4 weeks
Opening
May 2005

Tiberius
154
~
Architect
BEHF Architects
Client
Tiberius Leather &
Latex Tools

TroisO
22
~
Architect
Ito Masaru Design
Project / SEI
Client
TroisO
Lighting
H-Lighting Design
Graphics
Names+design complex
Total floor area
68.57 m²
Duration of construction
4 weeks
Opening
22 December 2004

Uniqlo Ginza
148
~
Architect
Klein Dytham architecture
Client
Uniqlo
Lighting
FDS Lighting Studio
Facilities
Sanyo Densyo, Takenaka
Corporation
Contractor
Tanseisha
Total floor area
2543.25 m²
Duration of construction
8 weeks
Opening
7 October 2005

Verso
244
~
Architect
Glenn Sestig Architects
Client
Verso
Colour consultants
BVARDK
Engineer
Janna Huyghe
Manufacturers
Descamps Dekoratie
Total floor area
2000 m²

Duration of construction
24 weeks
Opening
January 2003

Wayne Cooper
262
~
Architect
Hecker Phelan & Guthrie
Client
Wayne Cooper
Total floor area
76 m²
Duration of construction
12 weeks

Yoshie Inaba
220
~
Architect
Studio Power
Client
Yoshie Inaba

Dress Code
Interior Design for Fashion Shops

Publishers
Frame Publishers
www.framemag.com
Birkhäuser – Publishers for Architecture
www.birkhauser.ch

Compiled by
Tessa Blokland

Introduction by
Shonquis Moreno

Texts by
Joeri Bruyninckx, Sarah Martín Pearson,
Brigitte van Mechelen, Shonquis Moreno,
Edwin van Onna, Chris Scott, Matthew
Stewart and Masaaki Takahashi

Graphic design
Lesley Moore
www.lesleymoore.nl

Copy editing
Donna de Vries-Hermansader

Translation
InOtherWords
(D'Laine Camp,
Donna de Vries-Hermansader)

Colour reproduction
Graphic Link, Nijmegen

Printing
D2Print, Singapore

Distribution
ISBN-10: 90-77174-07-9
ISBN-13: 978-90-77174-07-4
Frame Publishers
Lijnbaansgracht 87
1015 GZ Amsterdam
Netherlands
www.framemag.com

ISBN-10: 3-7643-7560-4
ISBN-13: 978-3-7643-7560-7
Birkhäuser – Publishers
for Architecture
PO Box 133
4010 Basel
Switzerland
Part of Springer
Science+Business Media
www.birkhauser.ch

© 2006 Frame Publishers
© 2006 Birkhäuser – Publishers
for Architecture

A CIP catalogue record for this book is
available from the Library of Congress,
Washington D.C., USA

Bibliographic information published
by Die Deutsche Bibliothek.
Die Deutsche Bibliothek lists this publica-
tion in the Deutsche Nationalbibliografie;
detailed bibliographic data is available
in the internet at http://dnb.ddb.de.

Printed on acid-free paper produced
from chlorine-free pulp.
TCF ∞
Printed in Singapore
987654321